b2b brands

Table of contents

Introduction: How the B2B Brands playbook can work for you	2
Why being a beloved brand matters	12
How to use strategic thinking to help your brand win	20
How to build your brand around your core strength	33
How to build a tight bond with your most cherished customers	39
How to win the competitive battle for your customer's heart	47
How to address your brand situation before you make your next move	57
How to define the ideal target market to build your B2B brand around	63
Mapping out the B2B customer journey to set up your brand to win	76
How to define your brand positioning to help your brand win	83
How to create a brand idea you can build everything around	98
How to use your brand idea to organize everything you do	111
How to build a brand plan everyone can follow	121
How to build your brand's execution plans	143
How to write a creative brief to set up brilliant execution	153
How to make marketing communications decisions to break through clutter	166
How to conduct a deep-dive business review to uncover brand issues	190
Marketing Finance 101 to help manage your brand's profitability	206
B2B Brand Toolkit	217
B2B Marketing Training	218

Introductory Chapter

How our B2B Brands playbook can work for you

It takes a fundamentally sound B2B marketer to figure out how to win with brand love to attract loyal customers. As marketing rapidly evolves, the fundamentals of brand management matter more now than ever.

Today's B2B marketers are so busy, running from meeting to meeting, they feel overwhelmed and confused. They have no time to think. Marketing is now about 'get stuff done'— never about taking the time to stop and ask if it's the right stuff to do.

Meanwhile, to build a relationship, you must take the time to genuinely court your customers. To move your customer from stranger to friend and onto the forever stage, you need to think all the time. With the focus on access to big data, marketers are drowning in data, that they do not even have the time to sort through it all to produce the analytical stories to help to make decisions. Marketers are so overwhelmed by the breadth of media choices and the pressure to be everywhere. As a result, the quality of B2B marketing execution has suffered.

If B2B marketers do not love the work they create, how can they ever expect the customer to love the brand? As the bestselling author of Beloved Brands, I recognized the need for a marketing book that focuses on B2B marketing. Many of the same tools work in both consumer and B2B marketing. My goal in writing this B2B Brands playbook is to make you a smarter brand leader so your brand can win in the market.

I know your role and the challenges you face. I have been in your shoes. I will share everything I have learned in my 20 years in the trenches of brand management. I want to help you be successful. This book is intended as an actionable "make it happen" playbook, not a theory or opinion book.

What is a B2B brand?

In the diagram, you will see seven types of brand models. For business-to-business (B2B) brands, we will cover four primary types within this book:

1. **B2C thru B:** Sell your products through a third-party partner, whose reps then sell your brand to consumers.
2. **B2B Products:** Sell your products as an ingredient or component your customers will use to make their brand better.
3. **B2B Services:** Sell your services to companies or individuals at the company who want help to achieve success.
4. **DTC:** Sell your products directly to specific B2B customers who are using the product in their jobs or companies.

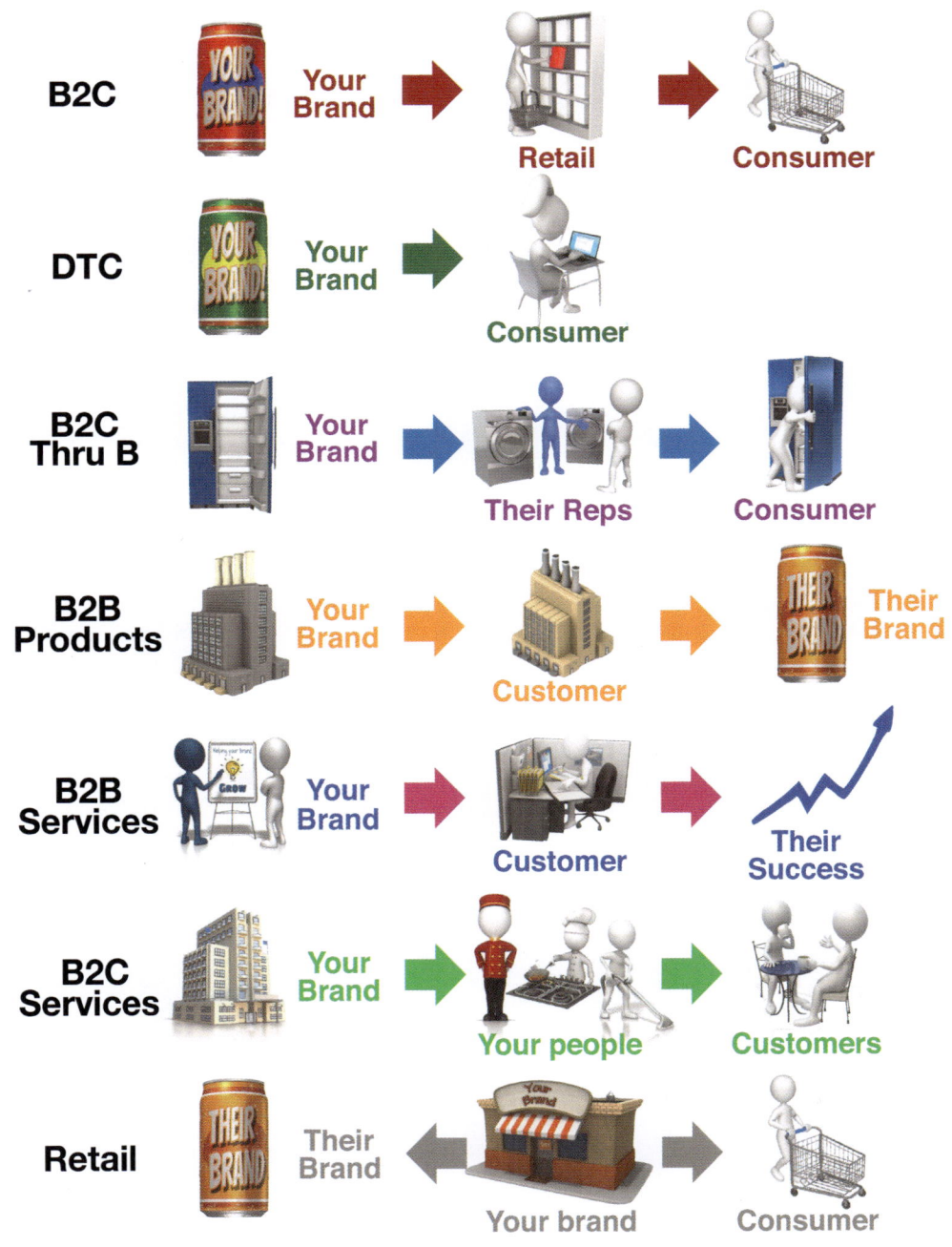

Choose your business model based on how your customer wants to buy, not how you want to sell.

A great case study is the Apple brand, which now uses all seven of these business models, as they sell to both consumers and businesses, sell both products and services, sell directly, through retailers, and through their own retail stores. Apple allows customers to engage the brand however the customers wish to purchase.

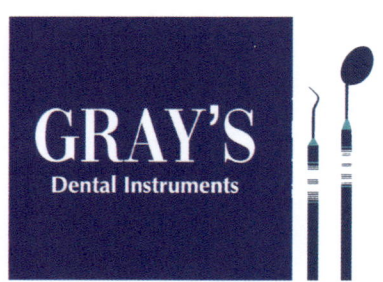
Medical Tools

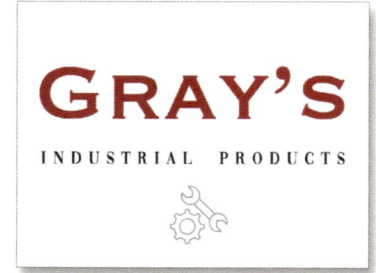
Industrial Tools

Administrative / Services

OEM ingredient

Packaging

Product Verticals

Scientific Discovery

SaaS / Tech

Manufacturing Equipment

Transportation

Professional Services

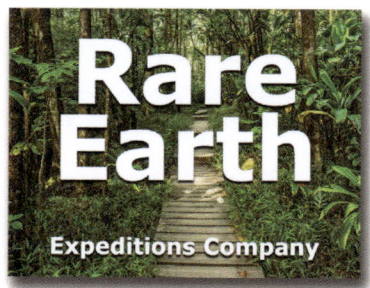
Vertical Search

B2B brands are moving closer to consumer marketing

I have worked in both consumer and B2B marketing, and the similarities are more than you think. I hear, "but we are not a consumer brand" all the time. Yes, you won't be doing a TV ad on the Super Bowl. However, the same principles that have been working in consumer marketing will have tremendous success with B2B brands.

My first job was at GE, working in the commercial and industrial lighting business. As a consultant for the last decade, I have worked on brands in oil and gas, financial services, medical products, commercial real estate, technology, and telecommunications. All of the models and secrets I share in this book have been used with my own clients.

Creating a bond with customers, to help win in the long-term

It is easy to get wrapped up with launching the new product for next week or trying to figure out a price that will help close a deal by noon. You forget to build your brand for the longer term. For customers, B2B decisions are much more emotional than you think, yet too many B2B companies focus on product features as the main differentiator and price as their usual deal closer.

The best B2B brands are building tight bonds with customers, so they feel more and think less. You want your best customers to become fans, who will be the first to try your new product and will want you to win the contract with their company.

Go beyond the product to create an exceptional experience

The best brands evolve into an experience-led brand, but it is not always a smooth transition. B2B brands face a much greater opportunity to win by adding vital services that elevate you beyond your products.

People who on your brand will make the most significant difference

B2B brands have the opportunity to build a culture with values and expected behaviors that can inspire everyone who works behind the scenes to deliver their greatest work on behalf of the brand. Make your best people the face of your brand whose "wow" personal stories showcase why they do what they do and the ways your people go over the top to surprise and delight their customers.

Your B2B marketing should connect with people, not companies

As media options expand, B2B brands can connect with specific customers at companies by communicating their beliefs. They can also make customers feel smarter with content that matters, and they can create emotion with stories of the greatness of their people. With account-based marketing (ABM) techniques, you can reach and build a bond with individuals within a company, even if you are not an approved vendor.

Balance efforts building your brand and transactional sales support

One-third of your marketing effort should be brand-building that creates a bond with customers; one-third is transactional sales support around new products and deal closing. If you keep saying "buy me now," customers will eventually forget why they should ever buy your brand. The remaining one-third might surprise you.

I want you to focus one-third on your employees who have to understand everything about your brand, including your brand idea, purpose, values, beliefs, and most motivating and ownable customer benefits. Your people are the face of your brand, and they are the ones who will deliver your brand reputation.

The fundamentals of marketing matter

When I see marketers jump straight to tactics, I know they are missing the underlying issues hurting their brand

Without taking enough time to think strategically, marketers fail to build on their brand's core strength, create a bond with customers, win the competitive battles, or improve the business situation of the brand. Our Strategic ThinkBox tool pushes B2B marketers to capture the unique circumstances before taking action.

When brands make the mistake of trying to be everything to anyone, the brand ends up being nothing to everyone

Without a clearly defined brand positioning, the brand never establishes the desired reputation with B2B customers. With a lack of clarity, the execution team lacks direction, so the brand messaging ends up random and confusing to customers.

Marketers should never allow competitors to define the brand because they certainly won't like how they define the brand. We will show how to define the target market and turn product features into customer benefits, with a balance of functional and emotional benefits.

When marketers try to do too many things in their plan, none of the ideas end up with enough resources to make the impact they expect

Marketing plans that fail to make firm decisions spread their limited resources across so many tactics that none of the ideas create a big enough impact to make a difference. With a lack of vision, the plan meanders and confuses those who work behind the scenes of the brand. We will show how to build your plan with a brand vision, purpose, values, key issues, strategies, and execution plans.

When marketing execution is not organized and aligned to the strategy, everyone operates in silos. The customer sees a disjointed, confused brand.

The brand communication, new product innovation, and the sales team never benefit from working together. Customers get frustrated by the disjointed execution, and they never feel connected to the brand. Our playbook teaches everything that marketers need to know about writing a creative brief, giving valuable feedback for better work, and making decisions on marketing execution.

When marketers don't go deep enough on analytics, they speak with random opinions not connected to the reality of what's happening in the marketplace

They miss out on understanding the customer trends, competitive dynamics, evolving technologies, shopper channels, and brand performance. The problems fester, and competitors steal the untapped opportunities. As a result, the brand positioning, marketing plans, and execution are not good enough. You owe your business a deep-dive business review at least once a year. We show how to lead a deep-dive business review that looks at five areas: the marketplace, customers, channels, competitors, and the brand.

We will challenge the way you think, define, plan, execute and analyze

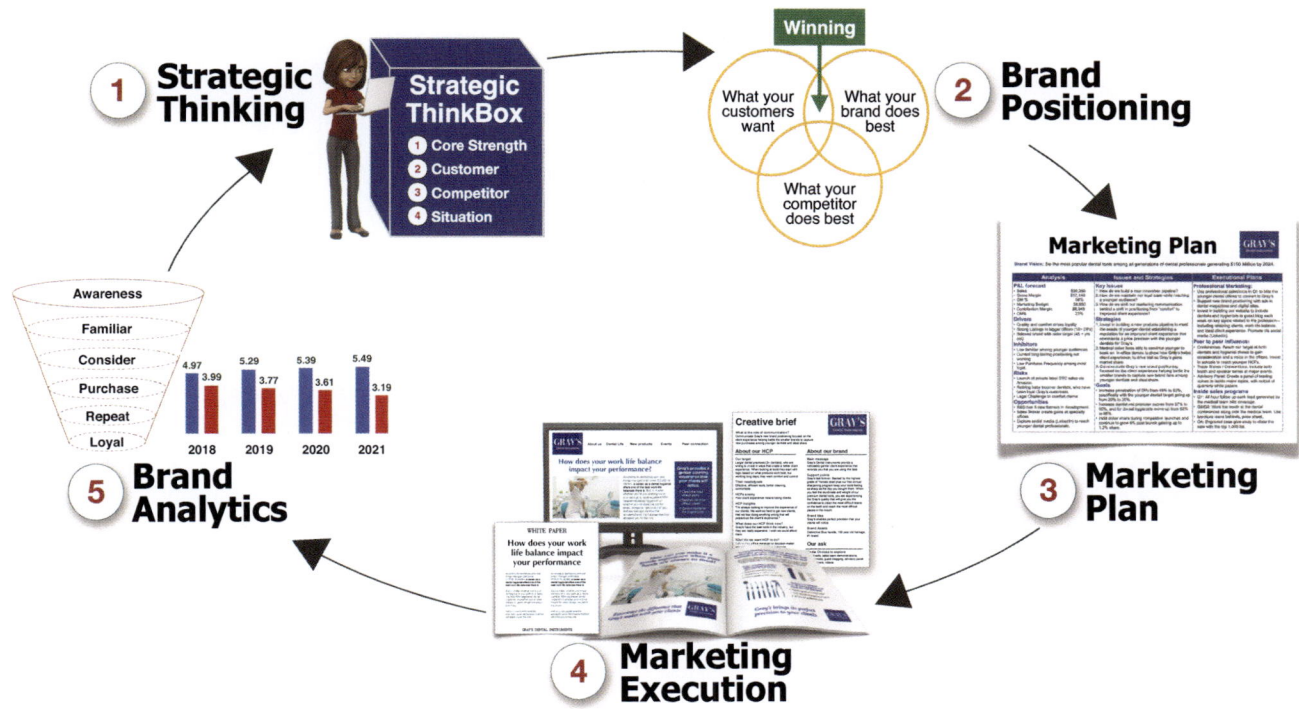

1. How to think strategically

Too many marketers are so busy they do not even have time to think. The best brand leaders do the necessary critical strategic thinking to find ways to win in the market. Strategic thinking is an essential foundation, forcing marketers to ask big questions to challenge and focus brand decisions.

I will show you four ways to enhance your strategic thinking, using the brand's core strength finder, customer strategy, competitive strategy, and situational strategy. You will learn how to set a vision for your brand, focus your limited resources on breakthrough points, take advantage of market opportunities, and find early wins to leverage to give your brand a positional power to drive growth and profits.

In our section on strategic thinking, you will learn how to:

✓ Use five elements of smart strategic thinking
✓ Engage our ThinkBox 360-degree strategic thinking model to trigger new questions
✓ Build everything around your brand's core strength
✓ Think strategically to tighten your brand's bond with customers
✓ Think strategically to win the competitive battles you face
✓ Think strategically within your brand's current situation
✓ Write strategic objective statements for each of the four strategies

2. How to define your brand positioning

Too many marketers are trying to be everything to anyone. This strategy is the usual recipe for becoming nothing to everyone. The best brand leaders target a specific motivated customer audience and then define their brand around a brand idea that is interesting, simple, unique, motivating, and ownable.

I will show you how to write a winning brand positioning statement with four essential elements: target market, competitive set, main benefit, and reason to believe (RTB). You will learn how to build a brand idea that leads every touchpoint of your brand, including the brand promise, brand story, innovation, purchase moment, and the customer experience. I will give you the tools for how to write a winning brand concept and brand story.

In our section on defining your brand, you will learn how to:

✓ Write brand positioning statements
✓ Define your target market, with insights, enemies, and need states
✓ Define customer benefits, both functional and emotional
✓ Come up with brand support points and claims
✓ Understand the relationships among brand soul, brand idea and brand reputation
✓ Develop your brand idea
✓ Write brand concept statements
✓ Turn your brand concept into a brand story
✓ Use the brand positioning and brand idea to build your internal brand credo

3. How to write brand plans

Too many marketers focus on a short-term to-do list, not a long-term plan. The best brand leaders write brand plans, so everyone in the organization can follow with ease, including senior management, sales, R&D, agencies, and operational teams. I will teach you how to write each element of the brand plan, including the brand vision, purpose, values, goals, key Issues, strategies, and tactics. Real-life examples will give you a framework to use on your brand. You will learn to build execution plans, including a brand communications plan, an innovation plan, and a selling plan.

In our section on how to write brand plans, you will learn how to:

- ✓ Use five strategic questions as an outline for your entire plan
- ✓ Write an inspirational brand vision statement to frame your brand plan
- ✓ Develop a brand purpose and brand values
- ✓ Summarize your brand's situation analysis
- ✓ Map out the key issues your brand faces
- ✓ Write smart, brand strategy objective statements to build your brand's core strength
- ✓ Write smart, customer-driven brand objective strategy statements
- ✓ Write smart, competitor-driven brand objective strategy statements
- ✓ Write smart, situational brand strategy objective statements
- ✓ Focus tactics to ensure a high return on effort
- ✓ Write specific execution plans for brand communications, innovation, and sales plan
- ✓ Develop profit statement, sales forecast, goals, and marketing budget for your plan
- ✓ Use an ideal one-page brand format for the annual brand plan and long-range strategic roadmap

4. How to inspire marketing execution

Too many marketing leaders are becoming task-masters and step over the line into execution. The best brand leaders need to inspire experts to produce smart and creative execution. I will provide tools and techniques for judging and making decisions on creative content marketing your agency creates.

For judging marketing execution, I use the ABC's tool, believing the best marketing executions must drive Attention (A), Brand link (B), Communication (C), and Stickiness (S). I will provide a checklist for you to use when judging executions, which will provide better direction to your agency to inspire and challenge great marketing execution.

In our section on how to lead the marketing execution, you will learn how to:

- ✓ Understand crucial role of the B2B brand leader in getting great creative execution
- ✓ Be the brand leader who can successfully manage all stages of the content process
- ✓ Write a brand communications plan
- ✓ Turn the brand communications plan into a creative brief
- ✓ Leverage smart and bad examples of the creative brief
- ✓ Use the ABC's marketing execution decision-making tool
- ✓ Give inspiring feedback on content marketing to push for great work
- ✓ Build your media planning with six media questions
- ✓ Align media choices with where customers are most willing to engage your brand

5. How to analyze your brand's performance

Too few marketers take the time to dig into data analytics. There is no value in having access to data if you are not using it to discover meaningful insights. The best brand leaders can tell strategic stories through analytics. I will show you how to create a deep-dive business review, looking at the marketplace, customers, competitors, sales channels, and brand. I will teach you how to turn your analysis into a presentation for management, showing the ideal presentation slide format. I will also provide a Finance 101 for Marketers, giving you every financial formula you need to run your brand.

In our section on brand analytics, you will learn how to:

✓ Analyze the marketplace your brand plays in
✓ Assess your customers
✓ Assess the channels you sell through
✓ Analyze the competitors
✓ Analyze the health of your brand
✓ Use 60 of the best analytical questions to ask
✓ Bring analysis together to summarize drivers, inhibitors, threats, and opportunities
✓ Know the financial formulas for compound CAGR, price increases, COGs, and ROI
✓ Prepare a deep-dive business review presentation

You will learn how to think, define, plan, execute, and analyze, and I provide every tool you will ever need to run your brand. We have translated most of our b2b brand tools from this book into brand management templates in downloadable PowerPoint presentations that you can find at **beloved-brands.com**

Every example in our B2B Brands playbook is a B2B brand. And, every tool we show you can be used at your desk to make your brand better. My brand promise is to help make you smarter so you can realize your full potential.

Graham Robertson

Founder and CMO of Beloved Brands Inc.
graham@beloved-brands.com

Chapter One
Why being a beloved brand matters

Even for a B2B brand?

I get so many B2B brands tell me, "That may work for a consumer-driven brand, but can our brand be loved?" I can hear the doubt and insecurity in their voice. I believe the best B2B brands must deliver on a promise, build a reputation for something specific over time, and create a deep bond with their most cherished customers.

If the best brands win because of the passionate and lasting love they have established with their most cherished customers, shouldn't that be even more important for a B2B brand?

Brands must treat their most cherished customers with the respect that establishes trust, enabling consumers to open up to a point where they replace thinking with feeling. The logic of demand evolves into an emotional state of desire, needs become cravings and repeat purchases progress into rituals and turn into a favorite moment in the day. Customers transform into the most outspoken and loyal brand fans and ambassadors.

The fundamentals of brand management matter more now than ever. Old-school marketers learned the 4Ps of product, place, price, and promotion. It is a useful start, but far too product-focused. New-school marketers have to deliver on customers insight that connect, both functional and emotional benefits instead of features, and focus on building a culture that delivers exceptionally happy customer experiences.

B2B Customers have changed

It takes a smart strategy to balance the rational and emotional management of the brand-to-customer relationship. The most beloved brands are so exceptional because of how well they treat their most loyal customers. They make them feel loved.

The customers of today must be won over. They are surrounded by the **clutter** of 5,000 brand messages a day that fight for a glimpse of their attention. That is 1.8 million per year or one message every 11 waking seconds.

Even B2B brands must compete for your customer's attention, as customers are **continuously distracted**—walking, talking, texting, searching, watching, replying—and all at the same time. Even at work, your customers are checking social media feeds and looking at their phone on a regular basis.

In a cluttered media world, customers glance past brand messages all day long. Their brain quickly rejects boring, irrelevant, or unnecessary messages. To succeed, B2B brands must capture the customer's imagination right away, with a brand idea that is simple, and unique. It must create as much excitement as a first-time encounter.

Customers are **tired of being burned** by broken brand promises. Once lied to, their well-guarded instincts begin to doubt first, test second, and at any point, they will cast aside any brand that does not live up to the original promise that captivated them on the first encounter. A brand must be worthy of love. The best brands of today have a soul that exists deep within the culture of the brand organization.

Brands must be customer focused. The brand's purpose must be able to explain why the people who work behind the scenes of the brand come to work every day so energized and ready to over-deliver on the brand's behalf. This purpose becomes a firm conviction with inner motivations, beliefs, and values that influence and inspire every employee to want to be part of the brand.

This brand conviction must be so firm that the brand would never make a choice that directly contradicts their internal belief system. Customers start to see, understand, and appreciate the level of conviction with the brand.

Brands must listen, observe, and know the thoughts of their customer before they even think it. Not only does the brand meet their functional needs, but the brand must also heroically beat down the customer's enemy that torments their life, every day.

The best brands must **show up consistently at every customer touchpoint**, whether it is the promise the brand makes, the stories they tell, the innovation designed to impress customers, the happy purchase moments or the delightful experiences that make customers want to tell their friends and colleagues the brand story. The customer keeps track to make sure the brand delivers before the customer is willing to commit. Only then will the customer become willing to open up and trust the brand.

The integrity of the brand's soul tightens the customer's unshakable bond with that brand. Brands have to do the little things that matter, to show they love their customer. Every time the brand over-delivers on their promise, it adds a little spark to the romance.

Over time, the brand must weave itself into the most critical moments of the customer's lives and business, and become part of the most cherished stories and memories within the customer's heart. In today's cluttered brand world, the pathway to brand success is all about building relationships with your most cherished customers.

A brand idea must be interesting, simple, unique, inspiring, motivating, and own-able. The brand idea must attract and move customers

The first connection point for customers with a brand is that moment when they see a brand idea worth engaging the brand. The brand almost jumps off the screen of a presentation, grips the audience's attention through content communications, or compels customers to click on a demonstration video. The brand has to generate interest very quickly.

When the brand idea is **interesting** and **simple**, it helps the brand gain quick entry into the customer's mind, so they want to engage and learn more about the brand. With the B2B customer bombarded by 5,000 brand messages every day, the brand has only seven seconds to connect or else customers will move on.

That is why the brand idea should be **unique** and **ownable** to stand out amid the clutter, and the brand can see enough rich potential to build their entire business around the idea. The idea should inspire the team working behind the scenes to deliver amazing customer experiences.

The brand idea must be motivating to customers, so the brand can move customers to see, think, feel, or act in positive ways that benefit the brand.

A brand idea must have enough longevity to last 5 to 10 years and enough flexibility to show **consistency** no matter what media options you choose. The idea must provide a common link across the entire product line-up. Everything you do should deliver the brand idea.

> **You have only seven seconds to connect with customers**

The brand has to show up the same way to everyone, no matter where it shows up. Even as the brand leader expands on the idea, whether telling the brand story over 60 seconds, 30 minutes or over the lifetime of the brand, it must tell the same story.

When the idea works best, the most far-reaching sales rep, the scientist in the lab, the plant manager, or the customer service rep must all articulate the brand idea, in the same way, using the same chosen words. Every time a customer engages with the brand, they must see, hear and feel the same brand idea. Each positive interaction further tightens their bond with the brand.

Use your brand idea to organize everything you do

As a brand leader, you have **five customer touchpoints** to align and manage, including the brand promise, brand story, product innovation, the path to the purchase moment, and the overall customer experience. The brand idea map shows you how to align all five customer touchpoints.

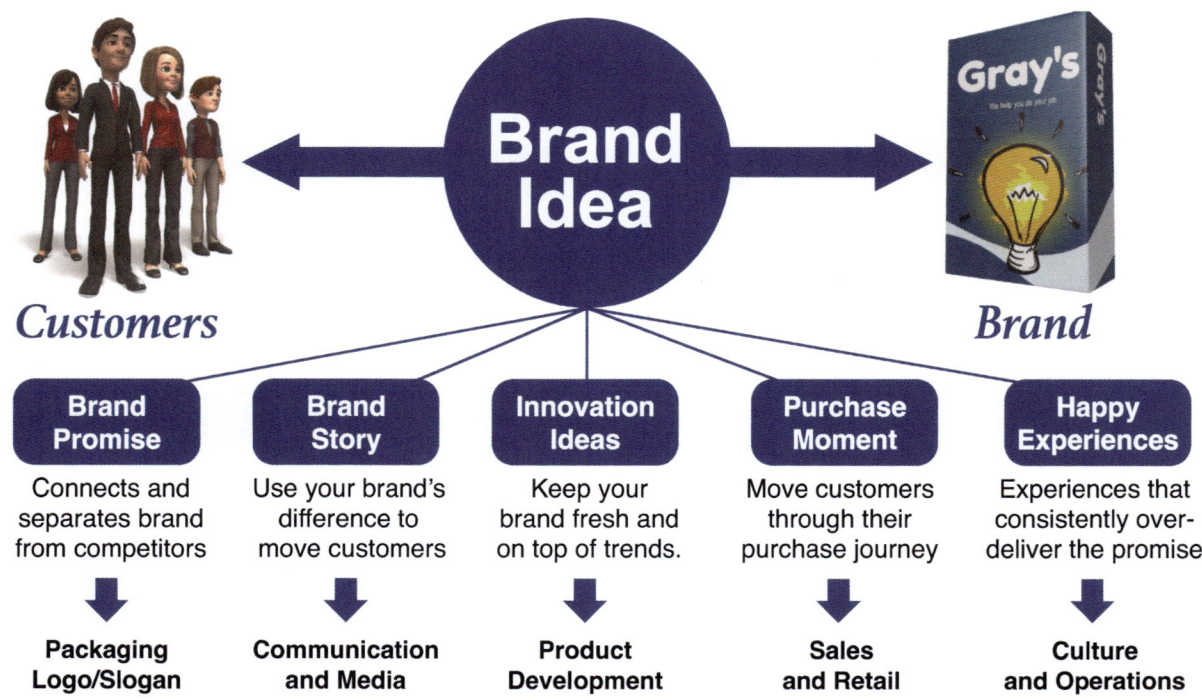

- The **brand promise** connects with customers and separates your brand from competitors. The promise must position the brand as interesting and unique, utilizing brand positioning work to define the target market, the balance of functional and emotional benefits, along with key support points.

- The **brand story** helps the brand stand out from the pack to gain the customer's consideration for purchase. It must push customers to see, think, feel, or act differently than before they saw the brand message.

- **Innovation** must help the brand stay on top of the latest trends in technology, customer need states, distribution, and competitive activity. A brand cannot stand still. The brand idea should act as an internal beacon to help inspire the product development team to come up with new ways to captivate customers.

- The **purchase moment** transforms the awareness and consideration into a purchase. The brand idea ensures everyone along the path to purchase delivers the same brand message, using retail and selling strategies to influence customers.

- Create **customer experiences** that overdeliver the promise, driving repeat purchase, and future customer loyalty. When you partner with HR, the brand idea inspires the culture and organization, influencing hiring decisions, service values, and motivation of the operations teams who deliver the experience.

It takes a strategic mind to figure out brand love

To show the differences in how customers feel about a brand as they move through five stages, I created the brand love curve. It defines customers' feelings as unknown, indifferent, like it, love it and onto the beloved brand status.

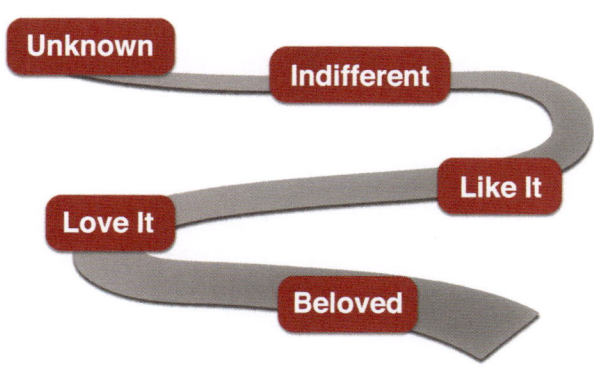

For **unknown brands**, the strategic focus should be to stand out so customers will notice the brand within a crowded brand world. For **indifferent brands**, the strategy must establish the brand in the customer's mind so they can see a clear point of difference. At the **like it stage**, the strategy is to separate the brand from the pack, creating happy experiences that build a trusted following. At the **love it stage**, the focus shifts to tugging at heartstrings to tighten the bond with the most loyal brand fans. At the **beloved brand stage**, the strategic challenge is to create outspoken, loyal brand fans who are willing to whisper to their friends on the brand's behalf.

The necessary ingredients to create brand love

- **Everything must be about the customer:** You need to know your customers as well as you know your brand. Dig deep to understand and appreciate the customer insights, enemies, and needs. Emphasize customer benefits, not features. Since customers always wonder, "What's in it for me?" communicate what they get from you and talk about how your brand makes them feel.
- **Dare to be different:** Your brand needs to stand out as being better, different, cheaper, or else your brand will not be around for very long. Be the brand that defines your unique value, rather than adding more clutter to the mountain of clutter.
- **Build everything you do around your brand idea:** Your brand idea is the first point of connection and creates a lasting impression. The brand idea is the reason customers first buy. Every time your brand delivers, the bond tightens just a little more. Whenever you fail to deliver, the customer goes into doubt mode, wondering if they will stay with your brand.
- **Breakthrough focus:** You must focus your brand's limited resources to key breakthrough points you believe will tighten the bond with your customers, putting the brand in a more powerful position to drive higher profits. You have to know your customer, know what your brand stands for, and be willing to focus on the strategies that will pay back in building the brand.
- **Passion matters:** You must exhibit incredible passion in the marketing execution, consistently focused on surprising your customers, to become one of their favorite brands. Always remember "I love it" is the highest bar you can set for achieving great work. If you do not love the work, how can you ever expect your customers to love your brand?

Brand love generates brand power

The tighter the bond a brand creates with its customers, the more powerful the brand will become with all stakeholders. Think of brand love as stored energy a brand can unleash in the form of power into the marketplace. You can use that power with customers, competitors, new entries, employees, influencers, media, suppliers, and channel partners.

These beloved B2B brands command power over the very **customers** who love them, as customers feel more and think less. These customers pay price premiums, line up in the rain, follow the brand as soon as it enters new categories, and relentlessly defend the brand to any attackers. They cannot live without the brand.

When B2B brands sell through **channel partners**, a beloved brand commands power over those partners. They know their customers would switch channels before they switch brands. They cannot stand up to the beloved brand; instead, they give the brand everything in negotiations. The beloved brand ends up with stronger loyalty among the partner's sales people, better trade terms, and better promotions.

The **competitors**, whether current competitors or new entries, cannot match the emotional bond the beloved brand has created with their brand fans. The beloved brand has a monopoly on emotions, making the customer's decisions less about the actual product and more about how the experience that makes customers feel. Unless a new brand has an overwhelming technological advantage, it will be impossible to break the emotional bond the customer has established with the beloved B2B brand.

The beloved brand also has power over the **media** whether paid, earned, social, or search media. With paid media, the beloved brand gets better placement, cheaper rates and they are one of the first calls for possible brand integrations. The beloved brand is considered newsworthy, so they earn more free media via mainstream media, expert reviews, bloggers, and user-generated content.

Beloved brands command power over customers, channel partners, suppliers, media, and employees

Being a famous and beloved brand helps bypass the need for **search engine optimization (SEO)**. The beloved brands become part of the conversation, whether it is through social media or at the lunch table at work. Beloved brands can use their homepage website to engage their most loyal users, inform the market of upcoming changes, allow customers to design their version of the brand and then sell the product directly to brand lovers.

Suppliers serve at the mercy of the beloved brand. The high volumes drive efficiencies of scale that drive down production costs, backing the supplier into a corner before they offer up most of those savings. Plus, the supplier becomes willing to give in, so that they can use the beloved brand as a selling tool for their supplier services to other potential brands.

Beloved brands even have power over **employees**, who want to be part of the brand. They are brand fans, who are proud to work on the brand. They embody the culture on day 1 and want to help the brand achieve success.

The beloved brands have power over **key influencers**, whether they are doctors recommending a drug, restaurant critics giving a positive review or salespeople at electronics shops pushing the beloved brands. These influencers become fans of the beloved brand and build their own emotions into their recommendations.

Brand love means brand profits

With all the love and power the beloved brand generates, it becomes easy to translate that stored power into sales growth, profit, and market valuation. Here are the eight ways a brand can drive profits:

1. Premium pricing
2. Trading up on price
3. Lower cost of goods
4. Lower sales and marketing costs
5. Stealing competitive users
6. Getting loyal users to use more
7. Entering new markets
8. Finding new uses for the brand

Beloved brands can use higher prices and lower costs to drive higher margins

Most beloved brands can use their loyal brand lovers to command a premium price, creating a relatively inelastic price. The weakened channel customers cave in during negotiations to give the brand richer margins. Satisfied and loyal customers are willing to trade up to the next best model. A well-run beloved brand can use their high volume to drive efficiency, helping to achieve a lower cost of goods structure.

Not only can beloved brands use their growth to drive economies of scale, but suppliers will cut their cost to be on the roster of the beloved brand. The beloved brand will operate with much more efficient marketing spend, using their power with the media to generate lower rates with plenty of free media. Plus, the higher sales volumes make the beloved brand's spend ratios much more efficient. The customer response to the marketing execution is much more efficient, giving the brand a higher return on investment.

Beloved brands use higher shares of a bigger market to drive higher volume

The beloved brands use their momentum to reach a tipping point of support to drive higher market shares. They can get loyal users to use more, as customers build the beloved brand into company's core business.

It is easier for the beloved brands to enter new categories, knowing their loyal customers will follow. Finally, there are more opportunities for the beloved brand to find more uses to increase the number of ways the beloved brand can fit into the customer's company's success and customer's work-life.

Chapter Two
How to use strategic thinking to help your brand win

Strategic thinkers see questions before they see solutions.

Ever hear someone say, "That's a good question." It usually means someone has just asked an interruptive question, designed to slow everyone's thinking, so they reflect and plan before they act. The strategic thinking side of marketing is logical and has to map out a range of decision trees that intersect, by imagining how events will play out in the future.

The risk of being only strategic is that, if you think too long, you may spiral around, unable to decide. Moreover, you may miss an opportunity window.

Opposite to a strategic thinker is the instinctual thinker who jumps in quickly to find answers before they even know the right question. Their brains move fast; they use emotional impulse and intuitive gut feel. They want action now and get easily frustrated by delays.

They believe it is better to do something than sit and wait around. They see strategic people as stuck running around in circles, as they try to figure out the right question. Instead, these instinctual leaders choose emotion over logic.

> **The best brand leaders are both strategic & intuitive**

While a "make it happen" attitude gets things done, if they go too fast, their actions may solve the wrong problem.

Brand leaders must be both strategic and intuitive. Learn to change brain speeds. Slow down the thinking when faced with challenging issue and move quickly with your best instincts on execution.

Our Strategic ThinkBox and Marketing PlayBox

I want to introduce you to my **ThinkBox** concept, which I have borrowed from sports. For instance, in golf, using a ThinkBox forces you to consider everything you are facing before taking the shot. Look at any lakes or bunkers in the way, the wind condition, or how well you are playing that day. Then, decide on your shot strategy. As you move to a **PlayBox**, visualize the ideal shot, think and feel your way through the mechanics of your swing, and trust you are making the right shot. Do not over-think the strategy during the execution.

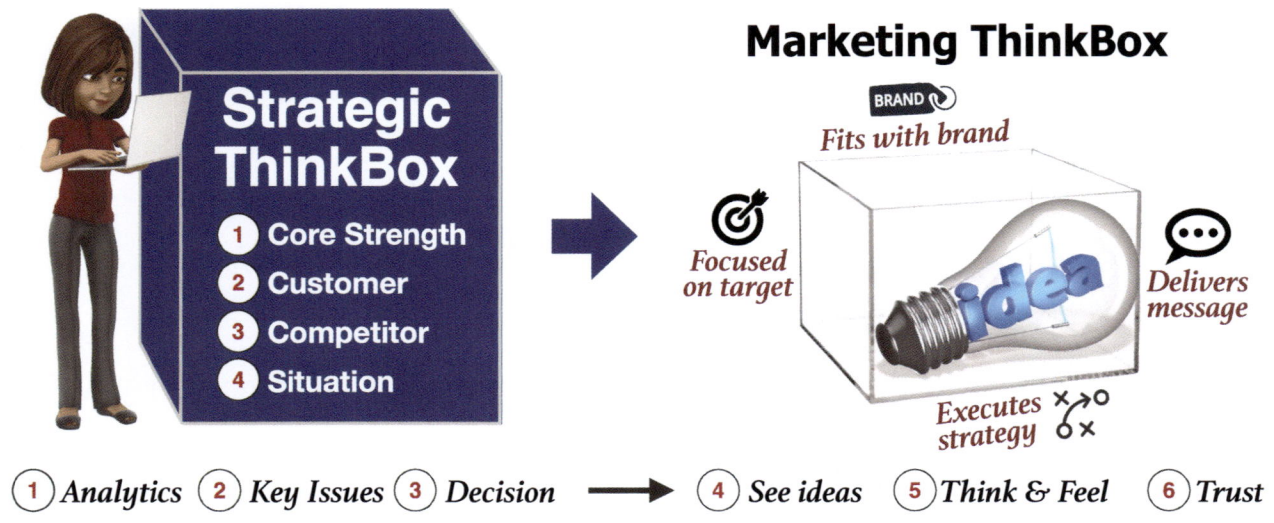

With your brand, you should use a **Strategic ThinkBox**, to get a 360-degree view of the situation, before taking action. Consider your brand's core strength, the bond you have with your customers, your brand's competitive position, and your brand's business situation.

Once you have completed your thinking, use the **Marketing PlayBox** to see the ideal execution, think and feel your way, then trust your instincts.

The four questions in our Strategic ThinkBox

As I created the Strategic ThinkBox, I made it so that each of the four questions uses a forced choice to make decisions, where you must focus on only one possible answer for each question.

1. What is the **core strength** that will help your brand win?
2. How tightly connected is your **customer** to your brand?
3. What is your current **competitive** position?
4. What is the current business **situation** your brand faces?

Strategic ThinkBox

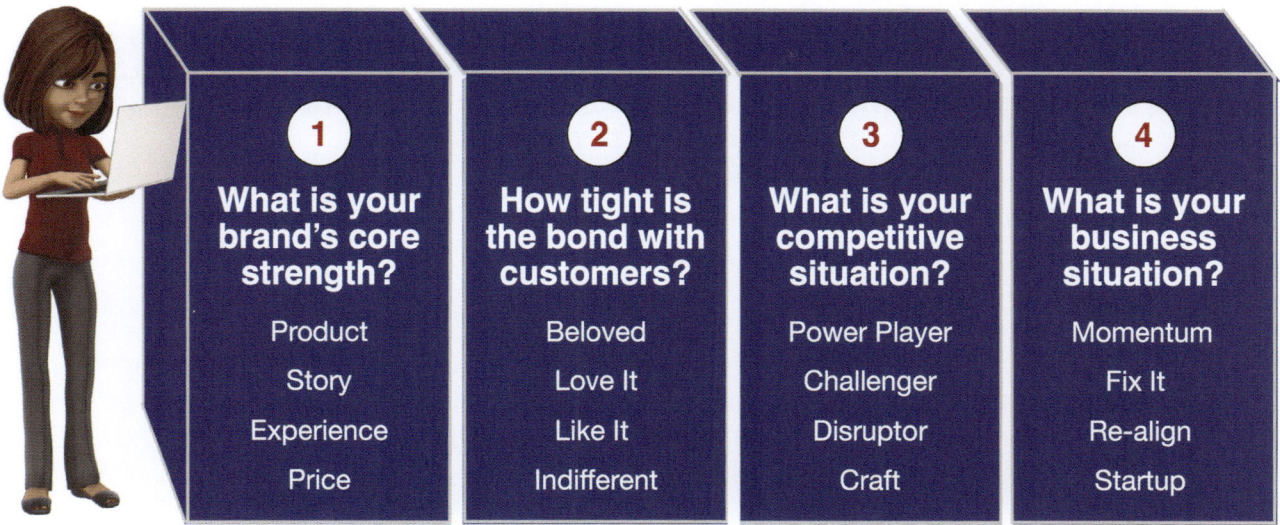

1. **Start with your brand's core strength. Decide which of four choices you will lead with:**
   - Product
   - Brand story
   - Customer experience
   - Price

   Your core strength will change your entire strategy, including the brand messages and the focus of your investment. In the next chapter, I show a unique process for how to choose your brand's core strength and then show you how to write smart, strategic objective statements around your core strength.

2. **Next, you have to look at your customer strategy. Start by determining where your brand currently sits on the brand love curve, whether your brand is:**
   - Indifferent
   - Like it
   - Love it
   - Beloved

3. **Regarding the competitive strategy, you must choose from one of four different types of competitive situations you find your brand operating within:**
   - Power players are the dominant leader in the category and take a competitive defensive stance
   - Challenger brands have gained enough power to battle head-to-head with the market leader
   - Disruptor brands have found a space so different they can pull customers away from any significant category players

- Craft brands aggressively go against the category with a niche target market and a niche customer benefit. They are small and stay far away from the market leaders

4. **A brand must look at the situational strategy, which starts with understanding your brand health, looking at both internal and external factors. Choose one of four potential situations:**
    - Keep the momentum going
    - Face a business turnaround situation
    - Realign everyone behind a strategy
    - Your brand is a start-up

As you put all four answers together, you start to map out the overall strategic direction where you should focus. When writing the brand plan, I recommend you map out a specific key issue question for each of the four strategic questions in your ThinkBox. Over the next few chapters, I will continue to go in depth on each of these strategies.

How our Strategic ThinkBox works with B2B brands

FedEx

FedEx's core strength has been its remarkable experience in shipping small packages overnight, which it pioneered in the 1970s. In terms of competitive strategy, FedEx entered the market as a classic disruptor, who made it impossible for any current alternative to compete and gave the company a significant competitive advantage over UPS. However, UPS caught up in the 1980s, and most customers view FedEx and UPS as equals.

In terms of customer strategy, FedEx remains one of the most trusted B2B brands, but UPS is almost as highly trusted. Yes, some loyal customers still love FedEx, but many are indifferent when they compare FedEx to UPS because there is no clear point of difference between them. FedEx's bond with customers is at risk, leaving the customer's decision to be made on price or availability.

Even with strong brand scores, the business situation is not great. With flat sales and pricing challenges, FedEx has seen its valuation fall 25% in the past few years. FedEx is stuck, wondering where to go next. E-commerce retailers and brands are building their own delivery systems for direct-to-customer service.

FedEx recently lost its deal with Amazon. FedEx is a classic case where its success is a burden. The challenge FedEx now faces is to find new revenue streams, or it will face a long, steady decline, and pinpoint where to attack itself to eliminate costs out of the system.

Boeing

Boeing is a product-led brand, now facing issues with their product due to recent crashes of the Boeing 737 MAX. For decades, Boeing has been one of the most respected and admired companies in the world. However, Boeing has completely mishandled its 737 MAX situation. It's a classic case of the PR misjudgment  of hoping the story goes away rather than address the root causes head-on. As a result, Boeing's reputation, sales results, and financial outlook have all suffered. As reporters look deeper, they question Boeing on its commitment to safety, suggesting the company is more focused on profits and cost efficiency than safety.

From a customer view, Ed Sims, the WestJet Airlines CEO, was quoted for his evaluation of Boeing saying, "I would grade it no higher than a B. I expect A-plus service from every supplier to WestJet, just as we expect our customers to evaluate us in the same way. I think Boeing has missed a beat, frankly, in the way that they have responded to this crisis." That is never a comment a brand wants to hear from their customer.

Boeing competes head-to-head with Airbus, similar to how Coke and Pepsi battle each other. Every loss by one brand is the other brand's gain. In the months following the 737 MAX crisis, Boeing's market capitalization fell by $30 billion, while Airbus quickly climbed $20 billion. Moreover, Airbus has used the crisis to race ahead of Boeing with new orders and deliveries. The challenge for Boeing is how to put the crisis behind it and refocus on innovation to get back into a competitive position with customers.

Microsoft

When it comes to enterprise software, Microsoft is the dominant power player B2B brand having achieved a near-monopoly in the PC market with core products such as Windows, Office, and Outlook. From 2000 to 2012, their valuation felt stuck, relying on a steady stream of sales for business offices. Microsoft didn't seem to know where to go next, with failures in mobile, music, and search engines. They needed a realignment for a better future.

Microsoft's growth has shifted investment and attention to its B2B enterprise business, behind the Azure cloud business, which includes on-premise servers, and software and enterprise consulting services. Arguably, Microsoft has shifted its B2B focus from product-led to experience-led.

The valuation for Microsoft is up four-fold, surpassing $1 trillion. Abandoning the monopoly mindset has opened up innovation with the Internet of Things (IoT), which will connect everyday internet connections with data collection and automation. As the business transforms, Microsoft needs to continue its momentum and competitively battle cloud offerings from Amazon and Google.

Marriott International

Marriott is the choice hotel of the business executive, not just because of the quality of its hotel rooms, but the exceptional Marriott Rewards program that makes staying in its hotels a must-have by making loyalty more enticing.

Following the acquisition of Starwood Hotels, Marriott is now the power player brand by adding Westin Hotels, Ritz Carlton, and the St. Regis brands. To the market, Marriott takes a house of brands approach, but internally, the Marriott Rewards program unifies the company as it approaches the business traveler.

The Marriott Rewards program is the company's secret sauce among B2B customers, shifting Marriott from a product-led brand into an idea-lead brand. While hotels will bid to procurement departments to be a preferred vendor, business executives have become so addicted to Marriott Rewards they insist on staying at a Marriott. With the stock up eight-fold over the last decade, Marriott needs to continue its momentum.

The recent launch of the Marriott Bonvoy Rewards program goes beyond just earning and redeeming free hotel stays, now including 40 airline partners, and the ability to book flights and cars using only points. This reward program is its new power play, as it beats any competitive offering. Marriott is a great B2B case study. It proves that, instead of treating a company as your customer, B2B brands should now manage every employee at a company as a potential customer.

Facebook

Although Facebook is primarily a customer-facing brand, all of its revenues come from B2B media sales. Facebook is an idea-led brand, and the dominant power player, willing to bully any competitor who threatens it.

In terms of its bond with customers, eight years ago, Facebook was on the verge of becoming a beloved brand. Facebook's arrogance and hunger for even more power have eroded its trust with users, and that puts its future B2B media revenues at risk. They keep copying every new player. However, they have yet to come up with an answer for TikTok.

There remains doubt about how Facebook will handle privacy, political interference, and concerns over the accuracy of its audience numbers – uncertainty that continues to cloud Facebook's trust. Mark Zuckerberg must be more forthcoming and honest in how he portrays his brand.
The question Facebook should focus on is how to tighten its bond with users. Looking at its business situation, Facebook appears to have peaked, with recent revenue declines and layoffs. Their stock price is plummeting. Facebook needs to regain its trust because the most significant risk to its arrogance is the threat of government regulations that would severely cut into future revenues.

Five elements of smart strategic thinking

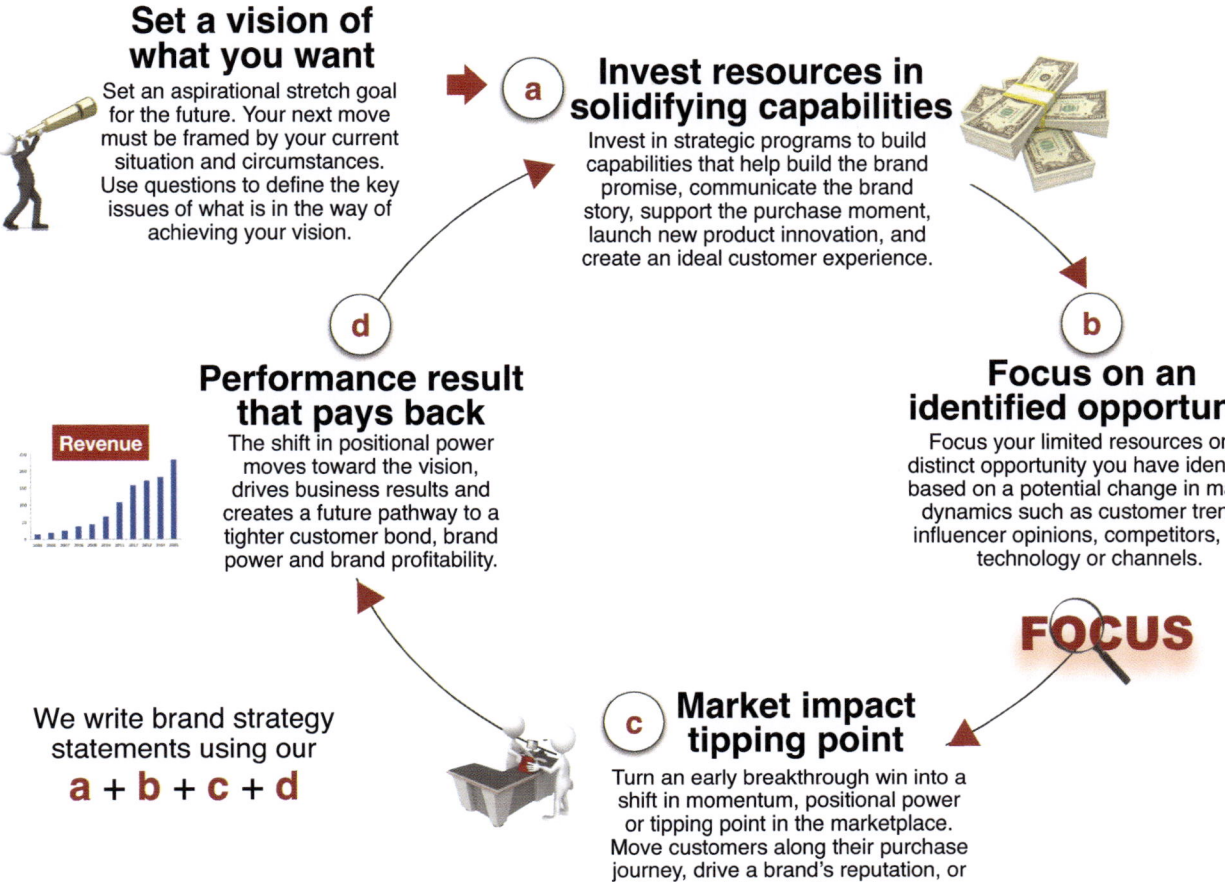

Slow down and organize our thoughts with five elements of strategic thinking, including the vision, investment in solidifying capabilities, focused opportunity, market impact and performance result. This creates a flywheel with the vision anchoring the strategy you keep investing behind to keep fueling more power and profit.

1. Set a vision of what you want for your brand

A vision sets aspirational stretch goals for the future, linked to a clear result or purpose. Write a vision statement in a way that scares you a little and excites you a lot. It should steer everyone who works on the brand to focus on finding ways to create a bond with your customers that will lead to power and profit beyond what the product alone could achieve.

As Yogi Berra famously said, "If you do not know where you are going, how will you know if you get there?" To be a visionary, you must be able to visualize the future.

Imagine it is five or 10 years from now and you wake up in the most fantastic mood. Visualize a perfect future and write down the most critical milestones you need to achieve. Even think about words that will inspire, lead, and steer your team towards your vision.

Key issues define what is in the way of achieving your aspirations. Brands need look at the gap between the current trajectory and the aspiring vision you have set. We use interruptive questions that frame the issues regarding what is in the way of getting what you want to achieve. By raising those issues early on, you can focus the team on the significant problems that need to be solved on the pathway to the stated vision.

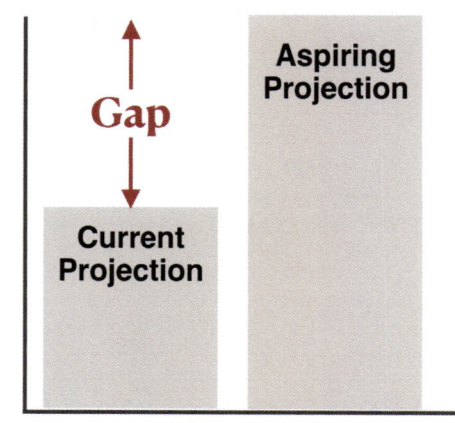

* Roger Martin "Playing to win"

2. Invest resources in solidifying your capabilities

Invest your limited resources—money, people, time, partnerships—in strategic programs that will build the capabilities to help close the gap between your current projection and the aspirational vision. From a brand viewpoint, align your investment to reinforce the brand promise, communicate the brand story, close the deal at the purchase moment, launch new product innovation, or create an ideal customer experience. These investments line up to deliver a brand's customer touchpoints so that you will tighten the bond with customers. The result of the investment will be a more powerful, faster-growing, and profitable brand.

3. Focus on an identified opportunity

Focus your limited resources on a distinct opportunity you have identified based on a potential change in the market, including changes to customers, competitive situation, technology, or sales channels.

In today's data-driven world, everyone has access to the equivalent information and, in turn, can see the same opportunities. Use speed to seize the opportunity before others can take action and before that opportunity is gone.

The best brand leaders never divide and conquer. They force themselves to focus and win. The smartest brand leaders use the word "or" more often than they use the word "and." If you come to a decision point, and you try to rationalize doing a little of both, you are not strategic. Force yourself to make choices.

Many marketers struggle to focus

Myth 1: The most prominent myth of marketing is to believe that your brand will get bigger if you have a broader target market.

- ✓ **Reality:** Too many marketers target anyone. I will always argue that it is better to be loved by a few than tolerated by many. You have to create a tight bond with a core base of brand fans, and then use that fan support to expand your following.

Myth 2: The second myth to becoming a more prominent brand is to believe a brand stands for everything. Some brands try to say everything possible with the hope the customer hears anything.

- ✓ **Reality:** Hope is never a strategy. To be loved by customers, a brand must stand for something with a backbone and conviction. Trying to be everything to anyone ends up becoming nothing to everyone.

Myth 3: Your brand will achieve higher sales if you try to be everywhere, whether in every sales channel or on every possible media option.

- ✓ **Reality:** If you went to Las Vegas and put a chip on every square, you would be bankrupt before midnight. The worst marketers lack focus because they fear missing out on someone or something. By trying to be everywhere, the brand will drain itself and eventually end up being nowhere.

Every brand has limited resources, whether they are financial, time, people, or partnerships. Marketers always face the temptation of an unlimited array of choices, whether in the possible target market, brand messages, strategies, or tactics. The smartest brand leaders limit their choices to match up to their limited resources, to focus on those that will deliver the highest return.

When you focus, five amazing things happen to your brand:

1. **Stronger return on investment (ROI):** When you focus your dollars on the distinct breakthrough point or against a program that you know will work, you will see the most positive and efficient response in the marketplace.

2. **Better return on effort (ROE):** You must make the most efficient use of your limited people resources. Find the Big Easy! Focus on the ideas with the most significant impact that is the easiest to execute. Avoid those ideas that are small and difficult to implement. While you may not always have the data to calculate your ROI, you should have the instincts to figure out your ROE.

3. **Stronger reputation:** When you limit your audience and brand message, you will have a better chance to own that reputation among that core target audience.

4. **More competitive:** When you focus your message to a specific target audience, your brand will start to create a space in the market, and you can defend against others from entering that space.

5. **More investment behind the brand:** When you focus and deliver business results, your management team will ask you to do that again. They will give you more money and more people resources. Even with increased resources, you must take the same focused approach.

4. Leverage the breakthrough market impact

A smart strategy turns an early breakthrough win into a shift in momentum, positional power, or tipping point where you begin to achieve more in the marketplace than the resources you put in.

Many underestimate the need for an early win. I see this as a crucial breakthrough point where you start to look at a small shift in momentum towards your vision. While there will always be doubters to every strategy, the results of the early win provide compelling proof to show everyone the plan will work. You can change the minds of the doubters—or at least keep them quiet—so everyone can stay focused on the breakthrough point.

The magic of strategy happens through leverage, where you can use the early win as an opening or a tipping point where you start to see a transformational power that allows you to make an impact and achieve results in the marketplace. A smart strategy should trigger the customer to move along the buying journey from awareness to buy and onto loyalty, and it can help tighten the customer's bond with the brand.

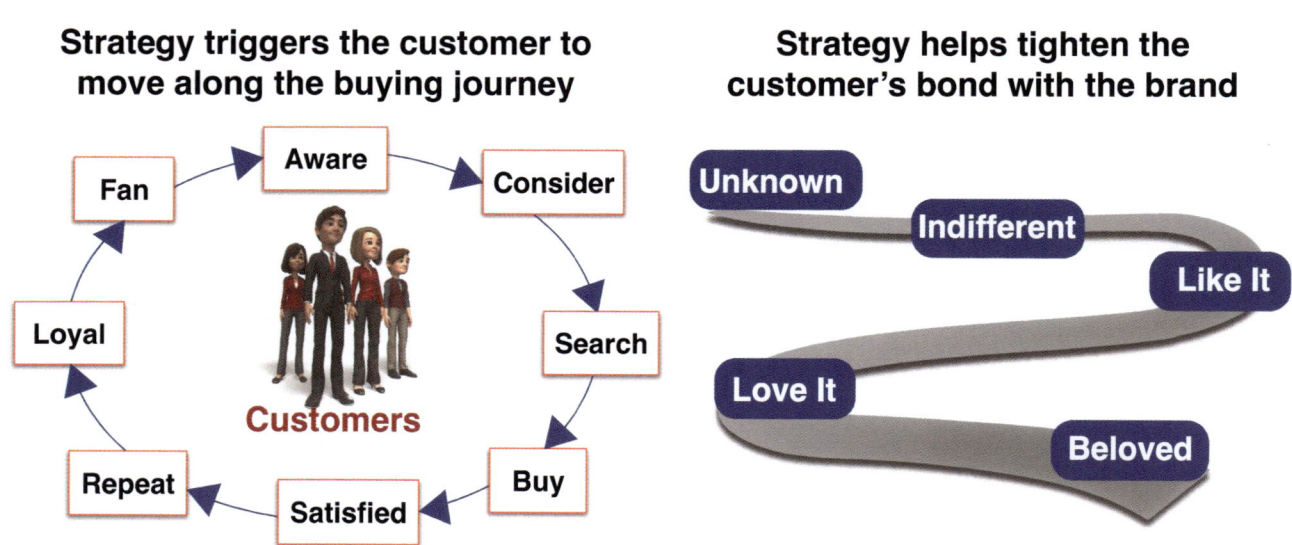

5. Performance result that pays back

The shift in positional power in the marketplace moves your brand toward your vision and creates a future pathway to building a customer bond, brand power, and brand profitability.

A brand can become **powerful** compared to the customer they serve, the competitors they battle, the channels they sell through, the suppliers who make the products or ingredients, the influencers in the market, any media choices and the employees who work for the brand. We explored these eight sources of power in the opening chapter.

You can drive **profit** through premium pricing, trading customers up on price, finding a lower cost of goods, using lower sales and marketing costs, stealing competitive users, getting loyal users to use more, entering new markets or finding new uses for the brand. We explored these eight ways a brand can add to their profitability in the opening chapter. For a strategy to work, what pays off in the marketplace must pay off in brand power or business results.

Using Gray's Lighting to demonstrate strategic thinking

We will use the fictional Gray's Lighting as a case study. Gray's Lighting is the ultimate stage lighting product, that brings the actors faces together so theater patrons can see the expression on their faces from the 40th row.

This lighting brand is battling the major mainstream competitors, starting from a small niche with a core target market of broadway theater director fans who are beginning to love the brand.

Five elements of smart strategic thinking for the fictional Gray's Lighting brand:

1. **Set a vision of what you want**
   - Gray's wants to bring magic to every theater, one director at a time. They want to make Gray's a $100 million brand by 2030. Like many new brands, Gray's needs to drive trial while closing gaps

2. Invest resources in solidifying your capabilities
- At the rapid growth stage, Gray's needs to build a strong bond with customers and address the distribution gaps while battling any mainstream brands who could enter the stage lighting segment.

3. Focus on an identified opportunity
- Gray's recognizes the opportunity to shift Gray's from a product-led launch into an idea-led brand to own "magic." The brand's content marketing strategy will include key influencers to speak on Gray's behalf to boost customer interest and build brand trust.

4. Leverage a breakthrough market impact
- As Gray's manages to get production houses to book a demo program, we know the demo trial will translate into purchases and successful theater implementation.

5. Achieve a performance result that pays back
- Gray's will gain market share that boosts volume, helping to lower the overall cost of its lighting products.

Our Strategic ThinkBox defines a brand's key issues

To me, the key issues and strategies are the guts of your strategic plan. Take all your thinking on your brand and start organizing the best strategic questions and answers.

The key issues answer, **"Why are we here?"** Take the summary findings of the deep-dive analysis. Draw out the significant issues that are in the way of achieving your stated brand vision.

Our methodology for finding key issues is to return to our **Strategic ThinkBox** with my four strategic questions model from the strategic thinking chapters. Our Strategic ThinkBox ensures you take a 360-degree view of your brand—your brand's strength, customer bond, competitive dynamic, and business situation.

What is your competitive situation?

What is your business situation?

How tight is the bond with customers?

What is your brand's core strength?

With each of these four questions, you need to decide on your main answer and see if your investments, communications, and execution deliver on that answer. Once we have the issues expressed as questions, we can provide our strategic solutions for Gray's Lighting.

1. What is your brand's core strength? (More details found in Chapter 3)

- Is your core strength the product, story, experience, or price? Are your capabilities lined up to deliver?
- Is your investment lined up to building capabilities that support your core strength? What has paid off or not?
- Are you communicating your core strength? Are you using your strength to move customers?
- What is working well? What needs fixing?

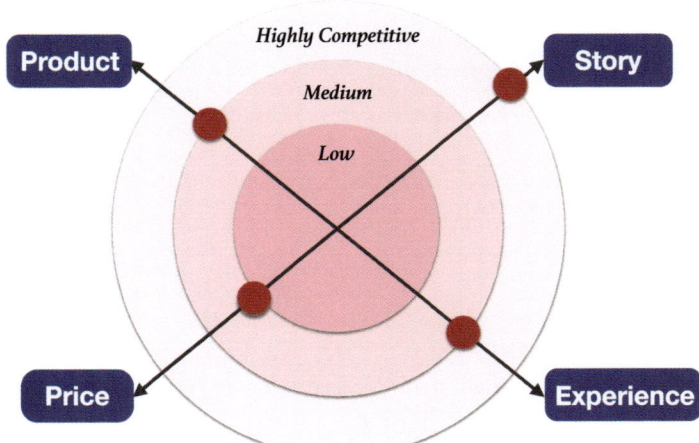

Gray's Lighting has taken a dormant HEX technology that had been used in automotive lighting, but failed due to the high price point, and has created a new stage lighting product. The product lights up the faces of stage actors in a way that captures their moods. To convey this difference, Gray's core strength is product but they use a "touch of magic" brand idea to breakthrough the clutter and tempt directors to request a 'see it for yourself' demo. The demo has been one of the deal-closers with directors.

2. How tight is the bond with customers? (Details found in Chapter 4)

- Where are you on our brand love curve; is your brand unknown, indifferent, liked, loved, or beloved?
- Who is the customer target, knowledge, insights, and how do they match with the brand's main benefits?
- Which capabilities do you need to invest in to tighten the brand's bond with customers?
- What does the funnel indicate? Penetration, frequency?

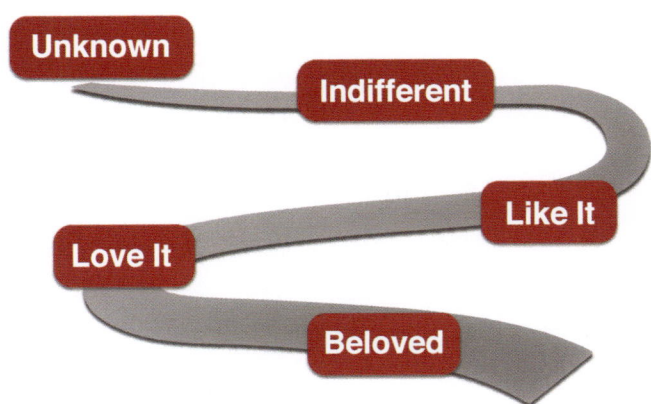

For Gray's Lighting, some of the more renowned broadway directors love this new product. They could become potential influencers with their peers. At the same time, they need them to push for our product, as they are a significant premium. The production houses set a budget for each show, and any added cost can cause tension with the owner who wants happy directors, and their buyer who watches every penny.

3. What is your competitive situation? (Details found in Chapter 5)

- Is your brand the power player, challenger, disruptor, or craft brand?
- What is the unique positioning space you win with?
- What is the intensity of competition? Are you attacking or defending?
- Winning battles: investment, messages, innovation, channels, location?

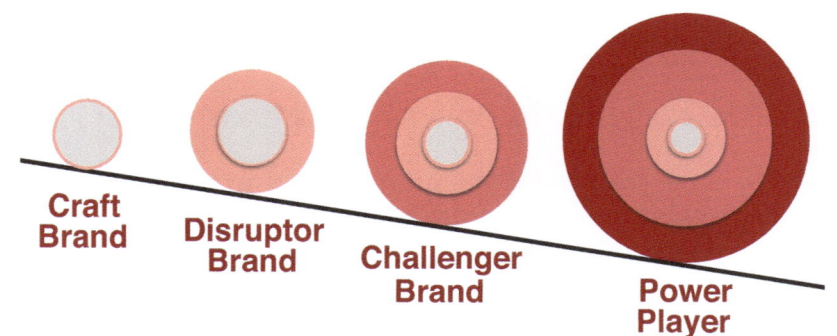

Gray's Lighting is a startup who has disrupted the theater lighting business. The big players (GE, Philips, Osram) will follow. They have a head-start, and since theater lighting is a small niche for the bigger players, it could be 2-3 years before they have a solution. With a tighter focus on one segment, they can invest in specific claims to defend against any new entrant.

4. What is your business situation? (Details found in Chapter 6)

- Continue momentum, turnaround results, realignment, or startup?
- Wealth: share, sales, profits? Health: reputation, distribution, pipeline?
- Significant gaps that need fixing: message, distribution, innovation?
- Current drivers and inhibitors? Future opportunities and threats?

Gray's is 2 years in, and just coming off the startup situation. Even after everything was set up (team, culture, positioning) Gray's need to look for new peripheral distribution channels, before the mainstream brands do. The options include off-Broadway, concert production or conferences. The challenge is which ones to go after next.

Transforming the thinking into key issue questions

Looking at the example on the next page, I have used the four Strategic ThinkBox questions to trigger my thinking, and then I developed four specific questions that fit the unique situation facing Gray's Lighting.

You may end up with multiple key issue questions matched up to one of the ThinkBox questions, or you may end up with redundant questions. With various ways to brainstorm and find the issues I recommend for the annual brand plan, focus on the **top three key issues**, which set up the **top three strategies**. A long-range strategic roadmap can typically handle five key issues and then five strategies.

Key issues for Gray's Lighting

360° ThinkBox Questions

1. What is the core strength your brand can win on?
2. How tightly connected is your customer to your brand?
3. What is your current competitive position?
4. What is the current business situation your brand faces?

Gray's Stage Lighting Key Issues

1. How do we shift Gray's from a product-led launch into an idea-led brand to own "magic"?
2. How do we use our loyal advocates to establish Gray's in the production house buyer's mind?
3. How do we defend against the entry of mainstream lighting brands into this stage lighting segment?
4. How do keep the early momentum going by filling the identified gaps in distribution?

Make sure you find the right level of the key issue

Keep asking the key question until it gets better. Tweak. Challenge. Debate. Refine. Perfect.

- **Too low:** How do we get customers to use more coupons? In this example, the key issue is too specific and too tactical to set up a strategic solution.

- **Too high:** How do we become the #1 brand? This key issue is too general and too broad of a question to lead to a pinpointed, strategic solution. It is more suited to a question on brand vision.

- **Just right:** How do we drive usage among loyal customers? With this example, the key issue does an excellent job of addressing an obstacle in the way of the vision, yet it is big enough to leave you sufficient room to explore various strategic solutions.

Once you nail the key issue question, move on to the planning stage, and build a brand strategy statement that answers the question. The better the key issue question, the better the strategy.

How to turn your thinking into strategic statements

Let's now look at how to turn your smart strategic thinking into writing a strategic statement that can provide specific marching orders to everyone who works on the brand.

The process covers all five elements of smart strategic thinking. You can see the brand vision, and key issue statement covers the first strategic element. However, you need the strategic objective statement to cover off the remaining four remaining strategic elements, including the program investment, focused opportunity, market impact, and the performance result.

Brand Vision
To be the lighting brand Broadway directors see as essential to their show. Make Gray's a $100 Million brand by 2030

➡

Key Issue
How do we shift Gray's from a product-led launch to an idea-led brand using "magic"?

➡

Strategy Statement
Content marketing to competitive customers, using key influencer directors to trigger theater production houses to book a demo program which will help close the deal.

Here's how that strategic objective statement breaks down:

a. **Program investment:** The statement calls out the investment in a strategic program, with crystal clear marching orders to the team, leaving no room for doubt, confusion or hesitation. In this example, the strategic program is to invest in "content marketing to competitive customers."

b. **Focused opportunity:** This is a breakthrough point where the brand will exert pressure to create a market impact. In this example, the focused opportunity is to "using key influencer directors."

c. **Market impact:** You must have a specific desired market impact to outline the market stakeholder you will attempt to move, whether it is customers, sales channels, competitors or influencers. In this example, the desired impact is to "trigger theater production houses to book a demo program."

d. **Performance result:** Finally, you need a specific performance result, linking the market impact to a specific result on the brand, either making the brand more powerful or more profitable. In this example, Gray's wants to "close the deal."

This unique strategic model will force you to pick answers to build a strategy statement with marching orders for those who follow your plan. As you build your brand plan, I recommend you use these four elements of smart strategic objective statements to structure your thinking.

Writing your brand strategy statements

Here is a cheat sheet to help you write your brand strategy statements.

a. Start by investing in capabilities, whether that delivering the brand promise, brand story, purchase moment, product innovation, or customer experience. And who will you target?

b. Choose your focused opportunity, whether you want to take advantage of the changing customer needs, competitive battles, influencers, new technology or new channels to sell through.

c. For the market impact, will you attract, inform, close, service or delight customers. What do you want them to do?

d. For performance result, choose one of four ways to get more powerful or wealthier, by pushing penetration, frequency, pricing or enter new markets.

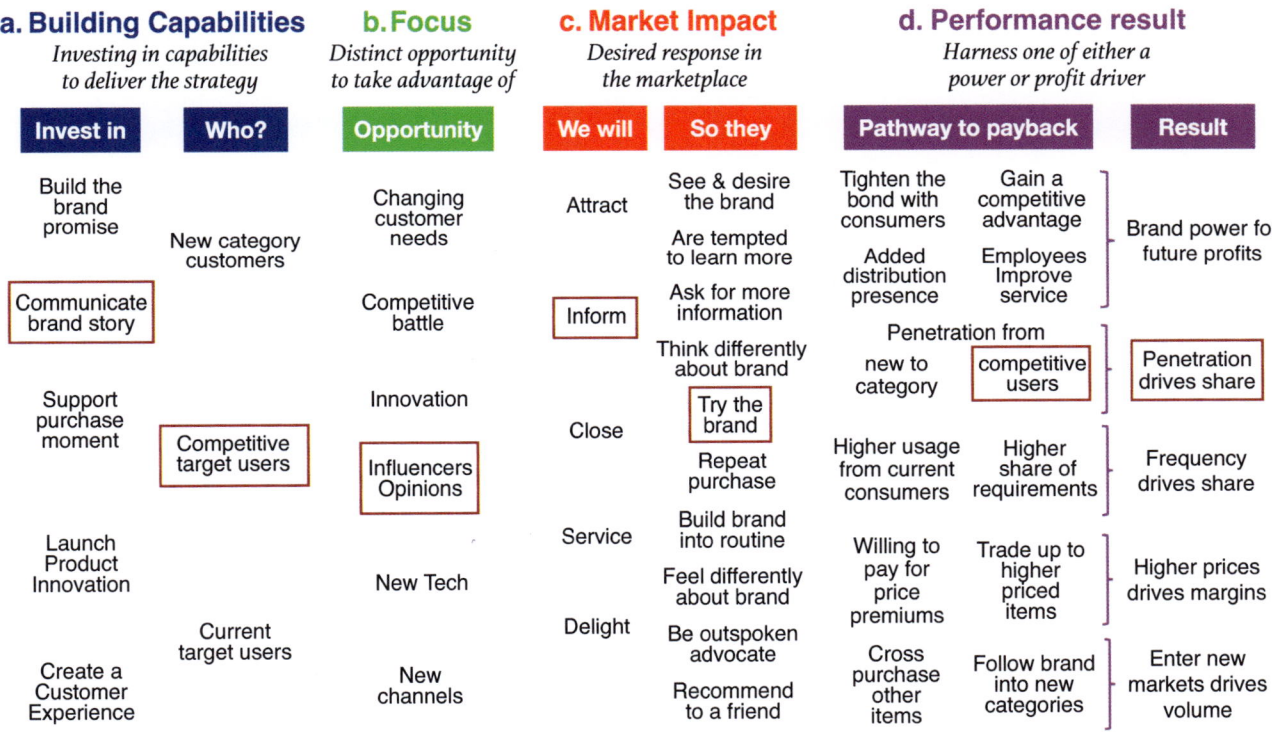

Structuring your brand strategy statement

Content marketing to competitive customers **(a)**, using key influencer directors **(b)** to trigger theater production houses to book a demo program with Gray's Lighting **(c)** which will help close the deal **(d)**.

Work exercise #1

Using these five elements of strategy, using the brands you are working on, map out one of their strategies and identify what is the:

1. Vision

2. Strategic program

3. Focused opportunity

4. Market impact

5. Performance result

Work exercise #2

Using the brand that you are working on, and see how you would answer the four questions from our Strategic ThinkBox.

1. What is the core strength your brand can win on? (Product, story, experience or price) Based on activity you see, are they living their strength?

2. How tightly connected is your customer to your brand? (Unknown, Indifferent, liked, loved or beloved) What is one thing you would do to move customers to the next stage?

3. What is your current competitive position? (Power player, challenger, disruptor, craft brand)

4. What is the current business situation your brand faces? (Keep momentum, turnaround, realignment or startup) How does the situation impact what you can do next?

Chapter Three
How to build your brand around your core strength

To be loved, brands must know who they are and then stand with pride, conviction, and confidence.

Too many brands try to have a few core strengths cluttering up their brand positioning, so they end up with no real perceived strength that stands out. Our core strength model forces you to select one of four possible options for you to win with: product, brand story, experience, or price.

For many marketers, their immediate response is an urge to pick two or three core strengths, believing the myth that having many strengths makes your brand stronger. Instead, committing to a clear focus will make your brand stronger.

Here is the game I have created to help choose your brand's core strength.

Brand's core strength

Product

Story

Experience

Price

- Using the diagram on the next page, start with four chips. You must place one chip where you believe you have the highest competitive advantage to win.

- Then put two chips at the medium level that backs up and supports the core strength.

- Finally, the game forces one chip to be at the low end, which is almost a throwaway weakness that will not be part of the strategy.

It is a great game to try with your team, as it sets up a great debate among your team members.

The Beloved Brands Core Strength Model

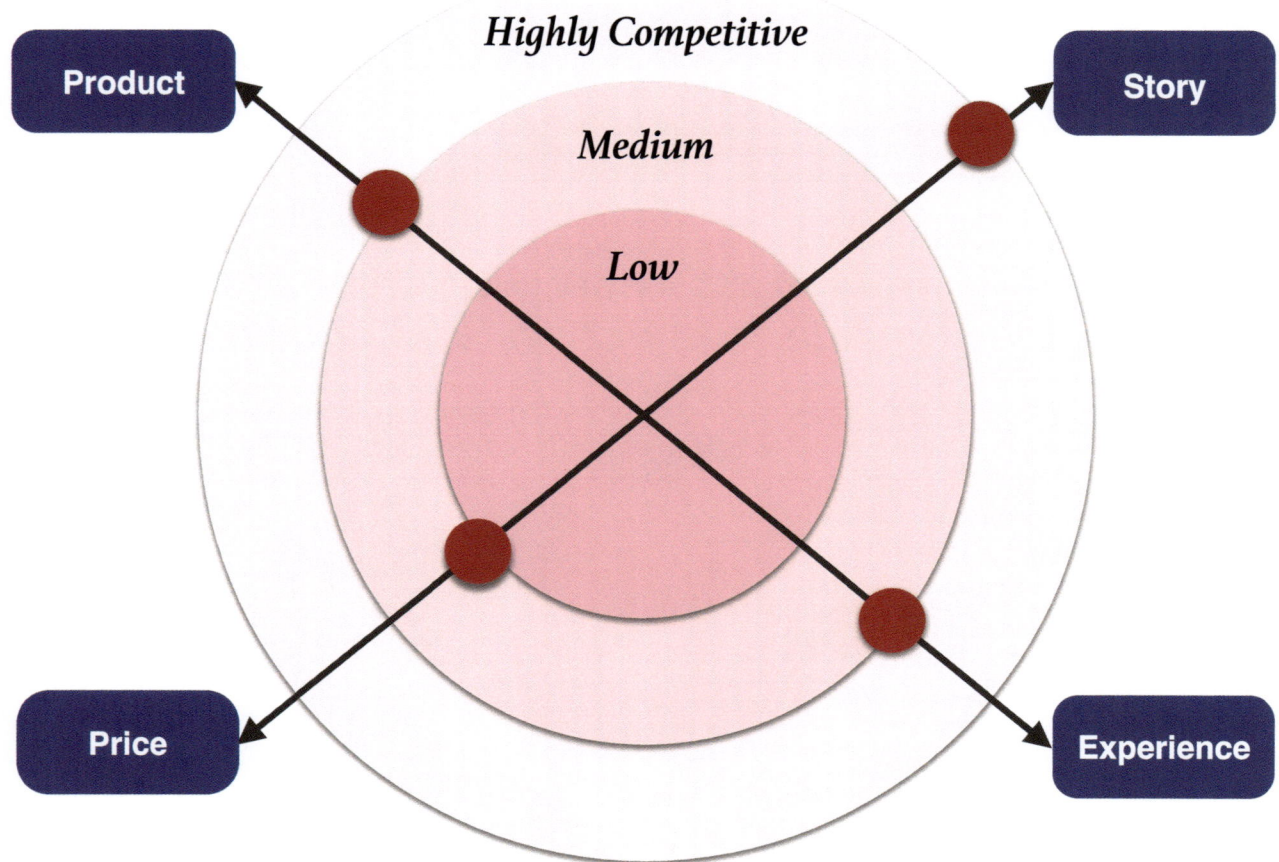

- **Product-led** brands should invest in R&D while communicating the customer benefits, features, and claims for what makes the brand better.
- **Story-led** brands need to invest in marketing communications, with the story, idea, or brand purpose communicating what makes the brand different.
- **Experience-led** brands have to invest in creating a culture with strong operations. Build your brand communications around the idea that, "Our great people make the difference in creating amazing experiences."
- **Price-led** brands must invest in operational efficiency with the brand communications explaining how "We are smarter and able to deliver the same quality at a lower cost."

Product-led brands

When you are a **product-led brand**, you must own the "better" position in your category. Invest heavily in continuous innovation to maintain category leadership in new technology, superiority claims, and the latest product formats. These brands must aggressively defend against any challengers. Leverage product-focused mass communication, directly highlighting the product's superiority and comparing product features to those of other competitors.

Within your mass communications, you can layer in "how the product is built" into the brand story to reinforce your brand's product point of difference.

Use online product reviews sites, bloggers, and expert influencers to reach the trend influencer customers on all new product innovations.

When selling to customers, use a rational approach, highlighting technical features, new claims, and the logic behind the purchase decision.

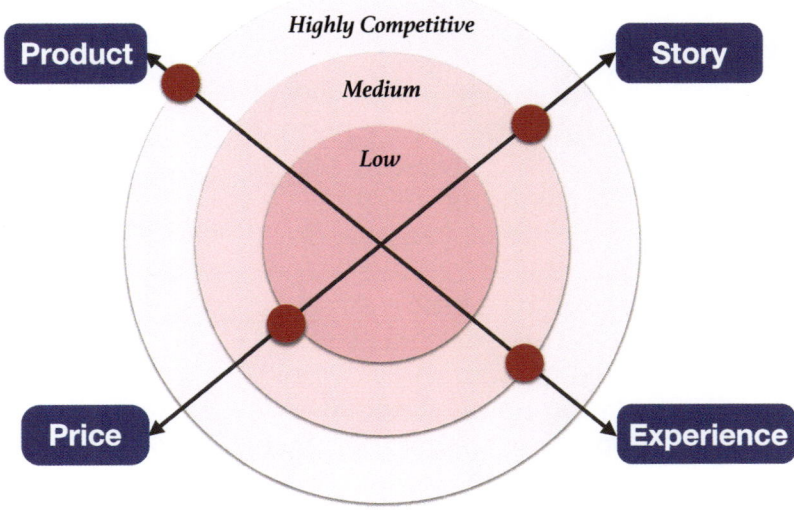

One issue to watch out for among product-led brands is the struggle to build and drive an emotional connection with customers.

As the brand matures, it must find ways to layer a brand idea on top of the product to inspire the customer to connect on a deeper level. Fantastic product-led brands include Intel, Samsung, Microsoft, Google, SAP and Gore-Tex as an ingredient that takes their customer's product and makes it suitable for the coldest wettest days.

The product manages to create a high degree of consumer loyalty, even if the brand struggles to project an emotional message.

Intel is an excellent example of a product-led brand that has done an incredible job of building emotion into their brand. With such a commitment to high speed and high-quality computer chips, Intel has made it nearly impossible for computer manufacturers to use anyone else.

"When you see Intel, you can be confident your computer will move faster." On top of that, Intel began layering in the latest chips with the i3, i5, and i7 chips, allowing their customers to charge higher prices for each chip evolution.

As we explore emotional benefits in later chapters, Intel plays with the customer benefits that focus on feeling in control, knowledge, and optimism.

Story-led brands

When the **brand story** is your brand's key strength, focus the strategy on ways to be different. Invest in gathering B2B customer insights, equal to how a product-led brand spends on patents. To tell the brand story, use emotional brand communication that connects the most motivated customers with the brand idea, lining up everything—brand story, product, and experience—under that brand idea.

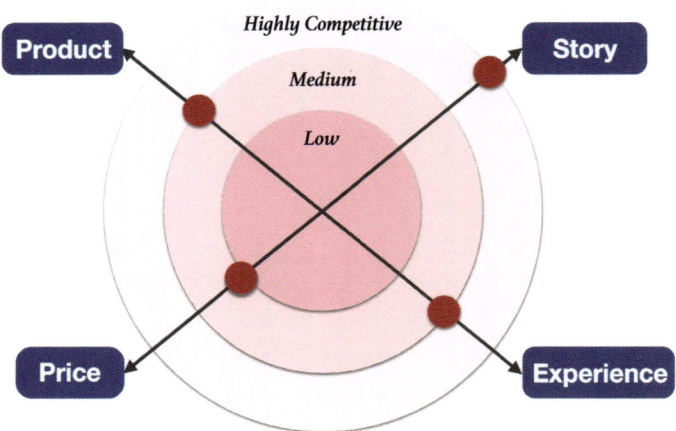

Story-led brands should cultivate a community of core "brand lovers" who can then talk about the brand story and influence others within their network. These brands should use a soft sell approach and never bring the price to the forefront, as it can take away from the idea.

Some of the more successful story-led brands include Kickstarter, United Way, Apple, LinkedIn, Shopify, Snap-On tools, John Deere, or Staples – which are also some of the most beloved B2B brands of our generation.

LinkedIn has become the modern networking gathering place where business is conducted. It may have started as a job site to post your resume, but has evolved into a place to share, explore, and engage with some of the best business opinion-driven content.

Like many social platforms, LinkedIn has continuously bounced around on how it looks or works. Early on, LinkedIn resembled a mere resume dump with personal updates on where you were flying. Then, it became all about Groups, resembling discussion boards that professionals use, with key influencers kickstarting the debate by linking opinion-based content from their website.

LinkedIn then got into a self-publishing tool, with individuals publishing 1,000-word opinion-driven pieces. Lately, LinkedIn has landed for now on using 300 character status updates that can accompany a website link, photo, video link or video file, or PDF file.

LinkedIn might wish it was an experience, but it's a collection of story-led brands linked to reaching your full potential. It helps B2B brands establish a leading voice for their business within their industry or among followers. LinkedIn serves people looking for a job and those hiring; it serves key influencers who provide free content to attract customers, and it helps those who use the content to improve themselves.

Customer experience-led brands

When the **customer experience** is your brand's lead strength, the strategy and organization should focus on creating a link between your culture and your brand.

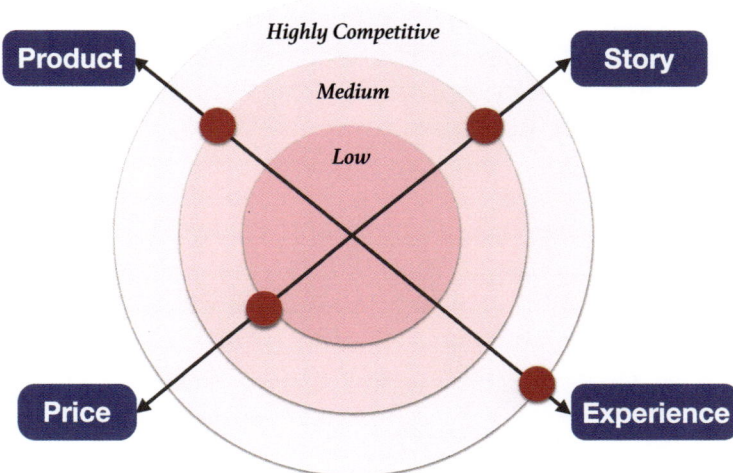

Your people are your product. Use your brand purpose ("Why you do what you do") and brand values to inspire and guide the service behaviors of your people. Then build a culture and organization with the right people who can deliver incredible experiences.

Experience-led brands need to be patient with how fast they build the brand, as the quick mass media approach might not be as fast or efficient as the product-led or idea-led brands. The most effective communication tools for customer experience-led brands include word of mouth, earned media, social media, online customer reviews, the voice of key influencers, and customer testimonials. These brands can make a mistake if they put too much emphasis on price, which can diminish the perceived customer experience.

Some of the best customer experience-led brands include National Car Rental, Emirates, Las Vegas for conventions and conferences, FedEx, Amazon, Salesforce, HubSpot, and American Express.

For business travel, **Las Vegas** puts an entirely different look for your conference or convention. Not only has Las Vegas become one of the top meeting cities, but it has also become a top destination for event planners from around the world. Vegas has three of the ten largest convention centers in the U.S., and everything lines up nicely for event attendees with 140,000 hotel rooms and an accessible airport. Vegas provides convenient access to event venues, iconic attractions, entertainment, nightlife, restaurants, shopping, and two major sports teams with its NHL and NFL teams.

Price-led brands

When **price** is your brand's lead strength, you must focus on ways to drive efficiency to ensure the lowest possible cost structure. These brands should invest in the fundamentals around production and sourcing to maintain a low-cost competitive advantage. They must use the brand's power to win negotiations.

These businesses have to drive cash flow with fast moving items that deliver high turns and high volume to compensate for their lower prices.

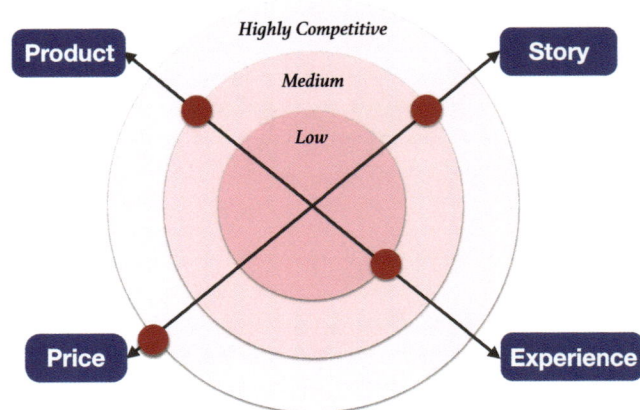

The winning price-led brands need to own the low price positioning by fiercely attacking any potential competitive challenges.

Regarding marketing communications, the smartest message explains your secret for how you are smarter than your competitors, and you can offer lower prices. Also, use call-to-action marketing to keep high sales turns.

There is a big difference between low-price and cheap. Price-driven customers are not always willing to sacrifice product quality. They expect lower prices but still want robust performance standards.

However, these price-driven customers have shown they are willing to accept a lower-quality customer experience. Since price is such a rational reason to buy, customers do struggle to love the price-led brands.

For price-led brands in the B2B space, you see quite a few DIY (do-it-yourself) offerings, whether involves doing your own accounting with **QuickBooks,** doing your own copywriting with **Open AI,** or doing your own artwork with **Canva**.

You can do your own e-commerce payments/transactions through **PayPal**. These companies have created great systems with limited service that helps these brands keep their price down.

Fiverr is a website that allows B2B customers to tap into low-priced independent contractors all over the world. As more workers in low-priced labour countries have signed up as contractors who offer their services, UpWork prices have gone down considerably. Instead of paying $75-100 an hour to an SEO expert in Florida, B2B customers can use UpWork and pay $9-12 an hour to an SEO expert in India or Thailand. This price point suits entrepreneurs just starting out, who are faced with limited funds and want to make sure every penny is spent wisely. Given the low price point and scattered quality risks I would consider UpWork one step above DIY.

Chapter Four
How to build a tight bond with your most cherished customers

"How tightly connected is your customer to your brand?"

I first came up with the idea of a brand love curve when I ran a marketing department with 15 different brands, which exhibited various degrees of success. Honestly, it was hard for me to keep track of where each brand stood. I did not want to apply a one-size-fits-all strategy to brands with dramatically different needs. I could have used some traditional matrix with market share versus category growth rates or stuck with revenue size versus margin rates. Every day on the job, I noticed brands that had created a stronger bond with their customer outperformed brands that lacked such a close connection. I started to refer to the high-performance brands as "beloved" because I could see how emotionally engaged customers were with the brand.

At the other end of the scale, I referred to the inferior performance brands as "indifferent" because customers did not care about them. They failed to stand for anything in the customer's mind; they were not better, different, or cheaper. I could see how these brands were unable to create any connection with their customers – and they faced massive declines.

Everything seemed to work better and easier for beloved brands. New product launches were more impactful because the brand's loyal customers were automatically curious about what was new. Retailers gave these the beloved brands preferential treatment because they knew their customers wanted them.

> **Brands with stronger bonds with their customers outperform rivals**

With a beloved brand, our channel partners knew their customers would switch channels before they switch brands. Everyone in my organization, from the president to the lab technician, cared more about these beloved brands. No one seemed to care about the indifferent brands. Internal brainstorm sessions produced inspiring ideas on beloved brands, yet people would not even show up for brainstorms on indifferent brands.

Our agencies bragged about the work they did on beloved brands. Even my people were more excited to work on these beloved brands, believing a move to the beloved brand was a big career move while being moved to an indifferent brand was a career death sentence.

These beloved brands saw a stronger return on marketing investment, with a better response to marketing programs, higher growth rates, and higher margins. The overall profitability fuelled further investment into beloved brands.

Why does brand love matter?

Brand building starts with cultivating close relationships with customers. The best brands of today follow a very similar path to the rituals of a personal courtship.

Through the eyes of customers, brands start as complete strangers, randomly purchased a few times without much thought. They become acquaintances and, when the brand successfully delivers on expectations, they move into something similar to a trusted friendship.

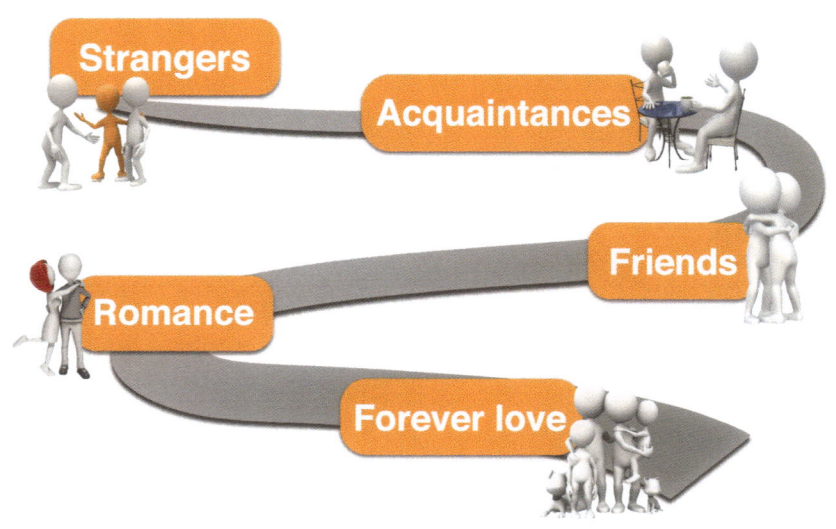

As the customer sees a consistent experience and trust, they begin to open up, and the romance begins. The customer allows their emotions to take over and, without knowing, they start to love the brand. As the brand weaves itself into the best moments of the B2B customer's own successes, the customer becomes an outspoken fan, an advocate, and one of the many brand lovers who cherish their relationship with the brand. As long as the brand delivers on the excitement of the original promise that attracted the customer on their first encounter, the brand moves into a position where the customer sees it as a forever love.

To replicate how brand building matches up with the building of a relationship, I created the brand love curve, which outlines how customers move through five stages: unknown, indifferent, like it, love it, and onto the beloved brand status.

The brand love curve

It takes a strategic mind to figure out brand love. For new brands, they were completely **"unknown"** to customers. Unless there were genuinely compelling messages, customers would walk past without even looking. To achieve some success, the priority for these brands is to get noticed within the clutter of the market.

At the **"indifferent"** stage, customers feel O.K. about the brand, similar to how they usually feel about commodities, like fruit and vegetables. These brands satisfy the customer's basic needs. B2B customers will only buy the brand when offered a special price, but switch back to their other brand choice when it is not. Make your brand more than just a commodity. Brands need to be better, different, or cheaper. Otherwise, they will not be around for long, and you waste your investment.

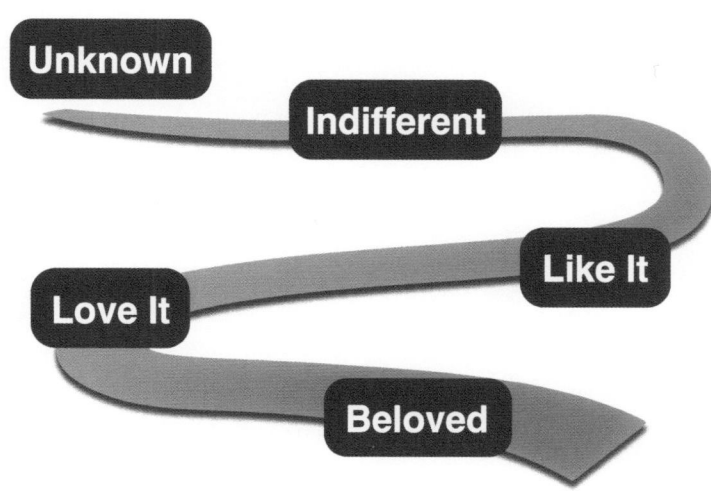

Brands that reach the **"like it"** stage experience the first sign of business success. Their customers see the brand as a logical, functional, and smart choice. However, the lack of any emotional connection leaves the purchase up to chance. Customers will still switch brands randomly. Brands at the like it stage stress the product performance so much they forget to trigger any emotions.

Brands at the **"love it"** stage start to see more emotionally engaged B2B customers. The rule of love you must follow: Customers must love the brand before you can tell customers you love them. Customers see the brand as a favorite choice, usually connected to a favorite part of their day. They are loyal and build the brand into a routine. These brands must also find a way to demonstrate their love toward customers and continue to tighten the bond with their most loyal brand lovers.

The **"beloved brand"** stage is where the brand becomes iconic, with a core base of brand lovers who cherish and defend the brand. These customers see the brand as a personal choice, a badge they proudly hold in their hand or wear on their feet. At the beloved stage, the brands must create magical experiences that inspire brand lovers to share with their friends.

How strategies match up to the brand love curve

Five major brand strategies help move your brand from one stage of the brand love curve to the next.

- For **unknown** brands, the strategic focus should be to stand out so customers will notice the brand within a cluttered customer brand world they live in, where they see an estimated 5,000 brand messages per day.
- For **indifferent** brands, the strategy must establish the brand in the customer's mind, so they can see a clear point of difference over other potential brand choices in their consideration set.
- At the **like it** stage, the strategy is to separate the brand from the pack, creating satisfied experiences that build a trusted following over time. Only after they trust the brand, customers begin to open up emotionally.
- At the **love it** stage, the strategic focus shifts tightening the bond with the most loyal brand fans.

- At the **beloved** stage, the strategic challenge is to create outspoken brand loyal fans, who are willing to serve as brand advocates willing to provide testimonials for a brand, that their peers will see.

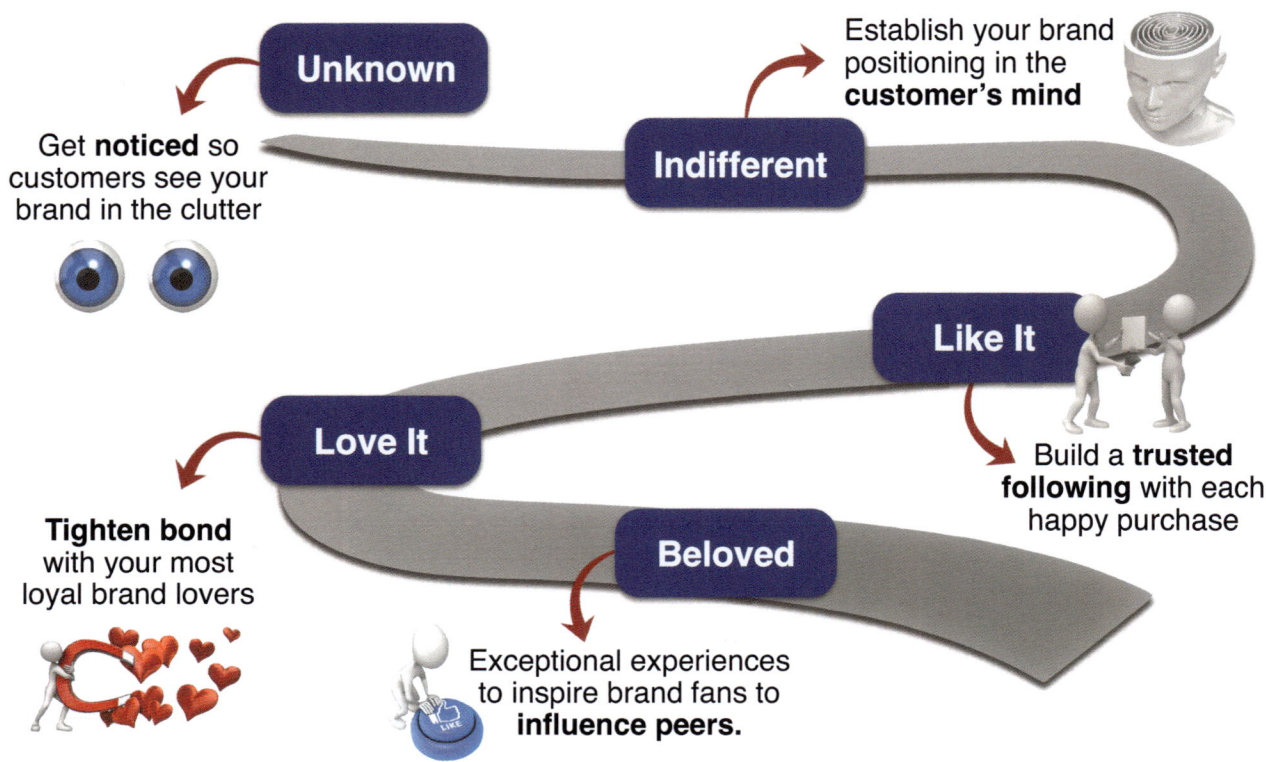

20 activities matching up to the brand love curve

The **brand love curve** guides strategic and tactical decisions that go into the writing of your annual brand plan. Here are **20 potential brand activities** that match up to where your brand sits on the curve and how to move your brand to the next stage.

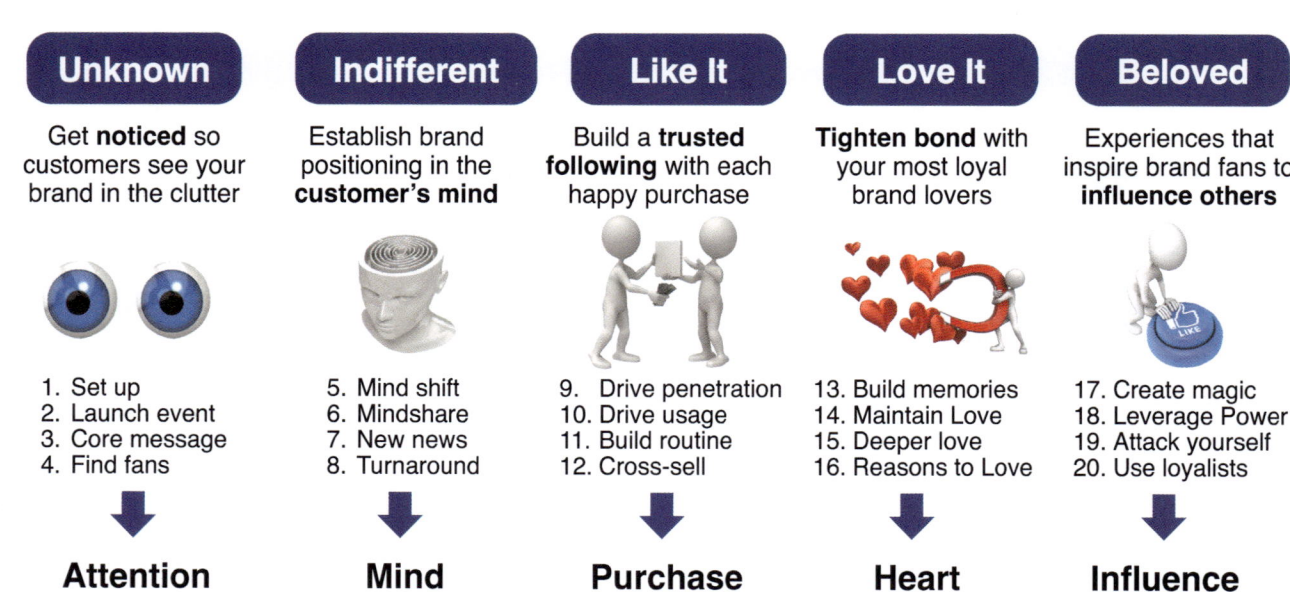

The game plan for unknown brands

All brands start at the unknown stage. Many new brands struggle to break through to reach customers or build the distribution due to doubting retailers. They face leadership team conflicts, confusion around the value proposition, inconsistent messages to customers, and everyone in the organization seems to move in different directions. The risk is that you will be seen as a product—not yet a brand idea.

Too often, companies at this early stage fixate more on selling with desperation to anyone who wants to buy. Sure, the cash flow helps. However, when the customer sees the brand as a commodity, the product has no real differentiation from competitors. This strategy will make it hard to command a price premium or gain any efficiency. Substantial investment is needed to establish both brand awareness and broad distribution. The unknown brands need to stand out in the crowd.

A three-point game plan for unknown brands:

1. Create a brand idea that expresses your customer benefit and build everything around that idea, both internally and externally
2. Focus your limited resources against a focused target, positioning, strategies, and activities.
3. Passionately express your brand purpose as a rallying point, both internally and externally.

Action plan for unknown brands:

- **Determine a target:** As a startup, you are launching into a space where no one knows you. Start by figuring out which segment of the market would be most motivated by what you have to offer.
- **Establish a framework:** Establish production, brand promise, communications, public relations, customer experience, distribution, and manage the purchase moments.
- **Brand message:** Build out your brand message with a brand idea that can steer everyone who works on the brand, from the name and logo to the brand story, how you present your product and service innovation, managing the purchase moment and driving the overall customer experience.
- **Brand culture** As a B2B brand, you need to get your people ready to serve and ready to deliver your brand. Use your brand purpose to drive a list of values, and lay out the expected leader behaviors that will help your brand win. With a B2B brand, your people will deliver your brand.
- **Find early brand lovers:** Find a small base of early adopters to drive trial among those who are already motivated by what you do. Use their energy to turn them into brand fans who can influence others.

The game plan for indifferent brands

Indifferent brands act like commodities. They are usually too product-focused and not yet able to find a way to separate the brand from competitors. These brands suffer from very skinny brand funnels with low awareness at the top of the brand funnel, with low purchase rates, low repeat scores, and low brand loyalty scores.

These brands struggle to gain new users or drive frequency. Without a brand idea or unique positioning, the marketing communications suffer from poor tracking scores, and the innovation shows little payback. Lower payback makes it hard to justify marketing investment in marketing communications and innovation.

Indifferent brands rely on price promotions to drive volume, resulting in a margin squeeze. They struggle to achieve the economies of scale needed to drive down the variable cost of goods. They have no power with retailers, so they are unable to get their fair share of shelf space, display, or price promotions. Private label brands threaten their sales levels. The indifferent brands need to establish the brand positioning and, in turn, the reputation in a customer's mind.

A three-point game plan for indifferent brands:

1. Focus your brand's limited resources on proving your brand has a point of difference in the customer's mind.
2. Create a brand idea to establish your brand's uniqueness to stand out in the cluttered market.
3. Put more passion, emotion, and risk into your work.

Action plan for indifferent brands:

- **Mind shift:** Drive a new brand positioning or reinforce current positioning to change your reputation.
- **Mindshare:** Draw more attention than competitors by being better or different.
- **New news:** Launch breakthrough innovation to enter the customer's mind.
- **Turnaround:** Focus energy on gaps or leaks in your brand's execution. Use the fix to shift minds.

The game plan for "like it" brands

Brands at the like it stage have established a degree of success in the market, and they have created a rational brand positioning with customers. However, they lack the emotional connection to build a bond with customers. They make gains during heavy marketing support periods but fall back down during the non-support periods. These brands appear content to hold onto their share and grow at the rate of the category.

These brands have awareness but they lose out to competitors as the customer moves to the purchase stage. As a result, they usually require a higher promotional trade spend to close the sale, which cuts into profit margins.

A vital customer tracking score to watch is "made the brand seem different," which will help separate your brand from the pack. The brand needs to begin to layer in the emotional benefits and focus on creating a stronger following with each happy purchase.

A three-point game plan for brands at the like it stage:

1. Focus resources to build a more significant following with happy purchases.
2. Leverage the brand idea to start making an emotional connection to build a following.
3. Increase customer engagement by adding more passion to your brand execution.

Action plan for brands at the like it stage:

- **Drive penetration:** Persuade new customers to try the brand.
- **Drive usage:** Get happy customers to use more or use it differently.
- **Build routine:** Get happy customers to build a routine around the brand.
- **Cross-sell:** Get happy customers to use your brand's other products or services.

The game plan for "love it" brands

Brands at the love it stage start to see a higher emotional connection with a base of brand fans. These brands also start to gain a stronger usage frequency, as the brand becomes a more significant part of the customer's life routines. With strong customer tracking results, the brand can leverage more efficient marketing spend. You will notice loyal customers are highly responsive to marketing communications and innovation. This thinking makes the marketing spend much more efficient, opening up a pathway to higher profits.

These brands should be able to leverage their power with retailers and influencers. Even in a competitive market, these brands should be able to gain share and widen their leadership stance. With high net promoter scores, they should be able to leverage word-of-mouth or social media recommendations, and positive online brand reviews (like Yelp or Trip Advisor) to influence new users. Brands at the love it stage must look for unique ways to reward customers and further tighten their bond with their most loyal brand lovers.

A three-point game plan for brands at the love it stage:

1. Tug at the heartstrings to help build a community of brand fans.
2. Shift to the creation of customer experiences that turn purchases into routines and rituals.
3. Turn the love for your work into a bit of magic for the customer.

Action plan for brands at the love it stage:

- **Build memories:** Create customer experiences that link the brand with life moments.
- **Maintain love:** Reinforce the brand strengths with your core base of brand fans.
- **Deeper love:** Match the passion of your customers to drive consolidation and get these customers to use your brand across a broader range of uses.
- **Reasons to love:** Reinforce brand messages among your most loyal users.

The game plan for beloved brands

Brands at the beloved stage are the iconic leaders in their category. These brands have an extremely healthy and robust brand funnel with likely near-perfect brand awareness (over 95%), high conversion to purchase, strong repeat, and very high loyalty scores. These brands have achieved desirable penetration and purchase frequency scores.

Tracking results show an immediate reaction to new marketing programs with high brand link scores on marketing communications and high trial on innovation. They have a dominant share position at least within a specific segment.

They have the power to take a dominant stance in the marketplace, to squeeze out smaller brands, and to reduce the influence of other competitors.

These brands have strong net promoter scores and have cultivated a community of outspoken brand fans. They can use their power with retailers to gain preferential shelf space and drive traffic. The company should manage the brand as an asset. These brands should work to create magical experiences that will inspire brand fans to talk about them and influence others.

A three-point game plan for brands at the beloved stage:

1. Focus on maintaining the love the brand has created with core brand fans.
2. Consistently challenge and perfect the customer experience.
3. Broaden the offering and selectively broaden your audience. Be careful.

Action plan for brands at the beloved stage:

- **Create magic:** Continue to surprise and delight your brand lovers.
- **Leverage power:** Drive growth and profit from your brand's source of power.
- **Attack yourself:** Continue to assess and close leaks to improve before competitors attack.
- **Use loyalists:** Leverage brand lovers to whisper with influence with their network.

Chapter Five
How to win the competitive battle for your customer's heart

You must decide if you will position your brand to be better, different, or cheaper. Otherwise, you will not be around for very long.

A winning brand position matches what customers want with what your brand does best, always better than your competitors. I will outline four types of competitive brand strategy situations: the power player, challenger brand, disruptor brand and the craft brand. You must identify and choose one competitive situation, which best fits where you are today, and where you want to go next.

How to find your space in the market to win

To find the competitive space in which your brand can win, on the next page, I introduce a Venn diagram of competitive situations that we will use throughout this chapter. The Venn diagram will resurface again, in the brand positioning chapter.

You will see three circles. The first circle comprises everything your customer wants or needs. The second circle includes everything your brand does best, including customer benefits, product features, or proven claims. Finally, the third circle lists what your competitor does best.

Your brand's **winning zone (in green)**, is the space that matches up "What customers want" with "What your brand does best." This space provides you a distinct positioning you can own and defend from attack. Your brand must be able to satisfy the customer needs better than any other competitor can.

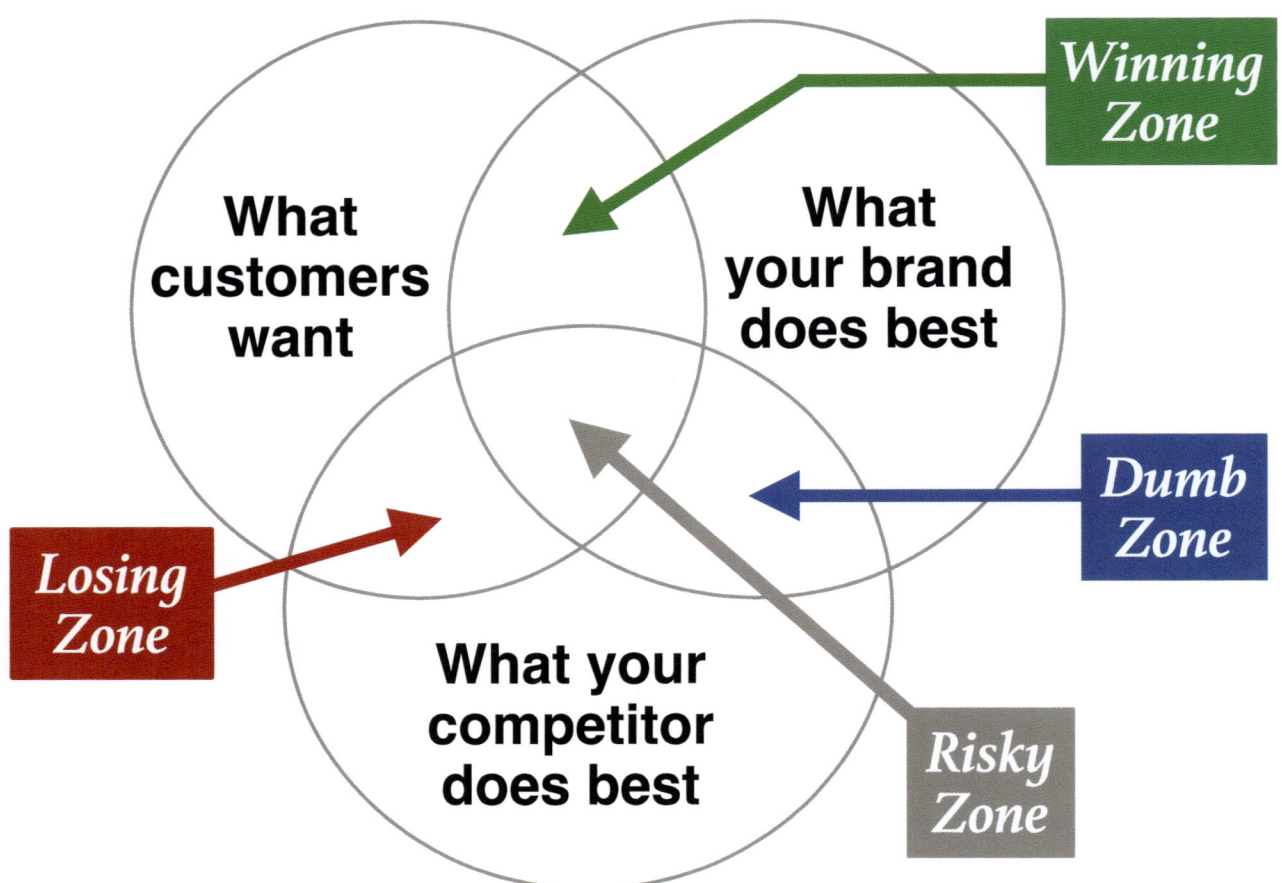

Your brand will not survive by trying to compete in the **losing zone (in red)**, which is the space that matches the customer needs with "What your competitor does best." When you play in this space, your competitor will beat you every time.

As markets mature, competitors copy each other. It has become harder to be better with a definitive product win. Many brands have to play in the **risky zone (in grey)**, which is the space where you and your competitor both meet the customer's needs in a relative tie.

There are four ways you can **win the risky zone**:

- **Dominate:** Use your brand's power in the market to squeeze out smaller, weaker brands.
- **Gain first-mover advantage:** Be the first to capture that space to earn a reputation you can defend.
- **Innovate:** Win with innovation and creativity to make your brand seem unique.
- **Captivate:** Build a deeper emotional connection to make your brand seem different.

Sadly, I always have to mention the **dumb zone (in blue)** where two competitors "battle it out" in the space customers do not care. One competitor says, "We are faster," and the other brand says, "We are just as fast." No one bothered to ask the customer if they care about speed. Both brands are dumb.

Competitive situations

Brands rarely experience competitive isolation. Even in a **blue ocean** situation, the euphoria of being alone quickly turns to a **red ocean**, cluttered with the blood from nasty battling competitors. The moment we think we are alone, a competitor is watching and believing they can do it better than we can. When you ignore your competition, believing only the customer matters, you are on a naive pathway to losing. Competitors can help sharpen our focus and tighten our language on the brand positioning we project to the marketplace.

Regarding **marketing war games**, I will use this Venn diagram to map out four types of competitive brands:

1. Power players
2. Challenger brands
3. Disruptor brands
4. Craft brands.

Power players

Power players lead the way as the share leader or perceived influential leader of the category. These brands command power over all the stakeholders, including customers, competitors, and retail channels.

What customers want
What your brand does best
What your competitor does best
Match 'what you do best' with the needs of consumers
Use your brand power to 'win the tie' and dominate the market

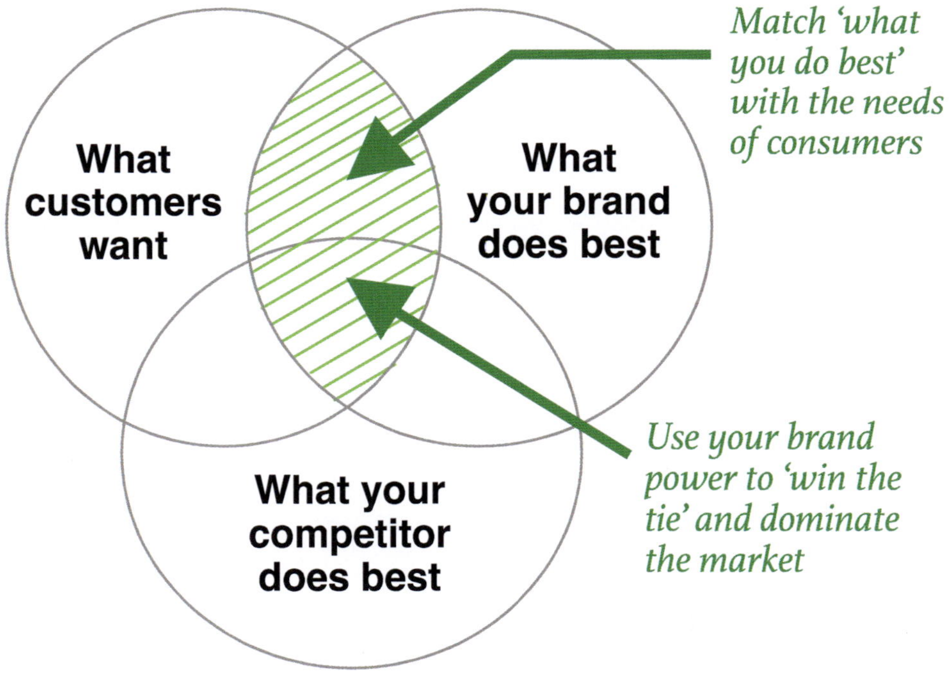

Regarding positioning, the power player brands own what they are best at and leverage their power in the market to help them own the position where there is a tie with another competitor. Owning both zones helps expand the brand's presence and power across a bigger market.

These brands can also use their exceptional financial situation to invest in innovation to catch up, defend, or stay ahead of competitors.

Power player brands must defend their territory by responding to every aggressive competitor's attacks. They even need to attack themselves by vigilantly watching for internal weaknesses to close any potential leaks before a competitor notices. Power player brands can never become complacent, or they will die.

One of the best contemporary power player brands is **Google**, which has managed to dominate the search engine market. The company's extreme focus and smart execution gained market power and squeezed out Microsoft and Yahoo. Focused on providing knowledge for customers, Google has continued to expand its services into a bundle of products with e-mail, maps, apps, docs, cloud technology, and cell phones.

Challenger brands

Challenger brands must change the playing field by amplifying what your brand does best while simultaneously repositioning the power player brand you want to take down.

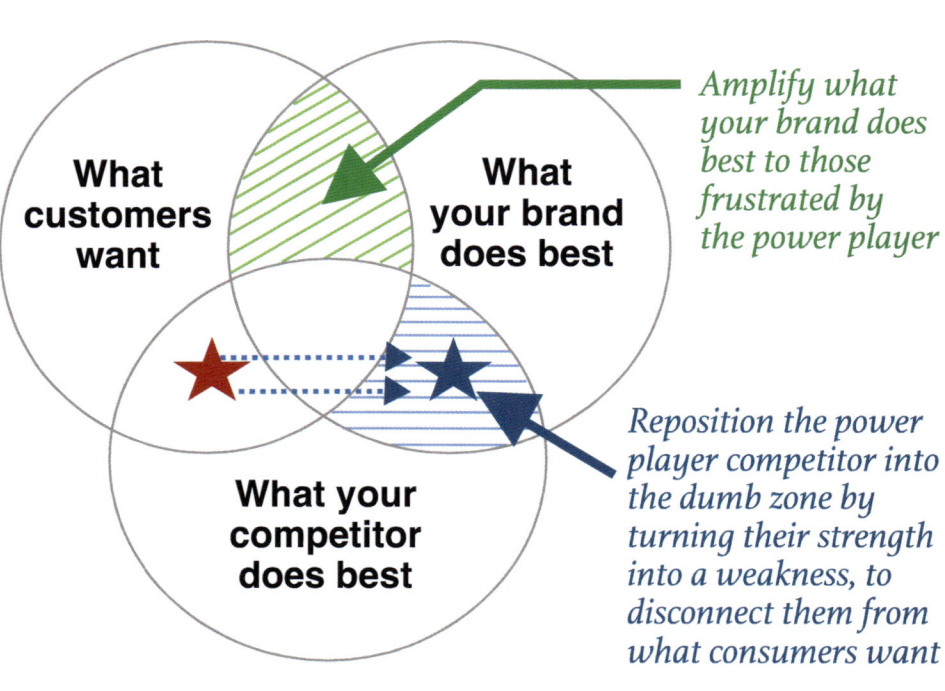

While your first instinct would be to attack the power player's weakness, the smarter move is to reposition one of the power player's well-known strengths into a perceived weakness. This strategy helps move the power player brand outside of what customers want.

When you attack a power player brand, be ready for the leader's potential defensive moves and anticipate a response with full force, as the power player brand has more significant resources than you. Be highly confident that your attack will make a positive impact before you begin to enter into a war.

The worst situation is to start a war, you cannot win, as it will drain your brand's limited resources, only to end up with the same market share after the war.
Since the power player leader tries to be everything to everyone, you can narrow your attack to slice off those customers who are frustrated with the leading brand. Tap into their frustration to help kickstart a migration of customers away from the leader. If you can gain these lost customers, you can quickly change share positions.

One of the best examples of a B2B challenger brand that made significant gains is **Apple,** which took on Blackberry as the B2B smart phone and destroyed them when Blackberry underestimated the needs of the B2B market beyond emails. Apple's iPhone enabled B2B users to browse, take photos, and engage on social media. Apple's MacBook Pro gained entry into the B2B laptop market, using a dramatically thinner laptop that made it easy to transport, and a harder shell making it more durable for travel. Laptop brands have since equalled the playing field with the MacBook Pro.

Disruptor brands

Disruptor brands move into a blue ocean space, alone. They use a new product, distribution channel, target market, or price point. They are so different that they appear to be the only brand that can satisfy the customer's changing needs. When successful, the disruptor brand repositions the major players, making them appear unattached to customers.

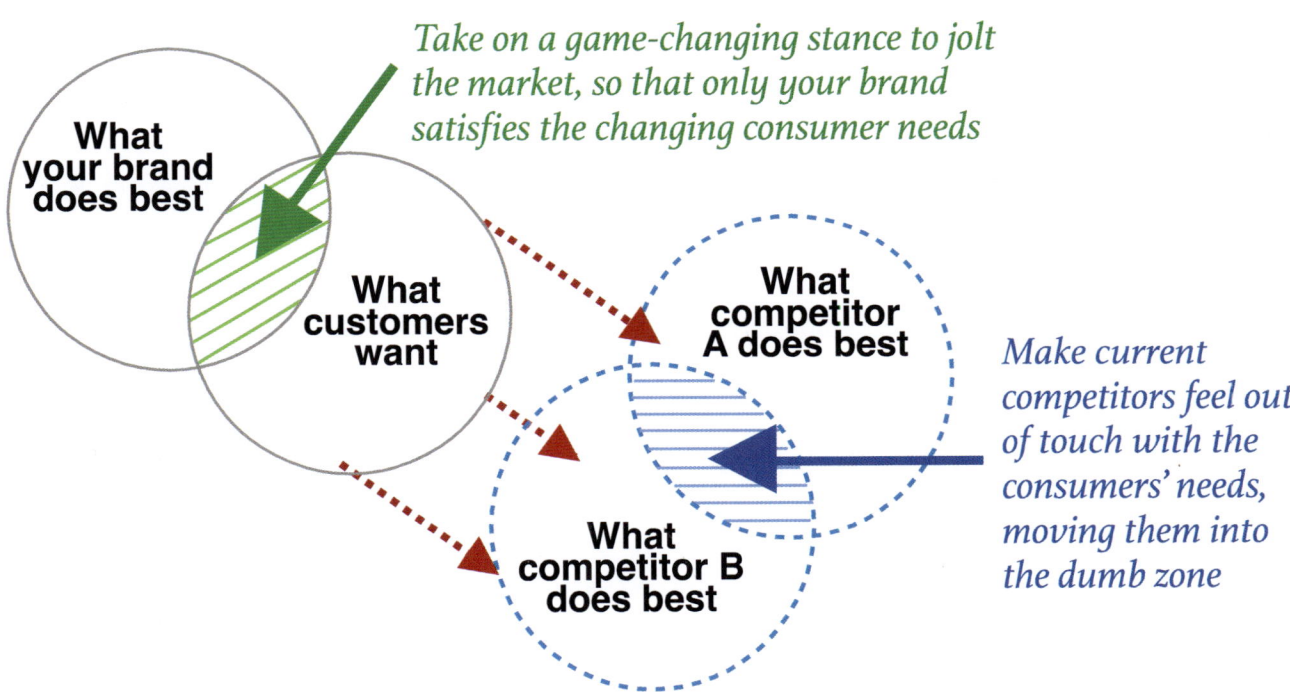

While everyone wants a game-changer, it is a high-risk, high-reward competitive situation. The trick is you have to be "so different" to catch the customers attention and mindshare. Being profoundly different increases the risk you may fail. Also, your success may invite other entrants to follow. At that point, you become the new power player of the new segment. You have to continue attacking the major players while defending against new entrants who attack your brand.

An excellent example of a B2B disruptor brand is what **Zip Recruiter** is disrupting the recruiter market with an artificial intelligence matching of companies and job seekers. The main customer benefit for Zip Recruiter is working faster and simpler, so businesses can stay in control of the hiring process.

With technology increasing at a rapid pace, we are seeing one year there is a disruptor like **Skype**, and then it is quickly replaced by another disruptor brand like **Zoom**, who added significantly more features.

Craft brands

Craft brands must win a small space in the marketplace that offers something unique to a highly engaged target. These brands succeed when they are far enough away from major competitors that the leaders ignore them because craft brands stay hidden away.

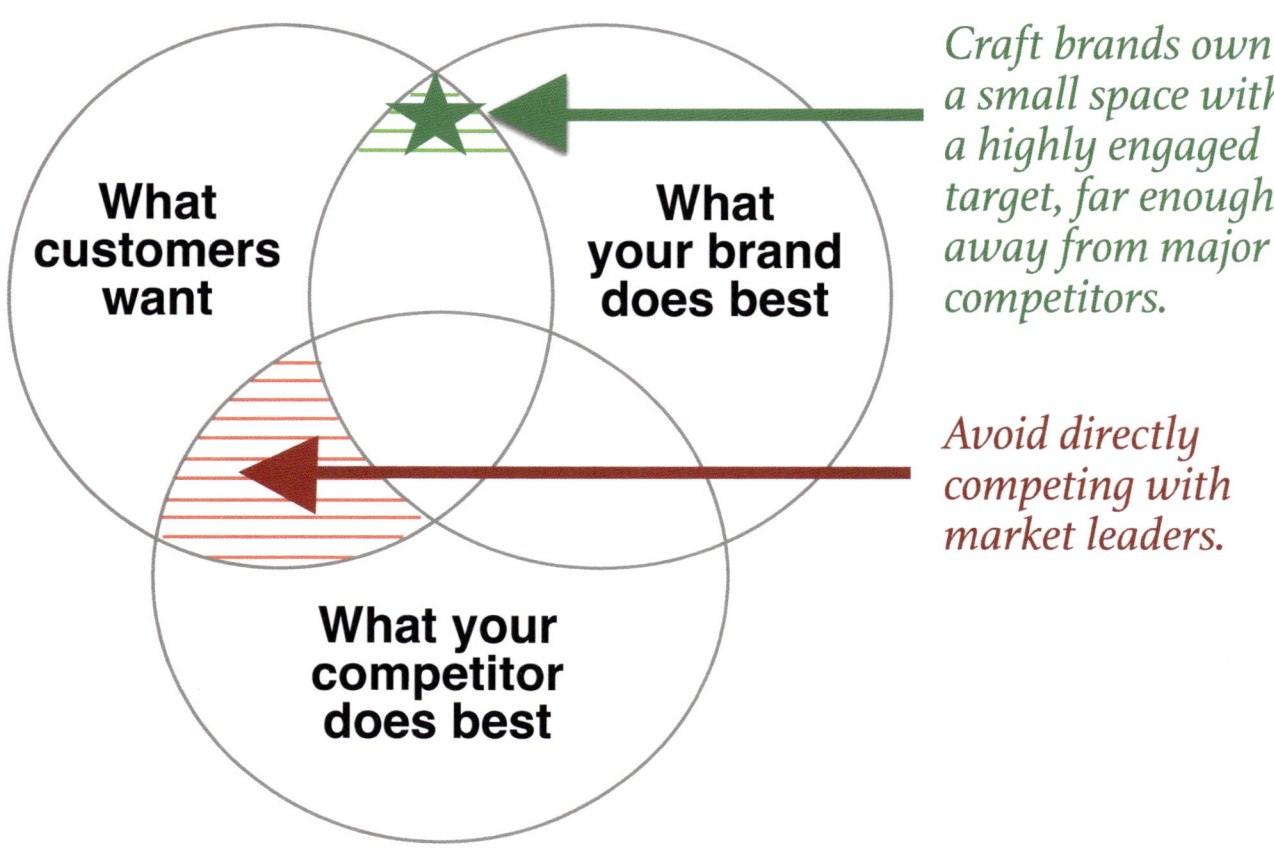

Craft B2B brands build themselves behind a micro-benefit, including freelance consultants, tax experts, content writers, media planners, lawyers, or social media experts. These craft brands take an antagonistic approach to the major players of the category, portraying every other brand in the category as old-school, overly corporate, unethical, or flawed in the overhead they provide.

Many times, these brands take a very aggressive marketing stance, calling out the other brands as expensive, tedious or clumsy. Craft brands believe it is better to be loved by the few than liked or tolerated by many.

As the business world has shifted towards freelancers who can either stay solo or link into a virtual agency model, which is a collection of remote freelancers, so the agency needs no headquarters.

By staying small, they can offer a high-speed, high-touch personalized service without the slowness of the bureaucracy. They can offer much lower overall costs, as customers are paying hourly rates to experts who do the work. These businesses sneak beneath the big agencies and firms, taking days or weeks to complete the projects that take months to complete with the larger companies.

The **freelancer** brand can charge a higher hourly rate, but only one person shows up, instead of a team of five with half the room taking notes. Because the freelancer is an expert with 15-20 years of experience, the quality is better, the timing is faster. The proposition to clients is "You only pay for the talent you need, not a room of note-takers" and "you are not paying the high-priced overhead of a fancy downtown office."

The customer adoption curve

In every category, a customer adoption curve maps out how various types of customers adopt innovation and new products. The curve divides customers into trend influencers, early adopters, early mass, and the late mass audience.

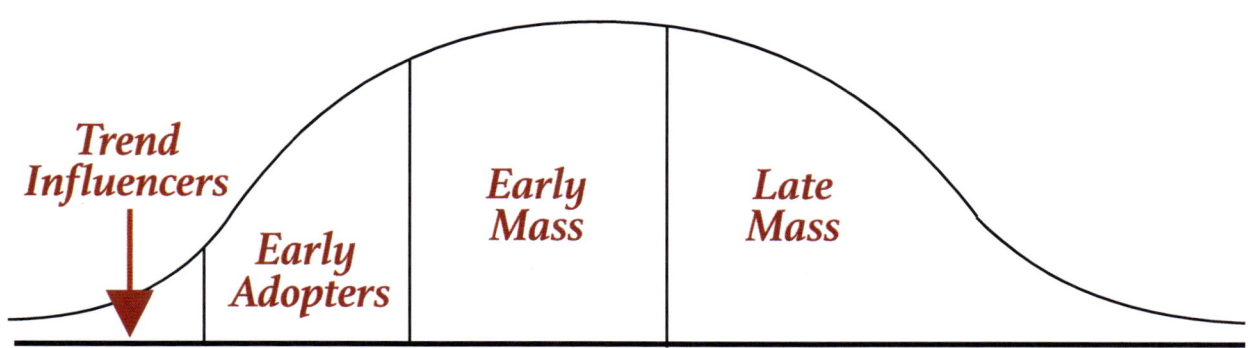

The trend influencer customers are at the beginning of the curve, representing 2-3% of the customers. They investigate every innovation in the categories they are interested in, right on the edge of what is new. They keep in touch with leading experts, love genuine leapfrog innovation, and despise the "death by incrementalism" approach of the safer and more prominent brands. They like to see themselves as experts, and they are always willing to share that knowledge with friends.

The early adopter group represents 10-15% of customers who play the bridge role between the trend influencers and the mass market. They try to keep up and enjoy being the first within their network to try the latest and greatest innovation. They loudly influence the masses of anything new and proven. They have a keen instinctual judgment of which products will succeed and use their influence to validate a new product poised to take off.

From there, the mass market customers represent 80% of the market, divided equally between early and late mass type customers. The early mass customers are willing to eventually take on new products when the products feel safe to use. The late mass customers are usually resistant to change, and they feel comfortable staying with out-of-date products.

We each fit into one of these types of customers, dependent on the category. You might be an early adopter of technology, but the early mass in fashion, late mass in music and yet a trend influencer in the best restaurants around the city. With our social network, we are starting to know who are the trend influencers or early adopters within a particular product category. When we buy something outside our area of expertise, we openly reach out to them for advice.

Brands must evolve their strategy as they move from the craft brand to the power player brand

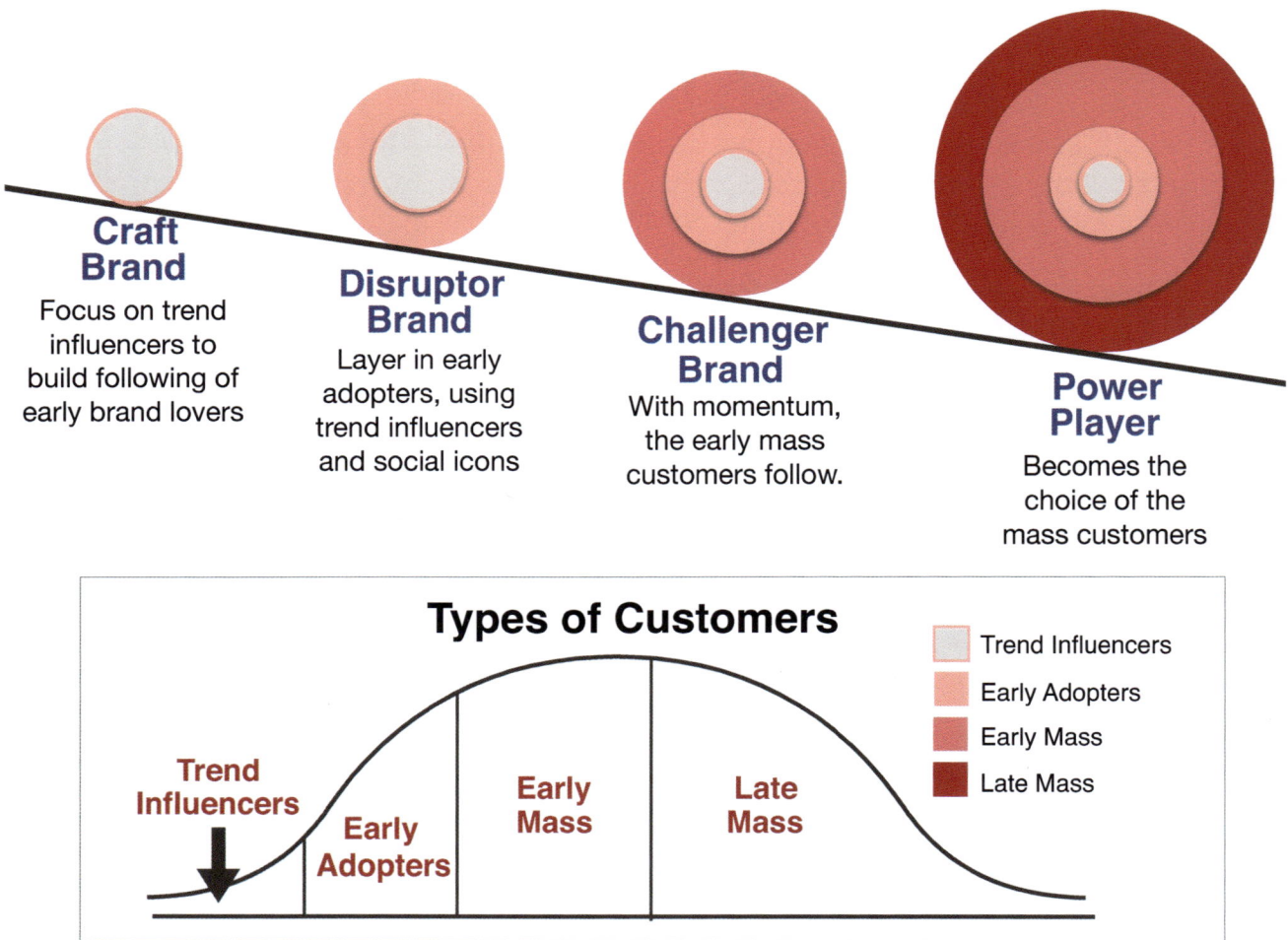

Many brands start in someone's garage or over a kitchen table at midnight

Start-ups should deploy a **craft brand strategy**. To stand out, you must be utterly different to a core group of trend influencers who are frustrated with the major competitors. You must be willing to take a "high risk/high reward" strategy.

It is O.K. if your brand alienates those who are not yet ready to take on something new. Playing it too safe will lead to your destruction. Do not worry about the mass audience, and avoid trying to grow too big, too fast.

As your brand grows, you can transition to a **disruptor brand strategy**. Utilize your core audience of trend influencers to gain a core base of early adopters. While a craft brand attracts the attention of trend influencers, the disruptor brand must dial up its aggressive stance and call out the major brands. Use your significant point of difference to pull customers away from the category-leading brands to make them seem detached from the needs of the customers.

As your brand continues to grow, you can use your increased resources and power to take on a **challenger brand strategy** against the leader. You can use the influence of the trend influencers and early adopters to attract the early mass audience. With a significant customer base, more brand power, and increased financial resources, your brand must gain hard-fought proximity, allowing you to go head-to-head with the power player leader. The challenger brand should turn the leader's strength into a weakness, pushing it out of what customers want, while creating a new customer problem for which your brand becomes the solution.

> **Brand strategies must evolve. Craft brands' needs are different from power players' needs.**

At the **power player stage**, the strategy shifts to maintaining your leadership position. You should take on a defensive strategy, to attack in response to any player who threatens your brand. While the trend influencers and early adopters played an essential role in making the brand a household name, you have to be comfortable that your earliest brand fans will eventually leave your brand and look for what is next. They may even call you a "sell-out." Stay focused on the mass audience.

Cluttered brands

I did say there are only four types of competitive brands. That is true. However, some brands are uncompetitive. I call these brands the **"cluttered brands."**

They get stuck in the cluttered mess of the market, without a defined target market or a defined point of difference. Customers cannot describe them and, even worse, the brands cannot express themselves.

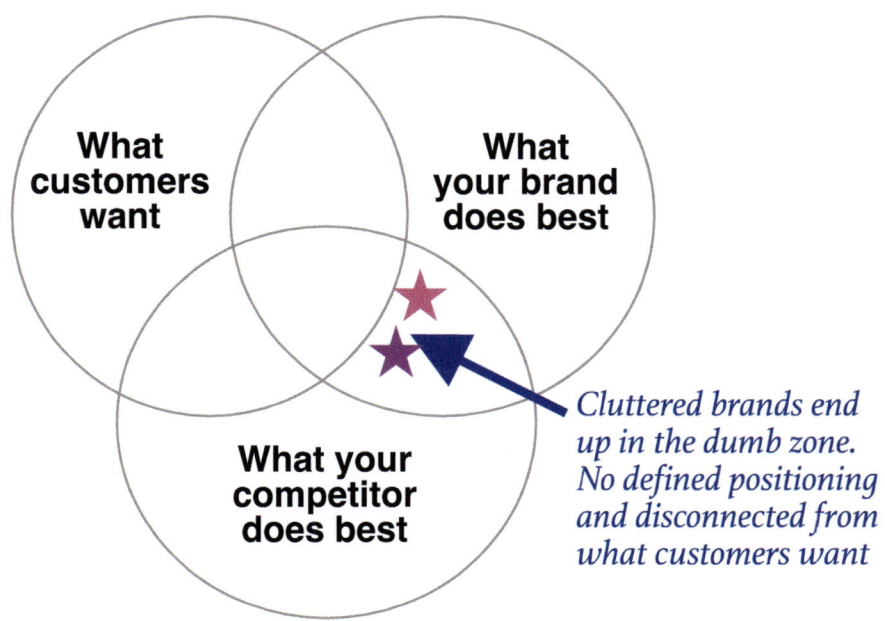

Cluttered brands end up in the dumb zone. No defined positioning and disconnected from what customers want

Competitive strategy attack choices

As you engage in competitive strategy, you must decide how **aggressive** you are willing to be, whether you wish to attack to gain share or defend to slow down any losses. The other dimension is the **focus of your attack**, whether you will build up the strengths of your brand or diminish the strengths of your competitor. That leaves your brand with four strategic attack options:

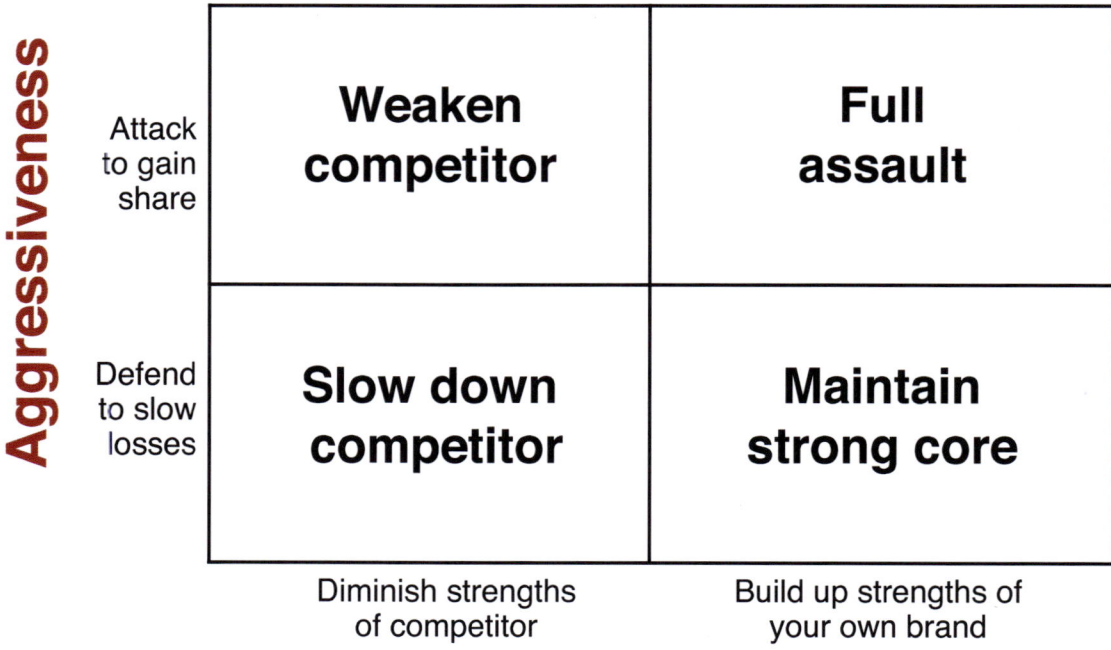

1. **Full assault:** You recognize an opportunity in the market where your strengths are considered superior to your competitor, and you see an opportunity to gain share. Focus on playing up your competitive advantage – whether you use your brand positioning, product innovation, or distribution channels – to enhance the purchase moment or the overall customer experience.

2. **Maintain strong core:** When you recognize attempts by an aggressive competitor, retreat and maintain your core audience by playing up the accepted strengths of your brand. This strategy can retain share against an aggressive competitor (or at least slow down the losses).

3. **Weaken competitor:** When you recognize a dramatic weakness in your competitor, this opens up the opportunity to gain share by attacking your rival.

4. **Slow down competitor:** When you recognize you are at a competitive disadvantage, attacking back on an element of your competitor can buy you time, so you can regroup behind the scenes to close the competitive gap. While you may lose share in the short term, once you have fixed that gap, you can look to rebuild your share by going back after any customers you may have lost.

Chapter Six
How to address your brand situation before you make your next move

Before moving towards a plan, you must fully understand the situation you face. Each year, conduct a deep-dive business review to assess the health of your branded business. A smart brand strategy is a smart business strategy. You are running a live business, with a need to drive sales, manage costs, and produce profits. Without addressing the competitive and customer factors you face; all your great strategic thinking will come collapsing down around you.

I will outline four distinct situations your brand could face:

- Fuel the momentum
- Fix it
- Realignment
- Start-up

Apply the right strategy and leadership to the right situation you face

When business results are healthy, fuel your momentum by staying on course and attacking small weaknesses. When things are going well, everyone within your organization will resist a change plan. When the external results are abysmal, your management team will look for opportunities to turn around those results quickly. They will be impatient.

Manage the short-term and long-term fix it plans at the same time. When different silos operate entirely autonomously within your organization, it causes unnecessary conflict and confusion that holds your brand back from maximizing its full potential. Build a realignment plan to get everyone moving in the same direction. Whether you are in an entrepreneurial start-up or entering into a new business from within a corporation, follow the plan for a start-up.

Fuel the momentum

Many marketers are notorious for wanting to make their mark. When they come into a brand situation, they see a long list of flaws left by the previous leader. They think it is time to do things right and change the way everyone operates. However, if you put a change plan in place when everything is going well, you will face significant resistance.

When brands have a strong market share position, steady sales growth,

> **Fuel the momentum plan:**
> - **Assessment indicators:** Steady sales growth, profitability, strong share position, and no looming competitive threat.
> - **Strategy:** Continue to fuel growth drivers, close any small gaps, and stay vigilant of looming threats to the current growth rates.
> - **Leadership style to engage:** Motivational leadership style that keeps everyone inspired, aligned, and focused.

strong profitability, strong underlying brand health measures, and they align the team on the direction for the future, the brand leader should keep the momentum going. It is harder than you think.

Your role as the leader should be to continue to fuel the growth drivers while resisting the temptation to make wholesale changes. Use the time to learn the success factors while looking at future scenarios that could threaten the current momentum.

You can attack what you see as smaller weaknesses and gaps that you feel will add to the overall growth rate. Use a motivational leadership style that keeps everyone inspired, aligned, and focused.

Fix it

When a brand faces poor external results with a decline in sales, shrinking market share, and lower profit margins due to lower prices or rising costs, the brand leader needs to create a turnaround plan that will fix it. From my experience, you will need both a short-term and long-term fix. The quick fix helps address the hemorrhaging results that harm the company's bottom line.

However, most fix it situations have a more in-depth cause, hidden beneath the surface level. You will need a change management leadership style that challenges everyone and everything. You will need a new plan, which includes a new vision filled with new ideas. Explore the need for different people to join the team. Losing can be contagious to the culture of a team. You will need to create a new, positive attitude to protect morale and engagement.

The quick fix can buy you time with management to implement what you see as the longer-term fix it plan. Any immediate wins also give the team a much-needed boost of motivation.

Dig deep into a full business review to understand the underlying market factors. Evaluate changing customer needs, new competitors, changes in the retail, economic, and political landscape, and changes in technology. Close leaks using a brand funnel analysis.

Go through every investment decision. Cut all spending that fails to drive results and reinvest in the new plan. Invest only in programs that give you an early breakthrough win and payback. Once you have the plan in place, make sure you have the right talent to make it happen.

The quick fix plan:

- Find early, and obvious potential wins to stop the hemorrhaging.
- Emphasize results to fuel a performance-driven culture.
- Use all early wins to boost team motivation.
- Celebrate every victory, big or small.

The long-term fix:

- Conduct a deep-dive business review of the market, customers, competitors, channels, and the brand. Focus on the top three issues emerging from the review.
- Invest in a new brand plan with a brand idea supported by a unique brand positioning.
- Make focused investment decisions, and take smart risks to fix the brand communication, product innovation, purchase moment, and the customer experience.

> **Fix it plan:**
> - **Assessment indicators:** Poor external results, declining sales, shrinking profitability, falling share position, and losing competitive battles.
> - **Strategy:** Quick wins stop declines and restores hope. Dig in deep to find underlying causes. Need long-term fixes for communication, innovation, selling and partnering
> - **Leadership style to engage:** Use a transformational change management style to challenge everything and everyone.

Realignment

A brand itself needs a consistent delivery of the brand promise. Issues arise when the brand promise shows up inconsistently across the marketing communications, new products, and the overall customer experience. It creates a confused and cluttered mess in the marketplace. You do not want the team behind the scenes of the brand moving in different directions.

When different functions operate in silos, you see the marketing and sales team each delivering their distinct brand messages, and the product development team invents products in a lab without any direction from brand or input from customers. The customer experience team lacks cohesion and consistency. The customers begin to notice a confused brand.

When I consult on a situation that looks splintered, I ask various leaders to describe the brand in seven seconds. The answers I get suggest a confused team. I hear:

- It depends on who you ask.
- It's complicated.
- I've never thought about it.
- I can't.

In situations like this, bring an energetic and focused leadership style to keep the team aligned. Use a highly participative leadership style to bring everyone together, to listen to all points of view and unite the team under a shared plan. Everyone on the team must move in the same direction to the same brand plan. A high-functioning team must agree on the following:

- Target market
- Main customer benefit
- An organizing brand idea
- Articulation of the brand idea for each function
- Brand vision
- Brand purpose and values
- Shared goals
- Key issues
- Strategies
- Execution plans and activities you will invest in

> **Realignment plan:**
> - **Assessment indicators:** Internal silos among functions behind the brand. Conflict over action plans. Confused messages.
> - **Strategy:** Realign the team by employing a cross-functional team to build a new brand positioning, an organizing brand idea, and a brand plan to get everyone on the same page. Build a shared vision, purpose, values, strategies, and execution.
> - **Leadership style to engage:** Participative leadership style to bring everyone together to listen to all points of view and unify them under a shared plan. Strive for cohesion and consistency in communications rather than a confused brand.

Each functional team should complete their plan to ensure it aligns with the overall brand plan. Each team needs clear marching orders, firm decisions, goals, budgets, and timelines.

Start-up

Start-up situations are either about the launch of a new brand in the market or the launch of a current brand in a new category. At this stage, you move quickly from blank slate to a new brand idea, a new brand plan, and a new team.

The first mistake many start-ups make is believing a product alone is good enough. Even at the start-up stage, you need a brand idea to help organize everything. Customers are more likely to buy into an idea than a product.

The second mistake is to sell to anyone and even adjust your product or service to fit every different type of customers who wants to buy. While you might feel desperate for revenue early on, you need to stay focused on your target and brand positioning. The goal for your brand is to build a reputation you can own. If you try to be everything to anyone, you will end up as nothing to everyone.

Build a "blowfish" brand plan.

Start-up plan:
- **Assessment indicators:** New product, yet to launch in the market or a new segment of the market.
- **Strategy:** Blowfish marketing plan, with a focused target market, a targeted main message, focused strategy and focused executions. Make the brand appear bigger than it is to those who matter the most.
- **Leadership style to engage:** Entrepreneurs need a participative and transactional style to roll up the sleeves and get the necessary tasks done, especially for those customers or influencers who matter the most.

To build intrigue and credibility, start-ups can build a "blowfish" brand plan. A blowfish can make itself appear bigger than it is. The idea of a blowfish brand plan is to make focused decisions and investments, so the brand appears bigger.

The idea of a blowfish brand plan is to make focused decisions and investments, so the brand appears bigger than it is, especially to those customers or influencers who matter the most.

For instance, when you focus and invest in a tight target market, those customers will begin to think the brand is bigger than it is. On the other hand, resist the temptation of going after a broad target market too early, or you will stretch your dollars so thin no one will even notice you.

Go after a niche customer benefit, so your brand can eventually own a trusted reputation in narrow competitive space.

Resist the temptation to try to be everywhere at once, as it spreads your resources so thin you will have a small presence anywhere. When you focus, your brand can start to dominate a focused distribution channel or media channel.

Focus! Focus! Focus!

Build the right team that fits the people to the strategy, not the strategy to the people. Build out the team's capabilities by acquiring the skills, behaviors, relationships, and capacity to fit the needs of the brand plan and execution. As start-up brands are continually learning, keep in mind that it is okay to maneuver and adjust your strategies – but do not change your overall vision.

Strategic Thinking Exercises

Work Exercise #1

Using the brand that you are working on, try out the game from this chapter. Place one chip where you have the highest competitive advantage to win. Then put two chips at the medium level that backs up and supports the core strength. Force one chip at the low end. What is your brand's core strength? Product, story, experience, or price? Are you lined up with it? Based on the core strength you chose, where should you invest and what should be your main message of communication?

Work Exercise #2

Where does your brand sit on the brand love curve? Unknown, indifferent, liked, loved, or beloved? What is your customer target, knowledge, insights, match with benefits?

Work Exercise #3

What is your competitive position? Power player, challenger, disruptor, or craft brand? What is the unique positioning space you win with? What is the intensity of competition? Are you attacking or defending? Winning battles: investment, messages, innovation, retail, location?

Work Exercise #4

What is your business position? Continue momentum, fix it, re-alignment or a startup?

Chapter Seven
How to define the ideal target market to build your B2B brand around

Instead of asking, "Who do we want?" you should be saying, "Who wants us?" Most B2B marketers think of the type of customers they want to attract.

Why not change your thinking and go after those customers who are already motivated by what your brand offers?

I use **eight fundamental questions** to define and build a profile of your ideal B2B customer target:

1. What is the description of the customer target?
2. What are the customer's main needs?
3. What are the goals of their business?
4. Who is the customer's enemy who torments them every day?
5. What are the insights we know about the customer?
6. What does the customer think now?
7. How does the customer buy?
8. What do we want customer to see, think, do, feel or whisper to their peers?

B2B Customer Profile

Using a fictional B2B brand, Gray's Stage Lighting, we will show an example of how these seven questions come to life in building a customer profile for broadway theater directors.

Target	Broadway Theater Directors
Target Description	• "Discerning Theatre Companies" with directors who are willing to do whatever to win the war on broadway or wherever they compete. There is a competitive fire everyone on the production team feels, and on-going battle to be the hit show and fill the seats.
Their needs	• Customer experience, positive reviews, intimate theater experience, latest technology.
Their enemy	• Experts not paying attention to details, noticeable flaws that get talked about, flat show.
Insights that tell their story	• "Of course directors are crazy perfectionists. We have to be to keep up with the crazy perfectionist down the street. We rely heavily on experts to do their part."
What do they think now?	• Many familiar with Gray's, but more fixated on show than the changes in lighting technology. Willing to listen to what's new, as long as it is significantly better. They need to convince production group that the Gray's price premium is worth it. Their buyer will review the deal.
How are they buying?	• **User:** Directors focused on getting the best, will need to influence the production company. • **Decision-maker:** Producers who want to drive early gate receipts and overall profit. • **Buyers:** Detailed before making decisions. Always compare brands and push for low price. • **Influencers:** Mentors and peers who constantly push each other to make production better.
We want them to think/feel/do	• **See:** Use lighting tests to get directors excited and imagine impact on their shows. • **Think:** Review Gray's lighting technical data comparisons with current brand choice. • **Do:** Bring in Gray's for a test run to see the difference, and convince production company. • **Feel:** Get current customers to know how Gray's lighting makes them feel more inspired. • **Whisper:** Get outspoken brand lovers to talk about the difference Gray's made on their show.

Who is your customer target?

One of the biggest mistakes I see B2B marketers make is picking too broad of a target market. A tight target market decides who is in the target and who is not in the target.

There is a myth that a bigger target will make the brand bigger, so the scared marketer targets "everyone." There seems to be an irrational fear of leaving someone out. Spreading your brand's limited resources across an entire population is completely cost-prohibitive.

While targeting everyone "just in case" might feel safe at first, it is riskier because you spread your resources so broadly you never see the full impact you desire.

A good target not only decides who is in your target but who is NOT in your target.

This fear of missing out (FOMO) gives your brand a lower return on investment and eventually will drain your brand's limited resources. Please focus.

Every time I go to the airport, I see the shoeshine person looking down at people's feet, qualifying potential customers based on whether they are wearing leather shoes. It reminds me of how simple it is to target those who are the most motivated by what you do.

Sure, they could be missing out on the very few people who have leather shoes in their suitcase. However, using a focused approach to profile customer is a smart way to maximize your return on effort.

If shoeshiners can narrow the focus of their target to people wearing leather shoes, why is it so difficult for you to narrow down your target to those who care the most about what your brand does?

Instead of going after who you want, go after those who want you

To illustrate this point of focus, I look at three types of potential target markets:

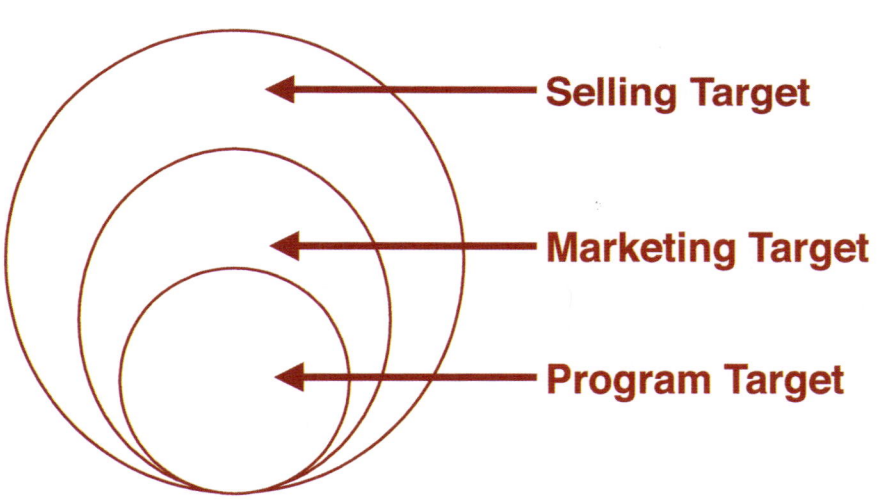

- **Selling target:** This is pretty much everyone, as you sell to anyone who comes in the door and wants to buy, regardless of whether they fit the ideal target. However, "everyone" should never be a marketing target, because you risk spreading your resources so thin your message will miss a chance to capture those potential customers who are most likely to respond, and provide the most impactful and efficient payback.

- **Marketing target:** Focus your limited resources on those customers who have the highest likelihood of responding positively to your brand positioning, communication, and new product innovation. A tighter target market provides the fastest and highest return on investment.

- **Program target:** When working on a specific campaign, narrow the target even further. Focus on customers you want to stimulate to see if you can get them to see, think, feel, or do things that will benefit your brand. A specific program target is smart when launching a new product or aligning with a promotional time of year.

Who is most likely to try your brand or love your brand in the future?

There are various ways to divide up the market to identify the most motivated possible audience. Here are three main ways to segment the market:

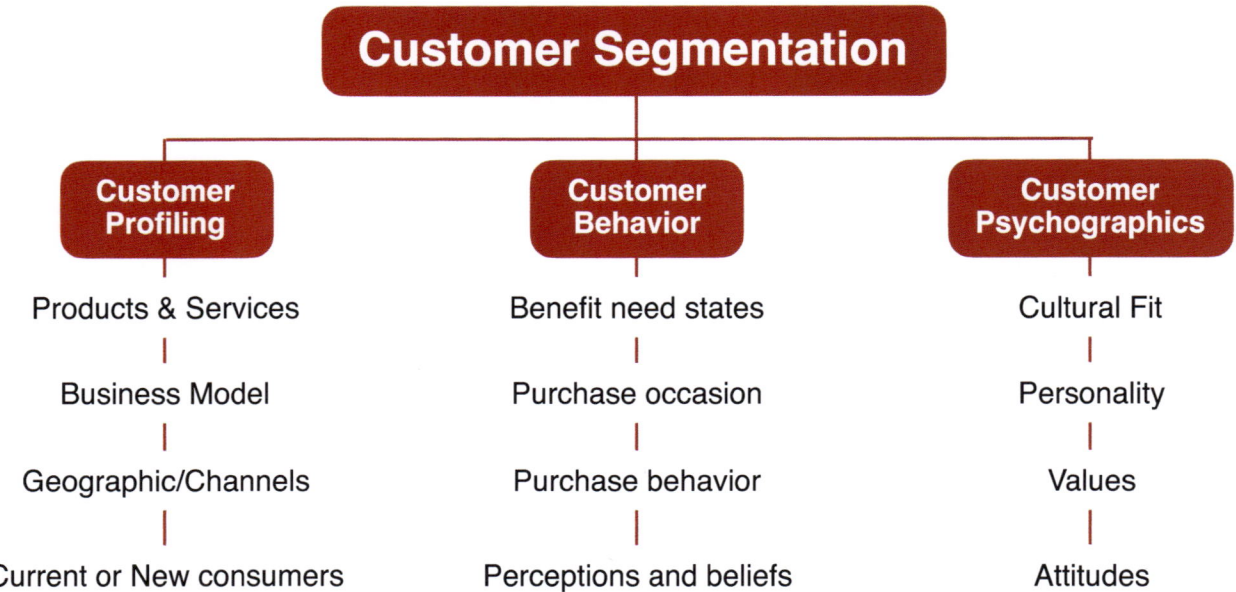

1. **Customer profiling:** Starting with the types of products and services is the easiest way to segment. Then add in the B2B customer's business model to figure out how they make their money and the underlying motivation of what they are looking for in a partner. You can segment customers using geography, company size, and the selling channels they play in. Focus on either current customers or new customers, but never both at the same time. Trying to drive penetration and usage at the same time will drain your resources.

2. **Customer behavior:** Divide the market based on benefit need states, and purchase occasions. You can also divide the market based on purchase behavior, perceptions, or beliefs.

3. **Customer psychographics:** Psychographics look at commonly a shared cultural fit with partners, such as the customer's shared corporate personality, values or attitudes.

Segmentation forces you to focus. Please do not spend tons of money on a segmentation study and then try to figure out how to go after each segment with a completely different brand message. I have seen marketers do this, and it is borderline crazy. That is not the right way to use these studies. A brand can only ever have one reputation.

While this shows 12 different ways you can segment, a good starting point is to use a combination of three or four segmentation elements to narrow down your target. The choice depends on the category.

What are your customer's needs?

If you can make customers buy, you will never have to sell. The best brands do not go after customers; they get customers to crave their brand and come after them. The process I will take you through involves matching up what your customers want and need with what your brand does best.

Possible functional needs

To help get you started, I have mapped out nine functional need states to help you understand the potential spaces your brand can play in:

Stay Connected	Sensory Appeal	Experience comes to life	Works better for you	Helps you be healthier	Helps your family
Makes you smarter	Saves you money	Simplifies your life	Enhances professional standing	Drives business results	Helps you execute

Possible emotional needs

I have also mapped out eight emotional need states your brand can play in. These need states mean something different for each category of brands, but they are a good starting point for you to brainstorm where you can add specific words that fit your brand situation.

Curiosity for knowledge	Sense of optimism	Feel comfortable	Stay in control	Fits with values	Self assured
Feel free	Get noticed	Feel liked	Sense of belonging	Feeling Revitalized	Sense of pride

Moment of accelerated needs

At certain moments in our customer's life, their physical and emotional needs will accelerate their consideration certain products or services. Brands can win by capturing customers at these moments when their motivation is very high and their knowledge remains low.

If you are selling a payroll system, look at potential moments when customers are more open-minded such as rapid expansion of the company, changing overall software, or when they are looking for major cost saving.

For a packaging company, look at moments such as a new manufacturing plant, environmental pressure, or when a competitor has launched new product technology.

Who is your customer's enemy?

While products solve small problems, the best brands beat down the enemies that torment their customers every day. Put yourself in the shoes of your customer and find their most significant frustration or pain point they feel no one is even noticing or addressing.

Shifting from solving a rational customer problem to beating down an emotional customer enemy is the starting point to reaching into the emotional need states of your customer. The customer enemy helps you connect with your customers on a deeper level.

Dentists
Problem: With dull tools, I can't get to the hardest to reach spots

Enemy: My clients secretly hate me because they think I'm too rough. Then they switch dentists without saying why.

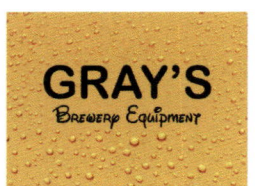

Craft Breweries
Problem: First 5 years of a start up is non-stop investing

Enemy: I live in fear of going bankrupt, and every mistake I make, I think this is it, I'm done.

Manufacturing
Problem: Competitors come up with packaging innovation before us.

Enemy: We love new ideas, but we find more reasons to reject cool ideas than approve and move forward

Examples of customer enemies brands beat down on their behalf

For example, Marriott's international hotels are loved by their B2B customers because they fight off the enemy of "taking a chance on a local hotel." Las Vegas fights the B2B customer enemy of "boring and predictable conferences." Apple fights off the B2B customer enemy of "frustration with computers."

While your instincts tell you to comfort your customers, you should always leave a doubt in your customer's mind of what life would be like without you.

Customer insights

Customer insights are little secrets hidden beneath the surface, which explain the underlying behaviors, motivations, pain points, and emotions of your customers. Your customers may not even be able to explain the insight until you play it back to them. When they say, "Yeah, that is exactly how I feel" you know you have the insight nailed.

Brands should think of customer insights as a potential competitive advantage, equal in importance to intellectual property.

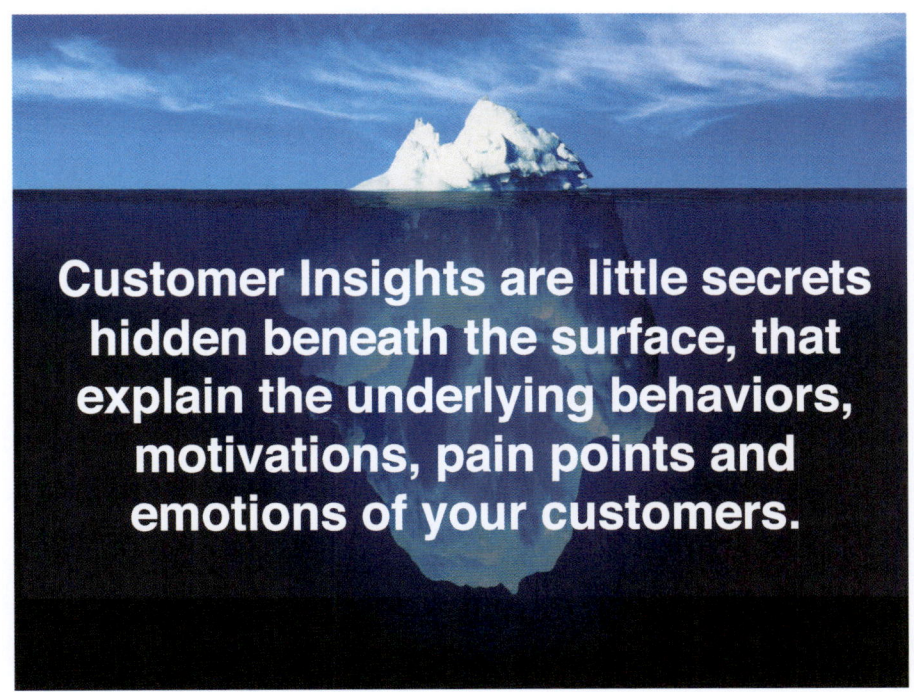

Avoid relying too heavily on facts and data alone without any context or story. Too many marketers think that data, trends, and facts are insights.

Here is a data point: "People in Brazil brush their teeth four times per day, compared to 1.7 times per day for North Americans." Do you think that is an insight? Some people do. But when you think of how little you know about this data point, you realize you need to go deeper into the context to gain an understanding. You must start to ask more questions, by asking who, what, when, where, or asking how and even why, that's when we begin to turn the fact into an insight.

Stereotypes and clichés are dangerous.

I once heard someone say, "Women over 50 are stuck in their ways and unwilling to change their routines." That is not a valid statement for many categories. Here are two examples of women over 50 making dramatic changes: a) Women take 8x more vitamins at 55, compared to 50 and b) The fastest growth for the Apple brand has been businesswomen over 50. Be careful you don't stereotype – especially when you are not in the target market you are going after.

Common knowledge offers no competitive advantage.

I hear insights all the time that are not unique secrets. For instance, "Customers wish there was a way they could drive more sales and profits" offers no competitive advantage. Everyone in the golf industry knows this. Dig deeper.

Watch out that you don't use insights just related to your product rather than about the customer's LIFE! Too many marketers use insights like, "Whenever I get frustrated on my computer, I love calling my IT consultant." This type of statement is too blatant to be an insight, yet people put stuff like this all the time.

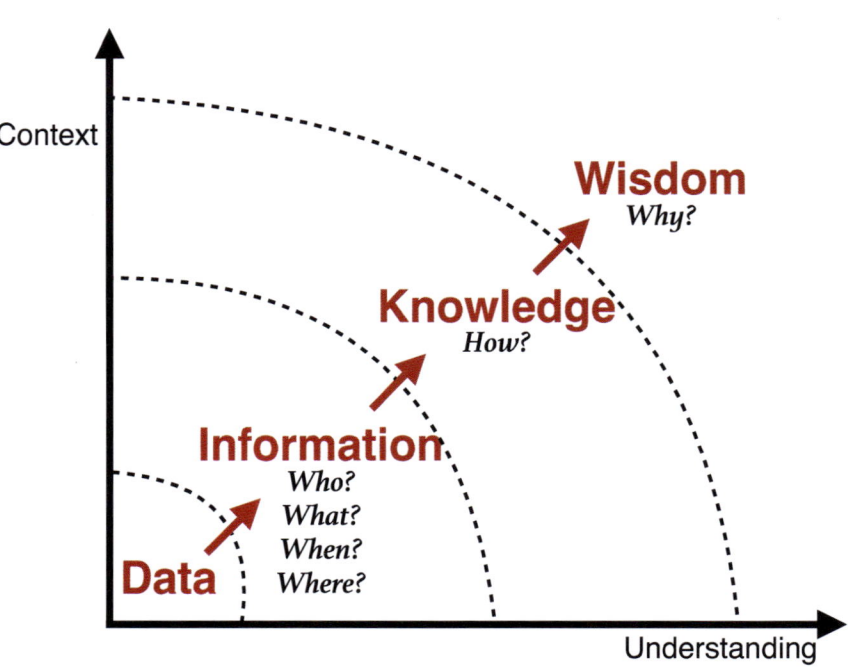

Go deep to understand and explain trends lying beneath the data. Think like a therapist: Listen, observe, collect, challenge, and carefully draw conclusions you can play back to the customer for assurance. Use the voice of the customer, social media, to listen and use our emotional cheat sheet to draw conclusions.

Hunt through the data to draw hypothetical insights. The dictionary definition of the word insight is "seeing below the surface." Sort through every data point, including market share information, panel data, testing and tracking results, brand funnel, customer sales, etc. With each data point, keep digging until you see a data break that needs explaining. Ask yourself, "So what does that mean for the customer?" over and over until you see the "Why it matters" come to life and explain the cause of the customer's behavior.

Make sure it fits with your customer's life. Try to map out a day-in-the-life, weekly life, or even the life stages your customer goes through to understand their insights and pain points. Take a holistic view of the customer to ensure you figure out where your brand fits in with their life. Ask questions that force you to go deeper, avoiding clichés that keep you stuck at the surface level and stop you from getting to the sincere, rich, and meaningful customer insights.

Find something that is an inspiring connection to engage and move customers. We need to find that magic secret, going deep below to show the customer we get them. Insights enable brands to connect with their customers on a deeper emotional level, showing 'we get you.'

When you do it right, smart consumer insights **get customers to stop and listen** to your brand's promise or brand story, engage in the latest innovation and believe the customer experiences fits perfect with their life.

Take a 360-degree approach to customer insights

Building a complete picture of your customer by looking at multiple sources is an excellent methodology to find customer insights. Start with market data, and then add your observations, the voice of the customer, emotional need states, and life moments:

1. **What we can read:** Explain data breaks, drivers, inhibitors, trends, sales changes, personnel change with customers, channels, and competitors.

2. **What we see:** Observe customer reactions in focus groups, product tests, ad testing, and direct customer engagements.

3. **What we sense:** Listen to the Voice of Customer (VOC) with comments on social media, product reviews, and market research. Look for word choices and tone.

4. **What we feel:** Use observations and listening to match the emotional need states with how the use of your brand makes them feel.

5. **Relationship moments:** Gather insights from your sales team, understanding the customer's business goals, motivations, beliefs, positive and negative experiences, frustrations, and successes.

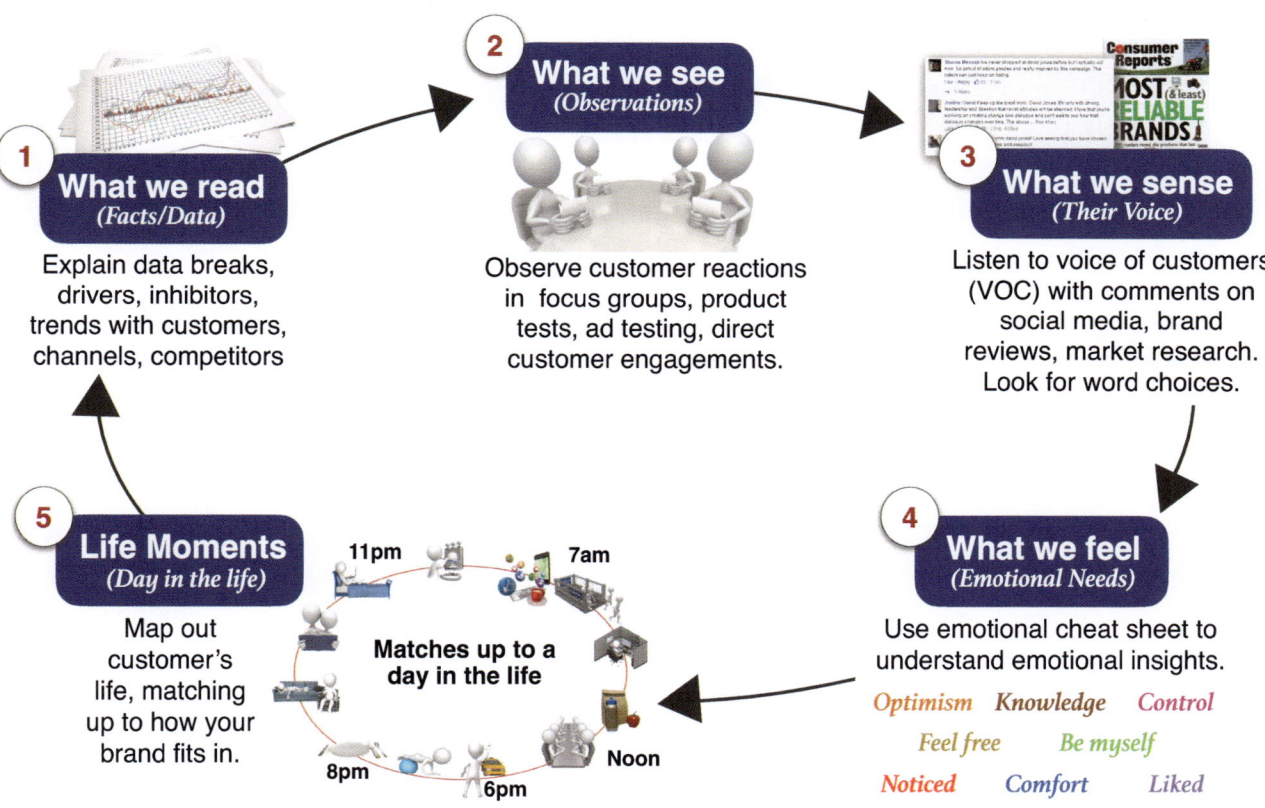

Once you have completed all five areas of the 360-degree mining process, get in the customer's shoes, observe, listen, and understand how they think, act, feel, and behave. Be empathetic to their fears, motivations, frustrations, and desires. Learn their language and use their voice.

Learn the secrets that only they know, even if they cannot explain. Insights are a great way to demonstrate "We know you" because the number one reason customers buy a brand simply that "It is a brand for me."

Case study: Selling dental Tools to dental professionals

Gray's Dental is a 100-year-old company, who is the market leader with a great reputation and a premium price.

They face an investment decision, whether to continue steady 3-5% growth but risk losing younger generation or invest significantly in innovation to grow at 8-10% higher level.

Below is how our customer insights process looks for Gray's Dental instruments. Do all the fact-gathering, observing, listening, understanding, and constructing the insights. For Gray's, the main connection point speaks to how they live in constant fear of doing anything wrong that jeopardizes the client experience.

The customer's enemy is that one bad experience and their client never comes back. And, they never tell you why they leave.

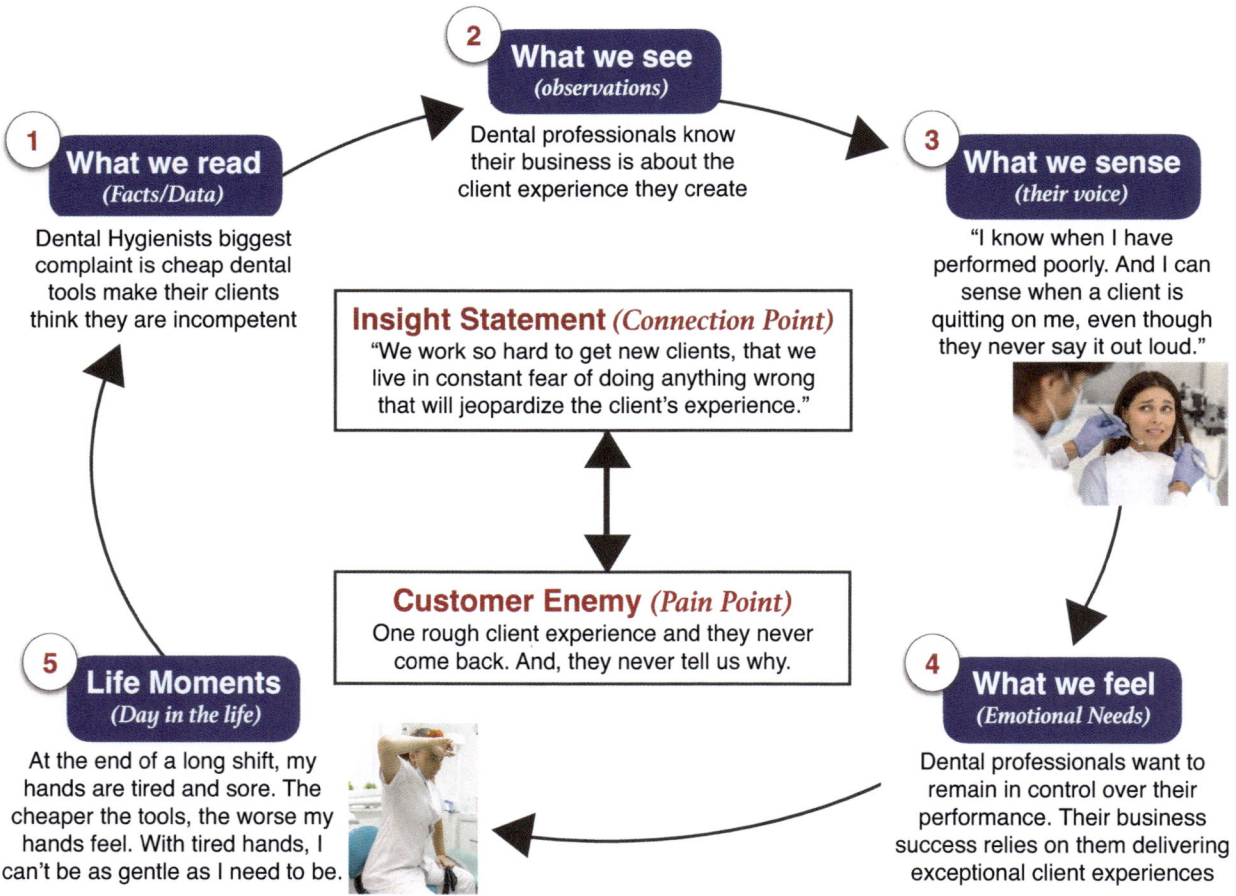

1. What we read *(Facts/Data)*
Dental Hygienists biggest complaint is cheap dental tools make their clients think they are incompetent

2. What we see *(observations)*
Dental professionals know their business is about the client experience they create

3. What we sense *(their voice)*
"I know when I have performed poorly. And I can sense when a client is quitting on me, even though they never say it out loud."

4. What we feel *(Emotional Needs)*
Dental professionals want to remain in control over their performance. Their business success relies on them delivering exceptional client experiences

5. Life Moments *(Day in the life)*
At the end of a long shift, my hands are tired and sore. The cheaper the tools, the worse my hands feel. With tired hands, I can't be as gentle as I need to be.

Insight Statement *(Connection Point)*
"We work so hard to get new clients, that we live in constant fear of doing anything wrong that will jeopardize the client's experience."

Customer Enemy *(Pain Point)*
One rough client experience and they never come back. And, they never tell us why.

How to write meaningful customer insights

Force yourself to get in the shoes of your customer and use their voice. Every customer insight should start with the word "I" to get into the shoes of your customer. I like to put the customer insight into quotes to force yourself to use their voice.

To kickstart your brainstorming, find the customer voice with our simple tool, "I feel _____ whenever I _____" with a human truth in the first blank, and a moment in your customer's life in the second blank.

Below is an example using Gray's Payroll Systems, a B2B brand helping small businesses with payroll software. It helps set up the customer insight of how accounting frustration can turn the customer into a monster.

Tool for writing a customer insight

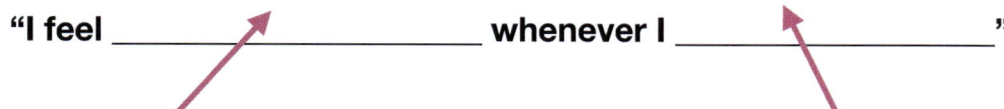

"I feel _____ whenever I _____"

A human truth based on one of:
- underlying behaviors
- motivations/inspirations
- values or beliefs
- pain points
- emotions

A moment in the target's life
- Business activity that happens at part of the day, week, year
- What triggers a re-look of the business
- A monumental time in their business life
- Moment of strength or weakness in their business

Example of a customer insight doing their own taxes

"I feel *I become a confused monster and the worst version of myself* whenever I *try to figure out my small business taxes on my own*"

B2B customers act like a four-headed monster with different roles of the people within your customers' companies

B2B follows a different type of targeting. First, while a B2B brand may start off thinking about selling to the entire market, then begin narrowing down based on the kind of customer or the subsegments of the category. As B2B marketers approach their customers, they must understand there are four types of people at the customer, including:

- **End-user** who has the immediate need
- **Decision-maker** who ultimately approves the purchase
- **Buyer** who performs the final sale
- **Influencing voice** somewhere in the organization

User	Decision Maker	Buyer	Influencer

Motivation	*Gatekeeper*	*Purchase / Fulfill*	*Deliver message*
Decision to use	*Decision to sign up*	*Doubts/Fears*	*Judge & Recommend*
Ritual / Routine	*Research*	*Keep buying*	*Trusted Advisor*

Depending on the size, power, and formality of the purchasing process of your customer, these four roles could be four distinct people who rarely engage each other, or for a simple purchase, it could be one or two people.

As you look at those **four roles** within your B2B customer audience, you have to understand how each role can impact your sale. I recommend you understand: a) each person's motivation behind a potential purchase, b) what it will take for them to see, think, do, feel, or whisper, c) what could go wrong that you need to watch out for, and d) where your sales team needs to focus.

The end-user

The motivation of the B2B end user is most similar to how a consumer would act with a brand. The end user focuses on how their personal experience will help them improve their performance in their role. Like a typical consumer, you want them to think about how the purchase will boost their performance, so they feel motivated to influence stakeholders to close the deal internally. It would help if you got them to use their motivation to fight for the purchase.

One major caution to watch out for is when the user is forced into a decision by the decision maker (their boss) or the buyer (due to savings), which they might naturally resist. It would be best if you had a personal connection with the end user to gain their trust. Focus your sales team on providing demonstrations or trials to show the end user the functional and emotional benefits related to their performance.

Decision maker

Usually, the decision makers' motivation will focus on understanding how your brand will add to their in-market performance impact and related business results. If they are a former user, they may bring their own bias to the decision, believing they know what is best for the end user. You will need a logical and quantifiable case for change to help them to think the impact and results will justify their decision.

When your entrance is through the end user, be careful they are not brought in too late to a potential decision, as it may frustrate them. A deal can fall apart if the user cannot build the case for change. Your sales team should involve decision makers early so you can understand their specific needs and requirements to build a case for change.

The buyer

Within an organization, the buyer's role is to focus on measures and control so they can find cost savings for the company. They focus on comparative price points and terms. What you want them to see are the savings to justify the purchase. As they are generalists covering so many different areas of procurement, you need to educate them on the technical aspects of products and services, so they feel in control of the decision.

The big caution is when the end user does not consult the buyer, it will frustrate them, and you may need to go back to the beginning and explain everything again. The buyer will need firm forecasted numbers to compare with other options. They may compare the metrics to the current status quo or other competitive brands. Your sales team should highlight comparative performance results and focus on the overall cost.

When possible, avoid the line-by-line comparison as the buyer may force you to deliver the lowest price on each line. That risks cutting into your overall profitability.

Influencing voice

The influencing voice is the hardest to manage, as it can come from anywhere in the organization. It could be a peer or mentor providing advice to your end user. Those individuals are the hardest for you to manage.

The influencing voices you should focus on are those peripheral leaders in other departments to your end user who will want to influence the purchase, so it can positively impact their vision and goals. For instance, when you are selling travel expense software, the sales leader might be an influential voice.

If you are selling new ingredient materials, then the marketing leader would want an influential voice for that decision. When they are highly motivated, they become an active voice, whispering to decision maker and user, almost selling internally on impact and performance. You want them selling for your brand, not against.

The most significant risk you need to manage is, when they see no personal benefit to their role, they turn into an absent voice, which is a passive non-supporter. You need to understand the influencer's motivation, so you can engage them when they are highly motivated, and yet manage them when they do not care.

Do you know your customers better than your competition knows your customers?

Brands should think of customer insights like intellectual property. Your knowledge of your customer is a competitive advantage. The deeper the love a brand can build with your most cherished customers, the more powerful and profitable that brand will be, going far beyond what the product alone could ever deliver. There is only one source of revenue: not the products you sell, but the customers who buy them.

Customer insights must show up at every customer touchpoint. Knowing the secrets of your customers can be a potent asset for your brand. The best brand communication should be like whispering an inside-joke that only you and your friend get. When the customer insight connects, it makes customers stop and say, "Hmmm. That's exactly how I feel. I thought I was the only one who felt like that." When portrayed with the brand's message, whether through sales messages, content marketing, or at the purchase moment, the customer will think the brand is made just for them. Selling to your customers starts by listening to their needs.

When you sell to many customers, you can narrow down the customer types or personas.

Target Name	Broadway Directors
Description	
Needs	
Their Goals	
Enemy	
Insights	
They think now?	
Buying process	
Desired response	

Target Name	Production Houses
Description	
Needs	
Their goals	
Enemy	
Insights	
They think now?	
Buying process	
Desired response	

Target Name	Convention Operators
Description	
Needs	
Their goals	
Enemy	
Insights	
They think now?	
Buying process	
Desired response	

Target Name	Concert Operators
Description	
Needs	
Their goals	
Enemy	
Insights	
They think now?	
Buying process	
Desired response	

Putting together your customer profile

For B2B brands that sell to specific customers, you can build a highly personalized profile.

Target	Connor Smith, Director of Wizzard of Oz at Toronto Theatre
Background	• He's a former actor, turned director, now with 20 years of experience, 3 Tony Awards. Has a reputation for being focused on dialogue, personality and humour. Married to a stage actress, with 2 kids. Connor works with TTI (Toronto Theater Inc.) production company.
Needs	• Wants production technology to create an intimate experience.
Goals	• Good reviews for a new production of a timeless classic. • Specific goals: 100% ticket for first 3 months, 90% ticket sales for 6 months.
Enemy	• Hates when noticeable flaws get talked about, embarrassed by a flat performance.
Insights that tell their story	• "Of course we are crazy perfectionists. We have to be to keep up with the crazy perfectionist down the street. We rely heavily on experts to do their part."
What do they think now?	• I have used Gray's Lighting in NY, and want them to help my Toronto shows. I need to convince my production group that it's worth it. Then use their buyer to close the deal.
How are they buying?	• Connor is tech savvy & influenced by trends. He cares about technology than most directors, and wants to really bring a high quality to his shows. Will help sell in ideas to buyers.
Role of decision makers	• **User:** Connor is an advocate we can use to influence the production company. • **Decision-Maker:** Pressure on TTI, to drive early gate receipts. Buyer drives costs/budgets. • **Buyer:** Anne Jones is very detailed before decisions. Good budget but pushes on price. • **Influencer:** Mentors and peers who constantly push each other to make production better.
We want them to think/feel/do	• **See:** Want TTI to see Gray's lighting test run from the back row of their theatre. • **Think:** Want Ann to review Gray's tech data production qualities. • **Do:** Get TTI/Connor to bring in Gray's for a test run inside their theatre to see the difference. • **Feel:** Once a fan, remind Connor to feel more inspired that he always reaches for the best. • **Whisper:** Trigger Connor to tell everyone about the difference Gray's made on their show.

We have customer profile templates as part of our B2B brand positioning presentation template on our website at **beloved-brands.com**

Chapter Eight
Mapping out the B2B customer journey to set up your brand to win

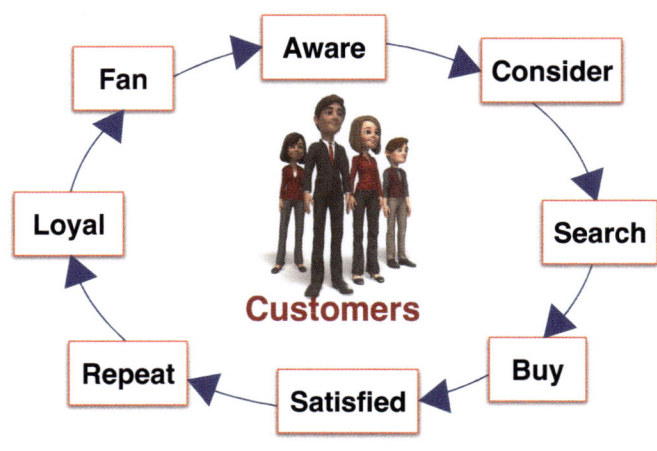

A typical brand funnel focuses on awareness, purchase, satisfied, and loyalty. In the last few years, the funnel has become a complete loop as we have seen the growth of search and the use of loyal brand fans to generate new awareness with influence to their network. Brands must understand how potential customers move from one stage to the next, as well as understanding why they exit the journey.

At the early stage of the B2B customer journey, the focus is on driving **awareness** and **consideration** to help the brand stand out and be seen in a crowd. Marketing options include LinkedIn, sponsorships, trade shows, events, engaging content videos, and blogs. To move customers to the consideration stage, use influencers to teach those seeking to learn more.

Use public relations to make the brand part of the industry news, whether through traditional, social, or blogger channels. Engage online user review sites or social media review sites.

For more complex or higher risk purchase decisions, customers will rely on **search** for almost everything, even if to confirm what makes sense. The strategy at this point is to solve questions or doubts in the minds of the customer.

Marketers can use search sites, such as Google, expert review sites, online content, or long copy print media. The brand website comes into play and should include the right information to close off gaps or doubts, then move customers towards the purchase decision.

As you move the customer to the **buying stage**, you must close the deal and trigger purchase, including highly personalized, one-to-one selling, backed by sales materials or credentials presentations to prompt customers at the purchase moment. It becomes crucial to understand the four potential roles of the user, decision maker, influencer, and buyer – some of whom you may never directly interact with. It may be essential to provide brand talking points to your contact to help them manage the others within their company.

After the purchase, make sure all your communications include the core brand messages and reinforce the purchase decision by outlining the expected customer benefits. Your customer service and operations teams will be the ones who deliver the happy customer experience. As your operations team continues to deliver on customer expectations, you can increase usage frequency among your most loyal users.

Among your base of **loyal** customers, it becomes important to cultivate a collection of **brand fans**, using VIP programs and experiential events with exclusive access to tighten the bond with brand fans who see your brand as one of their favorites. Once you have a strong base of brand lovers, by intentionally creating exceptional experiences inspires testimonials, to influence their peers.

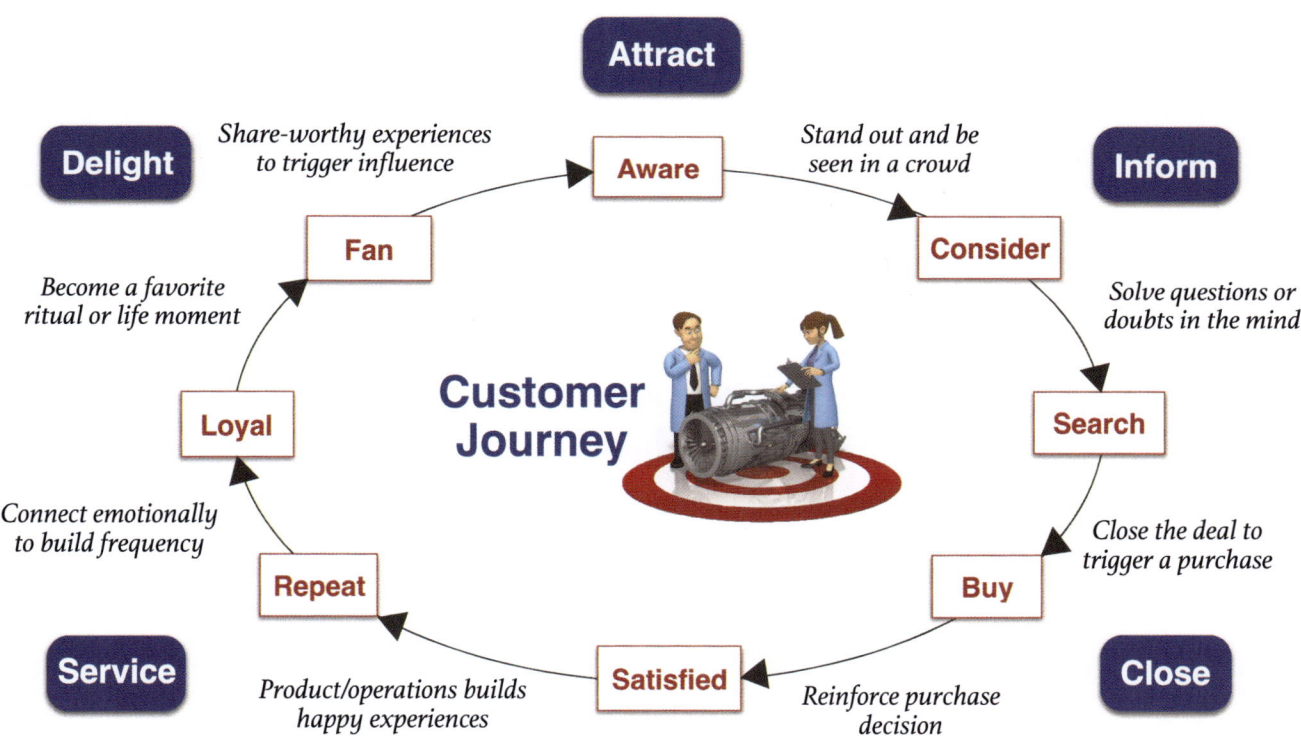

Awareness and Consideration stage

Awareness is the starting point of the B2B customer journey. We look at aided awareness to figure out if customers know of the brand name. Every brand starts as an unknown. Unaided asks customers to name brands without a list, which speaks to top-of-mind awareness and how familiar customers are with the brand. There is not always direct entry into the customer's mind. Many times, customers will overhear friends, see the brand through social media, or hear about it through influencers, including early adopters, category experts, or brand fans with prior experience.

When customers consider purchasing a brand, customers become motivated by something in the brand idea or promise. In more complicated or expensive categories, the risk of a purchase goes up, and customers will put multiple brands into a set of consideration choices they want to find out more information about. Brands need to use their positioning to enter the customer's mind, offering something new to stand out in the crowded marketplace. Customers need to see the brand as better than their current brand, or they won't consider it.

Questions to find out how customers become aware and consider

We need to understand where customers are most open to seeing and engaging with the brand. Then it is essential to understand the ideal customer benefits to make customers consider their brand.

1. How do you find out about most of the products or services you use to help your company achieve success? Are you actively engaged and looking to build a stable of choices, or is your decision more by chance?

2. How did you first find out about our brand?

    a. Sales rep first called our office

    b. Met a sales rep at a trade show

    c. One of my peers actively recommended it

    d. Searched for potential brands online

    e. Well known within the industry

    f. Other

3. How many competitors can you name? For each competitor, would you say you know the same level of detail, or more or less? Which competitors have you used in the past?

4. What are the factors which will make you consider using our brand? Product, brand idea or purpose, service experience, price? A personal relationship with the company? What do you see as the difference between our brand and our competitors?

Search and Buy stage

Search is a growing part of the B2B customer journey, giving the customer more control. They take action to learn more about the brand to fill in gaps or doubts the customers may have. They may use a combination of online, industry-specific publications or personal conversations with those they trust.

Customers will use a broad Google search, go to specific websites of brands within their consideration set, read well-known industry news, expert reviews, or browse online customer reviews.

The higher the risk of the purchase, the more in-depth the search, using comparisons and criteria to eliminate brands. You need to understand those risks and understand the online tools customers use, such as side-by-side comparisons, demonstration videos, detailed descriptions of ingredients or process, and a chat function to engage with questions and personalized answers.

When a purchase is large or complex, B2B customers will involve procurement or purchasing agents, and it may take weeks or months to complete. They may go through a formal request for proposal (RFP) to solicit a formal quote or written proposal. When the process is fair, customers will lay out the criteria for their decision, there will be a formal presentation, and then an official judgment will be made. Many times, pricing is intensely scrutinized and it overrides other criteria. B2B brands need to be careful not to waste resources when the potential is futile because the decision may already have been made and the company is following through with their required internal process.

With faster purchases, customers will complete a transaction through a purchase order, brand website, third-party distributors, or e-commerce sites.

Customers will usually make comparisons between brands to resolve any last-second doubts, comparing price to perceived value, using claims and product details to separate one brand from another, using customer ratings and online reviews, or reaching out for advice and details from the salespeople. Marketers need to understand which triggers effectively help to close the sale.

Questions to discover how customers search and buy

Brands need to understand the additional information customers are looking for during the search exploring both online and offline conversations they use.

1. When you are looking for a product or service to help you, how many hours do you usually spend searching online? What are you looking for that helps you decide whether to consider a brand? What doubts or questions do you need to cover off through your search process?

2. Which search tools do you use?

    a. 100% search online on your own, for reviews

    b. Go directly to the website of each potential company

    c. Balance your online search with peer conversation

    d. Reading industry publications

3. Can you think of examples of some of the best tools you have seen:

    a. Who has the best overall Website information?
    b. Who makes the best use of video demonstrations?

    c. Which brands are most active on social media (e.g., LinkedIn or Twitter)?

    d. Who writes the most engaging and interesting white papers?

4. How formal is the decision-making process? Do you use an RFP? Who are the decision-makers, influencers, purchasers, and project administrators in the process? What criteria do you use to evaluate the brands you work with? Can you lay out the top 2-3 criteria you use to assess those brands you engage in? During the search or evaluation stage, is there anything that would make you reject a brand?

Satisfied and Repeat stage

Every category will have unique criteria of customer satisfaction, and the best brands observe, listen, understand, close gaps, and track how well the brand is doing against these criteria.

The higher the risk of the purchase, the more susceptible brands are to post-purchase customer doubt. If a brand does not meet or exceed early expectations, customers will revisit the brands within their consideration set and question the decision they made. If issues remain unresolved, customers may not reconsider your brand at the repeat state. Marketers need to track performance gaps in both product or service and look to fix them.

While every brand has a different purchase cycle, ranging from hourly to five or ten years, repeat purchases are the most significant vote of customer satisfaction. For low involvement or low importance brands, customers can often repeat based on reasonable satisfaction. However, for the higher involvement and higher importance brands, customers go beyond their satisfaction and look at how those around them feel about their brand choice, helping add to the emotional experience.

With experience-led brands, customers will require a series of happy experiences and personal relationships with the company before they open up and begin to trust the brand fully.

Questions to find out how customers are satisfied and repeat

B2B marketers and sales need to figure out ways to over-deliver on the expectations their promise created with customers and track what issues cause customers to fall out of the purchase journey.

1. When you received your product, was everything you expected in the package? Did it arrive on time? Was there anything missing? What might you change? How were the delivery and service?

2. Did your overall experience match up to the criteria you set before the purchase?

3. Did you reach out to the brand after the purchase? Does the brand proactively reach out to you after the purchase? If so, was there outreach enough? Not enough? Just right?

4. How often do you purchase the products and services? How many brands do you keep in your consideration set for repurchasing? Do you have primary and secondary choices?

Loyal and Fan stage

When B2B customers use your brand for a higher share of their purchase requirements than competitors, they start to exhibit loyalty. As the connection shifts from functional to emotional, they begin to see your brand as a ritual or part of their work life.

The most loyal become outspoken advocates who influence their network through positive online reviews, social media recommendations to their friends or peers, and personal advice at the lunch table or direct conversations.

Many times, I ask brands if they treat their best customers better than they treat other customers. Sadly, the answer I get far too often is, "No, we treat everyone the same."

Questions to find out how customers become loyal and turn into potential brand fans

It becomes essential for marketers to know who their best customers are, and treat them better than they do other customers, to make them feel special, to help tighten the bond to turn them, into loyal brand lovers.

Marketers must know who they are and look for ways to cultivate their enthusiasm. Marketers must look to create shareable moments to trigger new awareness with influence. This influence can be potent when the brand fans denote the expert within their peer network.

1. Are you the type of person to recommend brands to your peers? When do you become an advocate?

2. Have you provided any testimonial or reviews? What is the tipping point for you to write a testimonial? What makes you an outspoken supporter, and how does that show up?

3. What does the brand do for you that makes you feel special?

Work Exercise #1

Using the brand that you are working on, start to define the target market:

1. Use 3-4 different demographic factors to write your target market description

2. What are the enemies that torment your customers?

3. What are the insights we know will connect?

Work Exercise #2

Complete the seven questions that make up the customer profile

1. What is the description of the customer target?

2. What are the customer's main needs?

3. Who is the customer's enemy who torments them every day?

4. What are the insights we know about the customer?

5. What does the customers think now?

6. How does the customers buy?

7. What do we want customers to see, think, do, feel or whisper?

Chapter Nine

How to define your brand positioning to help your brand win

Build your brand positioning around your core strength: product, story, customer experience, or price

If you do not define your brand, then you run the risk of the possibility that your competitors will define your brand. And you might not like it.

I will show you the homework you must do to figure out a winning brand positioning statement. The tools are designed to help decide who your brand will serve and what you will stand for as a brand. In the last two chapters, you narrowed the target to those customers who are most capable of loving what your brand does best.

In this chapter, I will show you how to find the ideal balance between the functional and emotional benefits, to find which ones are simple, interesting, motivating, and ownable for your brand.

Where to play and where to win

As you create your brand positioning statement, look for the ideal **space to play** and **space your brand can win.** As I showed in the competitive brand strategy, I will use that same Venn diagram to map out everything your customers want or need, what your brand does best and what your competitor does best.

The first step is always to find **where to play**, which matches up what your customers want with what your brand does best. This tool forces you to focus on meeting the customer's needs.

Next, you layer in what your competition does best, to narrow the space **where your brand can win**. Your brand might be fast, but if your competitor is even faster, then you will lose out if you try to play in that space.

Brand positioning statement elements

Four elements make up a brand positioning statement, including who you serve, where you play, where will you win and why customers should believe you. These are the customer target, marketplace definition, the customer benefit, and support points.

1. Who is your **customer target**? What slice of the marketplace is the most motivated by what your brand offers? Do not just think about who you want but rather who wants your brand.
2. Where will you play? What is the **competitive set** that defines the space in the market where your brand competes? Positioning is always relative to the other companies your brand competes against.
3. Where will you win? What is the main **customer benefit** promise you will make to the customer target to make your brand stand out as interesting, simple, unique, motivating, and ownable? Do not talk about what you do (features); instead, talk about what the customer gets (functional benefits) and how the customer feels (emotional benefits).
4. Why should they believe us? Understand what **support points** and features you need to back up your main promise. These support points should close any possible doubts, questions, or concerns the customer has after hearing your main promise.

Before you randomly write out a brand positioning statement based on your intuition, I will force you to think deeper to help focus your decisions on the best possible space for your brand to win and own.

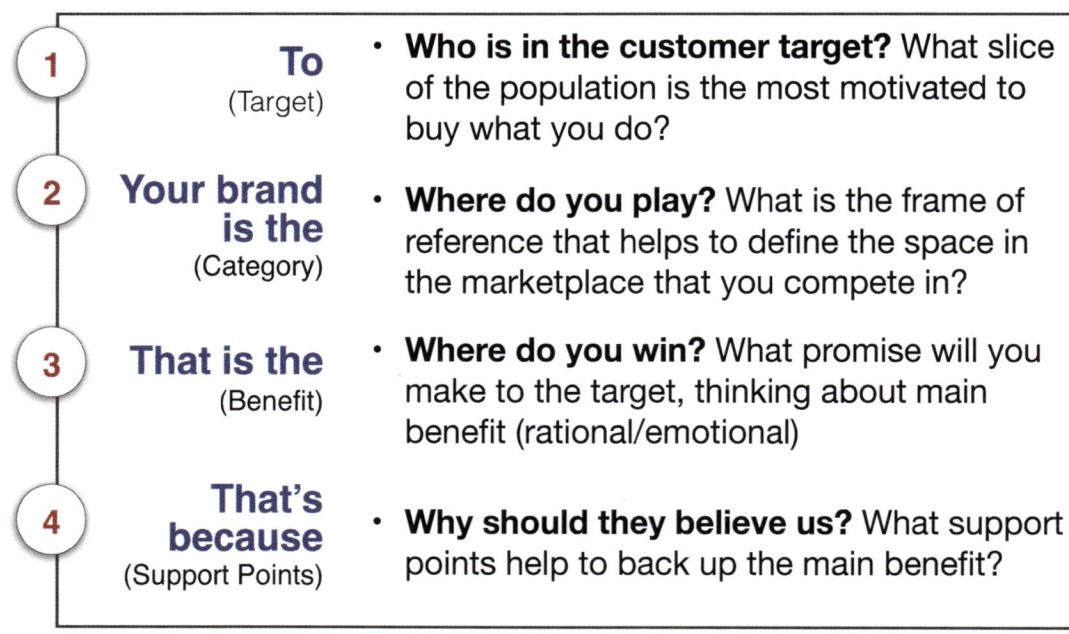

The customer benefits ladder

The customer benefits ladder helps turn your brand's features into customer benefits. Stop talking about what your brand does and start talking about what your customer gets. The four steps to building a customer benefits ladder:

1. Leverage all available research to define your **ideal customer target** profile with need states, customer insights, and the customer enemy.

2. Brainstorm all possible brand **features**. Focus on those features you believe give your brand a competitive advantage.

3. Move up to the **functional benefits** by putting yourself in the shoes of the customer. For each feature on your list, ask, "So, what do I get from that?" Challenge yourself to come up with better benefits by asking the question until you move into a richer zone.

4. Then move up to the **emotional benefits**. Look at each functional benefit and in the voice of the customer you should ask, "So, how does that make me feel?" As you did in step 3, keep asking the question until you see a more in-depth emotional space you can win with and own.

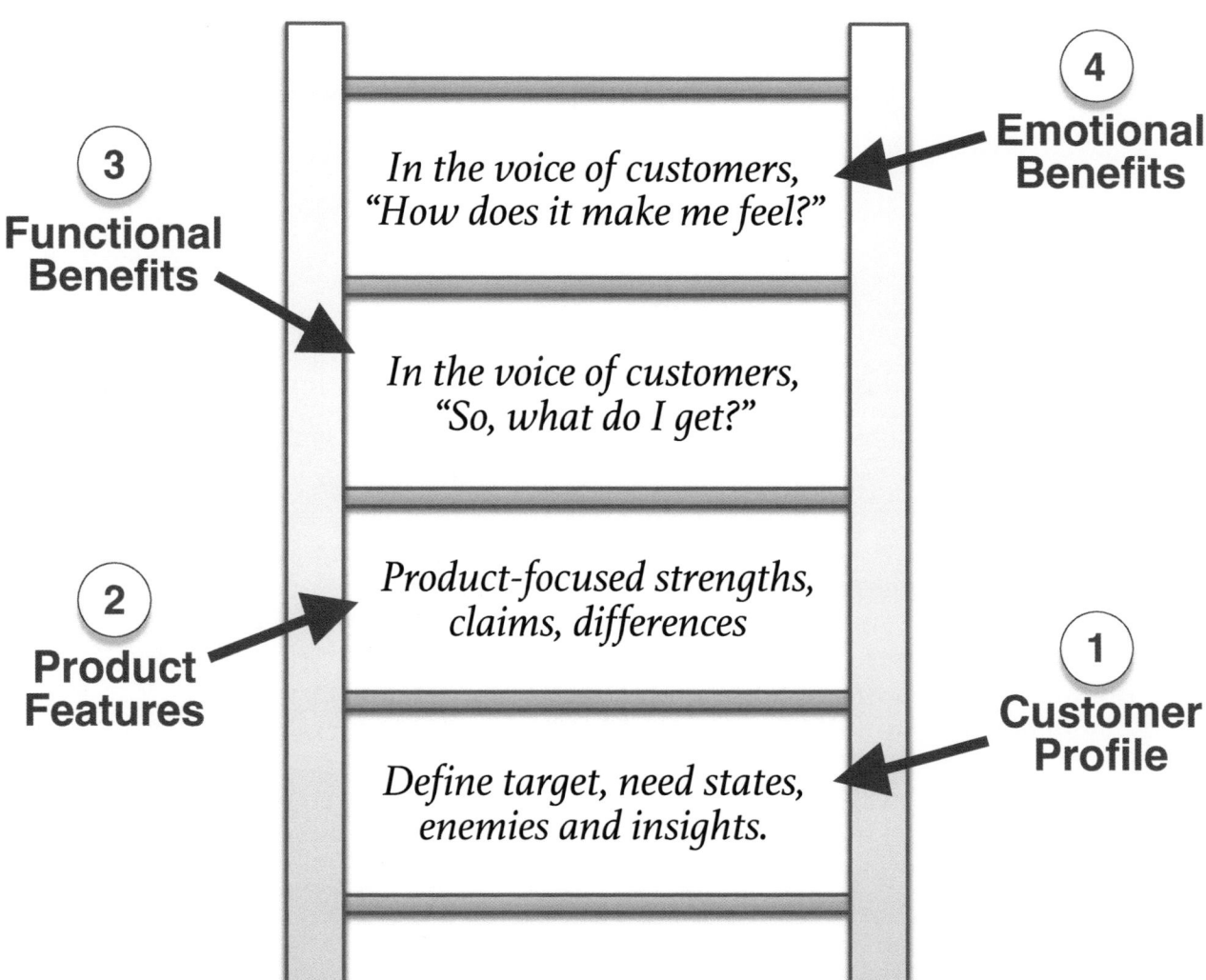

Functional benefits

To help brand leaders, I have taken **nine functional need state zones** and expanded the list to over 50 potential functional benefits your brand can build around. As you look through the list, gravitate to the functional benefits you think will fit the needs of your customers and where your brand can do it better than competitors. Start with the words on the cheat sheet below, then layer in your creative language based on specific category words or specific customer words and phrases they use.

The functional benefits cheat sheet

Emotional benefits

Below you will find a list of 40 potential emotional benefits. From my experience, marketers are better at finding the ideal rational benefits compared with how they work at finding the ideal emotional benefits for their brands.

As a brand, you want to own one emotional space in the customer's heart as much as you own a rational space in the customer's mind.

When I push brand managers to get emotional, they struggle and opt for what they view as obvious emotions, even if they do not fit with their brand. I swear every brand manager thinks their brand should be the trusted, reliable, and likable. Use our cheat sheet to dig deeper on emotions.

The emotional benefits cheat sheet

Our **emotional cheat sheet** has nine emotional customer benefits zones, which include optimism, freedom, get noticed, feel satisfied, comfort, fit with company, stay in control, self-assured, and curious for knowledge. Use the words within each zone to provide added context.

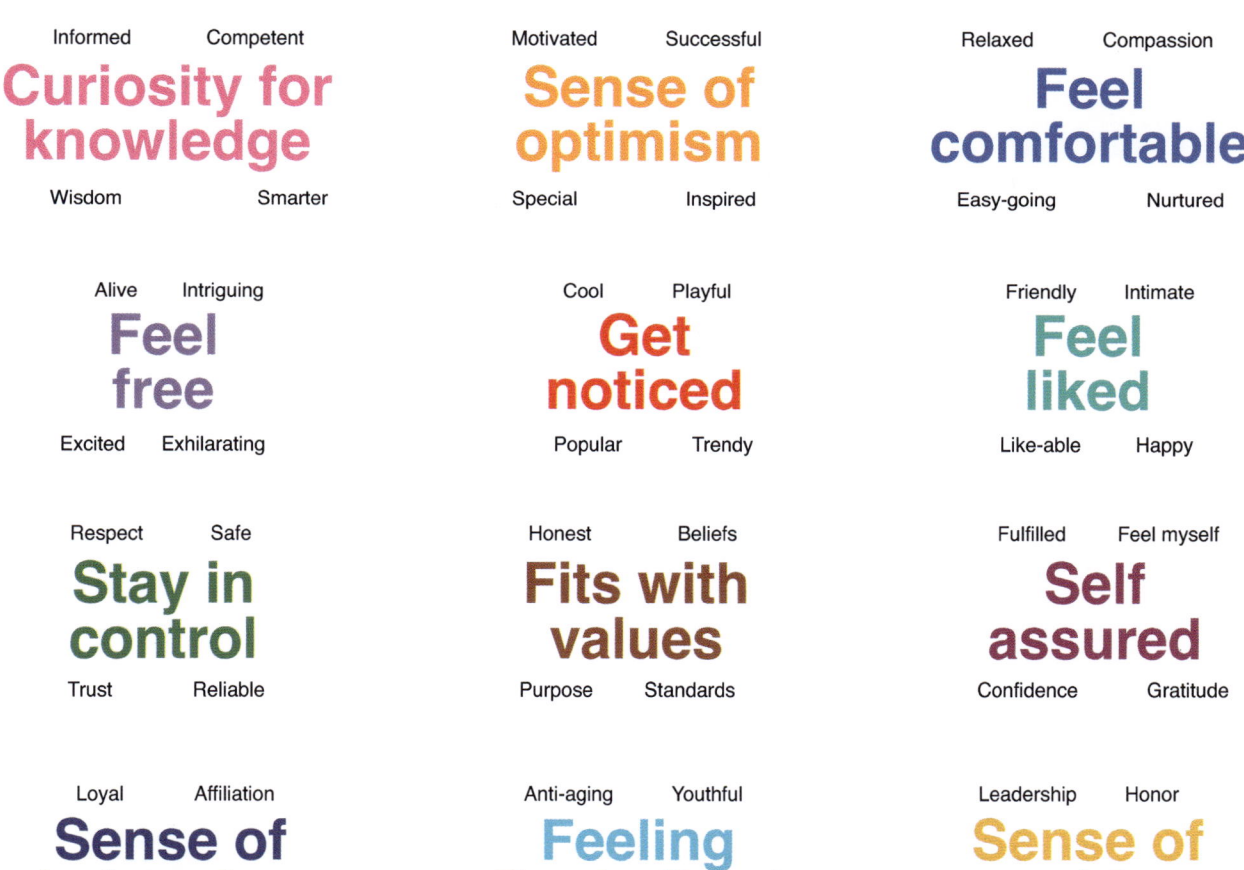

Build around benefit clusters

Start by looking at the two cheat sheets and narrow down to potential clusters of the functional and emotional benefits. Match what customers want and what your brand does best. I recommend that you take three of the zones from each of the two cheat sheets, and then add 2-3 support words per zone to create a cluster.

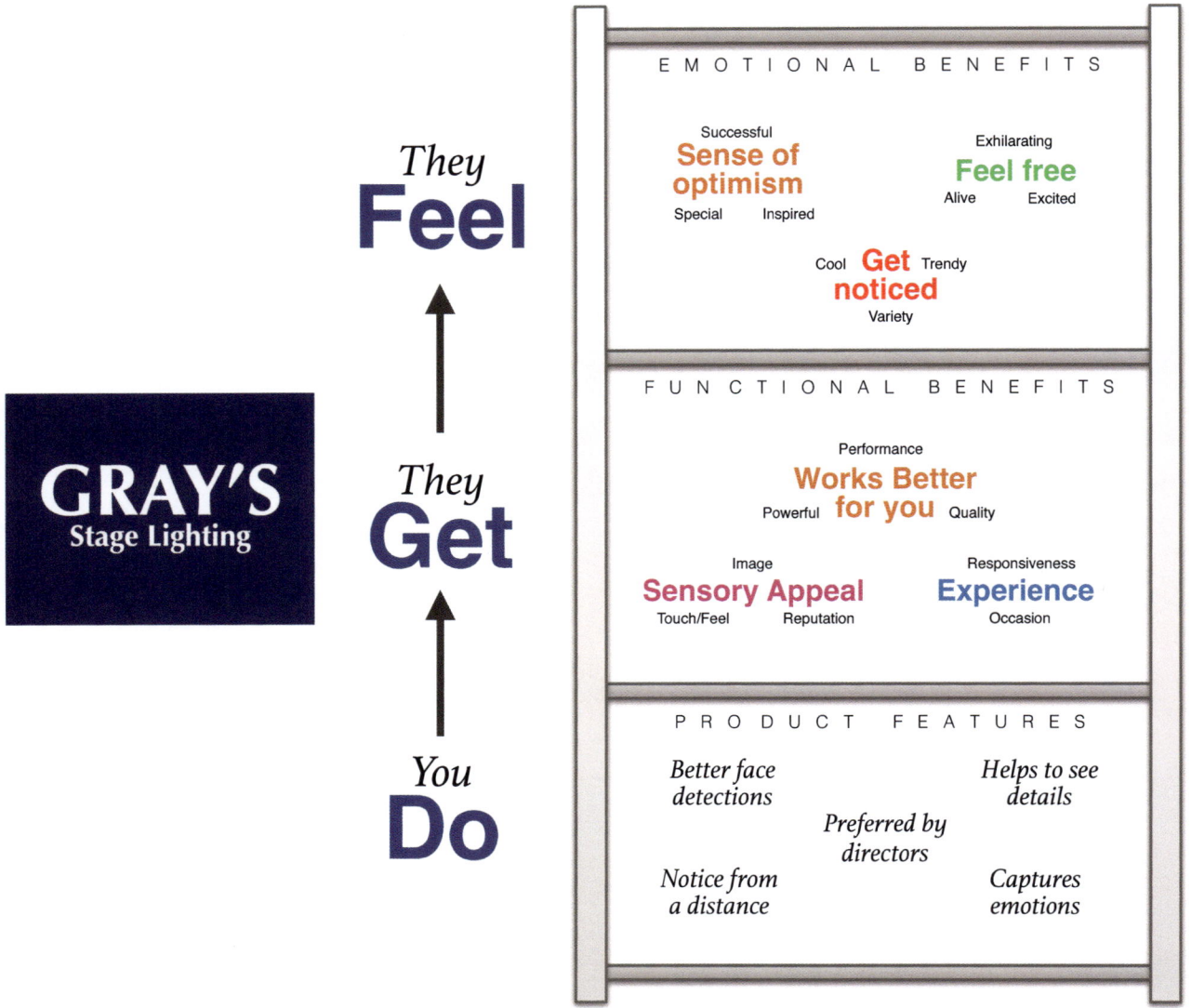

Customer benefits brainstorm

For each cluster, use the words to inspire a brainstorm of specific benefit statements that fit your brand, using the specific brand, customer or category words. For Gray's Lighting, a fictional stage lighting brand that provides such a high quality lighting that it brings out every detail on the face of actors.

Concerning functional benefits, I have chosen to build around functional clusters, such as works better for you, sensory appeal, and experiences, and the emotional clusters, such as optimism, feeling free, and getting noticed.

Once I made those choices, I began brainstorming 10-15 key benefit phrases that start with "I get..." for the functional benefits and "I feel" for the emotional benefits.

Functional Clusters

Performance
Works Better
Powerful Quality

Reputation
Sensory
Touch/Feel Image

Responsiveness
Experience
Occasion

Benefit statement brainstorm

- I get higher quality lighting to bring richness to the stage.
- I get better performance in bringing emotions into the show.
- I get lighting that brings facial expressions to life.
- I get responsive lighting systems with flexibility.
- I get lights that bring a better performance from my actors.
- I get to bring the actors faces to life for theatre patrons
- I get to see/feel every emotion on the actor's faces.
- I get lighting designed for actor expressions.
- I get to experience what it's like to sit in the front row.
- I get onsite installation from Gray's team.
- I get energy efficient lighting
- I get a trial test run of the lights before buying.
- I get a guaranteed satisfaction or replacement lights.

Emotional Clusters

Successful
Optimism
Special Inspired

Exhilarating
Feel free
Alive Excited

Cool
Get noticed
Trendy

- I feel more optimistic that patrons will love our show.
- I am inspired to showcase the facial expressions of our actors.
- I feel we are getting leading edge lighting before anyone else.
- I feel inspired to see the show from the back row.
- I feel free to direct, knowing I'm using the latest technology
- I feel special knowing I'm one of the first to try the latest.
- I feel the show will be more successful.
- I feel excited knowing everyone will see what I see.
- It will be cool to be on the leading edge of technology
- I am excited to see the impact on our actors faces.

Find the winning statements

After the brainstorm, you need a tool to help decide on which ones are the best for your brand positioning. Looking at the positioning Venn diagram we have been using, I have created a 2x2 grid to help sort through the potential benefits to find the winners, according to which are most motivating to customers and most ownable for your brand. You will see the same four zones from the Venn diagram are now on the customer benefits sort grid, including the winning, losing, risky, and dumb zone.

With Gray's Lighting, you can see that the "bringing the actors faces to life" customer benefit is most highly motivating and highly ownable benefit statement for the brand, helping it land in the winning zone.

On the other hand, the customer benefit of "energy efficient" is highly motivating but already owned by other companies, so it falls into the losing zone.

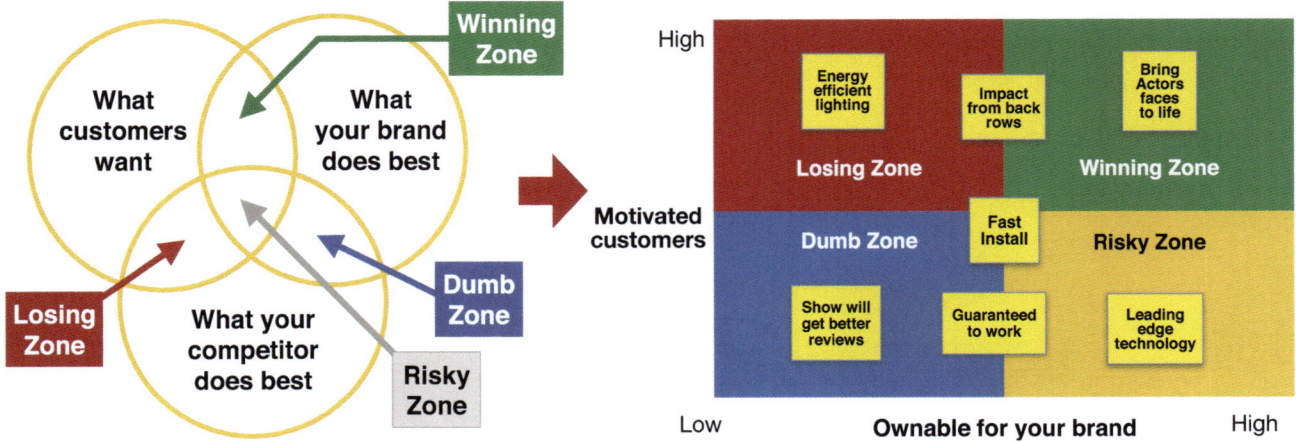

The "leading technology" benefit falls into the risky zone. The benefit of "better reviews" is likely unrealistic, making it neither motivating nor ownable, so it falls into the dumb zone.

Support points

I took one logic class at university, and the only thing I learned was "premise-premise conclusion." It was an easy class, but a life-long lesson that has stuck with me. Here is a classic logical argument statement:

- All fish live in water (premise)
- Tuna are fish (premise)
- Therefore, tuna live in the water (conclusion).

This example fits with my brand positioning statement model, as the main customer benefit is the conclusion with a need for two support points as the premises. If pure logic teaches us that two premise points are good enough to draw out any conclusion, then you only need two "reasons to believe" (RTB).

Brands that build concepts with a laundry list of RTBs are not doing their job in making focused decisions on what support points are required. Since customers seeing constant brand promises from sales reps, having a long list of support points risks making your brand communications a cluttered mess. Claims can be a useful tool in helping to support your RTB, yet an RTB should never be your main conclusion.

There are four types of claims you can use on your brand:

Process support
- How your product works differently
- What do you do differently within the production process
- Showcase what you do differently within the production process
- What added service you provide in the value chain

Product claims
- Usage of an ingredient that makes your brand better
- Process or ingredient that makes your brand safer
- Process that makes your brand cheaper

Third-person endorsement
- Experts in the field who can speak on your brand's behalf
- Past users/clients with proof support of stories or reviews
- Recognized awards, such J.D. Power

Behavioral results
- Clinical tests
- In market usage study
- Before and after studies

Brainstorm of the best claims and features for Gray's Lighting

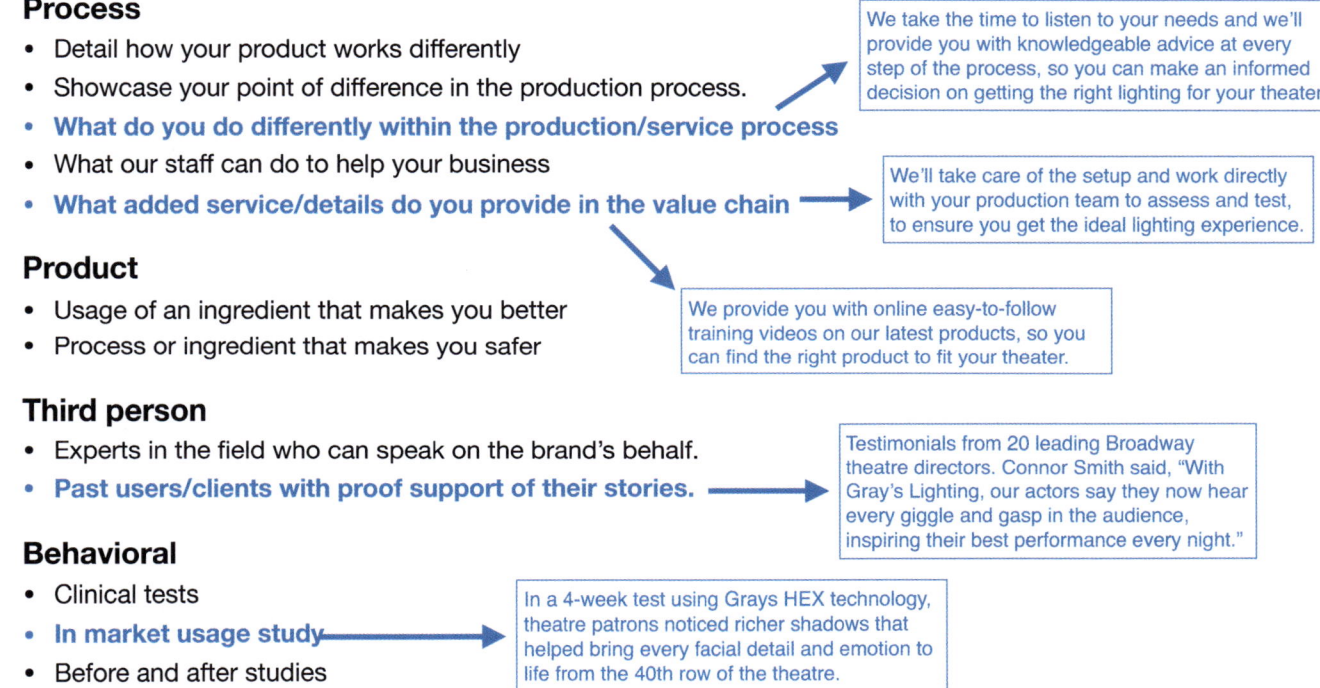

Process
- Detail how your product works differently
- Showcase your point of difference in the production process.
- **What do you do differently within the production/service process**
- What our staff can do to help your business
- **What added service/details do you provide in the value chain**

We take the time to listen to your needs and we'll provide you with knowledgeable advice at every step of the process, so you can make an informed decision on getting the right lighting for your theater.

We'll take care of the setup and work directly with your production team to assess and test, to ensure you get the ideal lighting experience.

Product
- Usage of an ingredient that makes you better
- Process or ingredient that makes you safer

We provide you with online easy-to-follow training videos on our latest products, so you can find the right product to fit your theater.

Third person
- Experts in the field who can speak on the brand's behalf.
- **Past users/clients with proof support of their stories.**

Testimonials from 20 leading Broadway theatre directors. Connor Smith said, "With Gray's Lighting, our actors say they now hear every giggle and gasp in the audience, inspiring their best performance every night."

Behavioral
- Clinical tests
- **In market usage study**
- Before and after studies

In a 4-week test using Grays HEX technology, theatre patrons noticed richer shadows that helped bring every facial detail and emotion to life from the 40th row of the theatre.

How to write the final brand positioning statement

Taking all the homework, here are some thoughts on bringing the brand positioning statement together:

1. **Who is your customer target?** Keep your target definition focused. Bring the target to life with need states, customer insights, and a customer enemy. You can have groups of customers, or specific customers.
2. **Where will you play?** Define the space you play in, measuring it against those brands you compete with.

3. **Where will you win?** Narrow your benefit down to one thing. Never try to stand for too many things at once—whether too many functional benefits or too many emotional benefits. You cannot be all things to all people. Make sure you talk benefits, not features. The ideal space must be unique and motivating to the customers while being ownable for your brand.
4. **Why should they believe us?** The role of support points is to resolve any potential doubts the customers might have when they see your main benefit. Ensure these support points are not just random claims or features that you want to jam into your brand message. They should support and fit with the main benefit.

The final brand positioning statement for Gray's Lighting

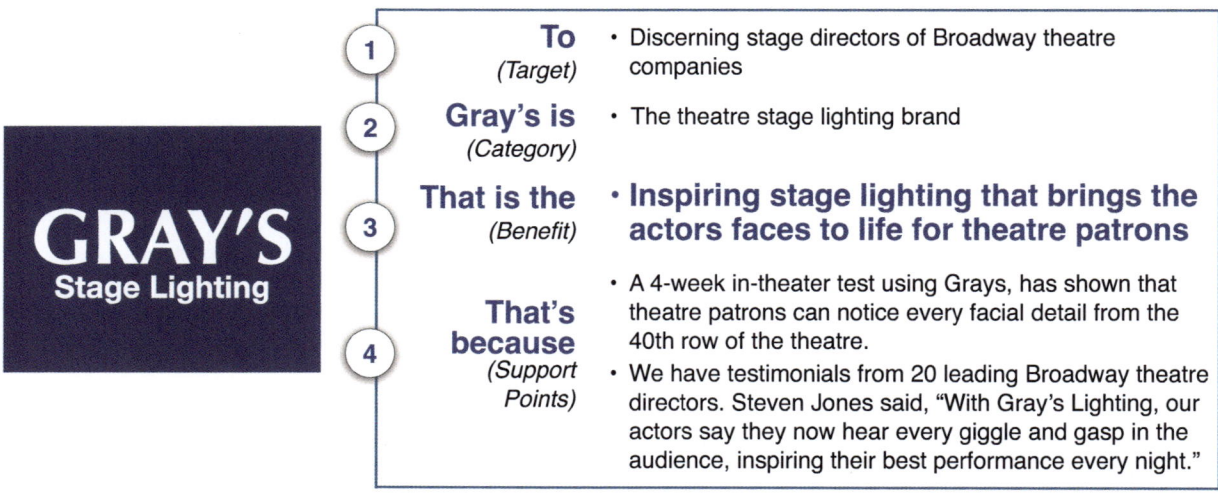

Brand positioning statement for an industrial product

Example of a B2B manufacturing equipment brand

1. **To** *(Target)* — Entrepreneurs, with an underdog, challenging spirit who is looking to launch an authentic craft beer that can take on the big guys
2. **Gray's is** *(Category)* — The brewery manufacturing equipment brand
3. **That** *(Benefit)* — **Is the helping hand so craft breweries can achieve a competitive advantage over the mainstream beers**
4. **That's because** *(Support Points)*
   - At Gray's, it is more about our people than just our products. We take the time to listen to your needs and we'll provide you with knowledgeable advice at every state of the process, so you can make an informed decision on getting the right equipment.
   - We take care of your brewery structure and work directly with your operations teams to make sure you make the highest quality beer.

Example of a B2B medical supplies

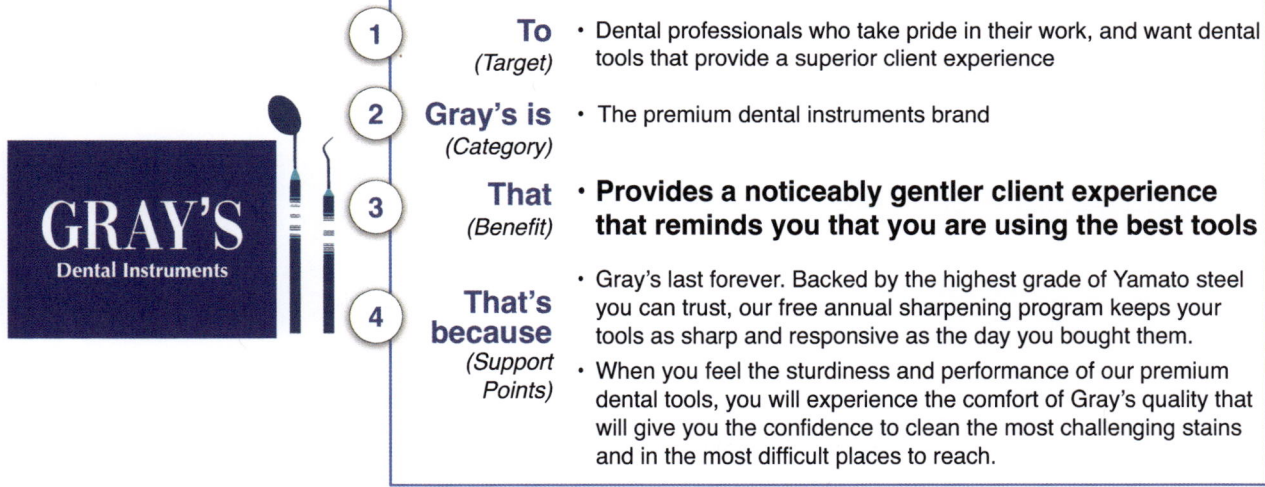

1. **To** *(Target)* — Dental professionals who take pride in their work, and want dental tools that provide a superior client experience
2. **Gray's is** *(Category)* — The premium dental instruments brand
3. **That** *(Benefit)* — **Provides a noticeably gentler client experience that reminds you that you are using the best tools**
4. **That's because** *(Support Points)*
   - Gray's last forever. Backed by the highest grade of Yamato steel you can trust, our free annual sharpening program keeps your tools as sharp and responsive as the day you bought them.
   - When you feel the sturdiness and performance of our premium dental tools, you will experience the comfort of Gray's quality that will give you the confidence to clean the most challenging stains and in the most difficult places to reach.

Work exercise #1

Using the brand that you are working on, map out the potential benefits clusters. What are the three functional zones, and 3-4 words in each zone? What are the three emotional zones, and 3-4 words in each zone?

Work exercise #2

Using your benefit clusters, conduct a functional benefits statement brainstorm and list out key "I get" phrases

-
-
-

Using your benefit clusters, conduct a emotional benefits statement brainstorm and list out key "I feel" phrases

-
-
-

Using the grid, sort \through all your functional and emotional benefit statements to see where they land on how well they motivate customers and how ownable it is for your brand.

Based on the grid, which are the best functional and emotional benefit statements:

What are your best support points

-
-
-
-

Work exercise #3

With your decisions on exercise #2 build your brand positioning statement

1. Who is the most motivated customer?

2. The space you play in

3. Combine functional and emotional in one sentence

4. Two support points that close off any gaps that customers might have

Chapter Ten

How to create a brand idea you can build everything around

Organize everything you do around a brand idea

You have to realize that your customers are bombarded with brand promises all day long. The first seven seconds a customer engages with a brand is a make-or-break moment, whether they listen or how they listen. The brand must captivate the customer's mind quickly or the customer will move on. The brand must be able to entice customers to want to find out more, then motivate them to want to see, think, feel, or act in positive ways that benefit the brand. I will show you how to develop a brand idea that serves as your brand's seven-second sales pitch

What is a brand idea?

To me, the brand idea simplifies everything, not just for your customer but for everyone working on the brand. The dictionary definition of the word "idea" means a thought, opinion, belief, or mental impression. A brand idea must be all those things.

A B2B brand must get customers to agree on the brand reputation and get employees who work behind the scenes of the brand to agree and deliver. Let's assume they are the same thing. What we are creating is the most significant, most prominent, and yet most succinct definition of the brand. To become a successful and beloved brand, you need a brand idea that is interesting, simple, unique, inspiring, motivating, and ownable.

The brand idea apparatus

In Psychology 101, they teach the three constructs of human personality as the ego, the id, and the superego. In our brand idea apparatus, I see three separate constructs that must all work together similarly:

1. The brand soul is a collection of the inner purpose, motivations, and values, which explains **"What you want your brand to be."** The complexity and mess of a large organization filled with silos lead to conflicting opinions and motivations, making it challenging to gain alignment around one brand soul.

2. The B2B brand reputation is the outside view of the brand, which explains **"What customers think of you."** Customers own your brand's reputation in their minds. The complexity of the marketplace has conflicting messages from competitors, expert influencers, and other companies within the value chain, each cluttering the opinion of your brand.

3. As the ego of the human mind works to regulate the id and superego, the brand idea works as the **stabilizer** between the inner motivations of those behind the brand and the outward reputation, which is a constantly-changing view of the brand. As a stabilizer role, the brand idea must adjust to the actual reputation yet send signals to steer the customer's mind towards the desired reputation, which helps to express the brand soul.

A brand is in equilibrium when the soul, reputation, and brand idea are equal

Inside your Company
What you want your brand to be

Stabilizer
Brand Idea summarizes brand soul, while influencing reputation

Outward Reputation
What your customers think of your brand

The brand idea must represent your brand soul

The brand soul defines the moral fiber for why everyone who works on the brand "wakes up each day to deliver greatness on behalf of the brand." The brand soul must be an inspiration to align the team behind a common purpose, cause, or excitement for why they do what they do. Just like the soul of a human, every brand brings a unique combination of unexplainable assets, culture, motivations, and beliefs. Support your brand purpose with a set of values and beliefs, deeply held in the heart of everyone who works behind the scenes of the brand.

From the outside eye, the complexity of an organization can appear to be a complete mess. Many organizations are filled with silos of conflicts that get in the way of what the brand stands for with varying opinions on where the brand should go next.

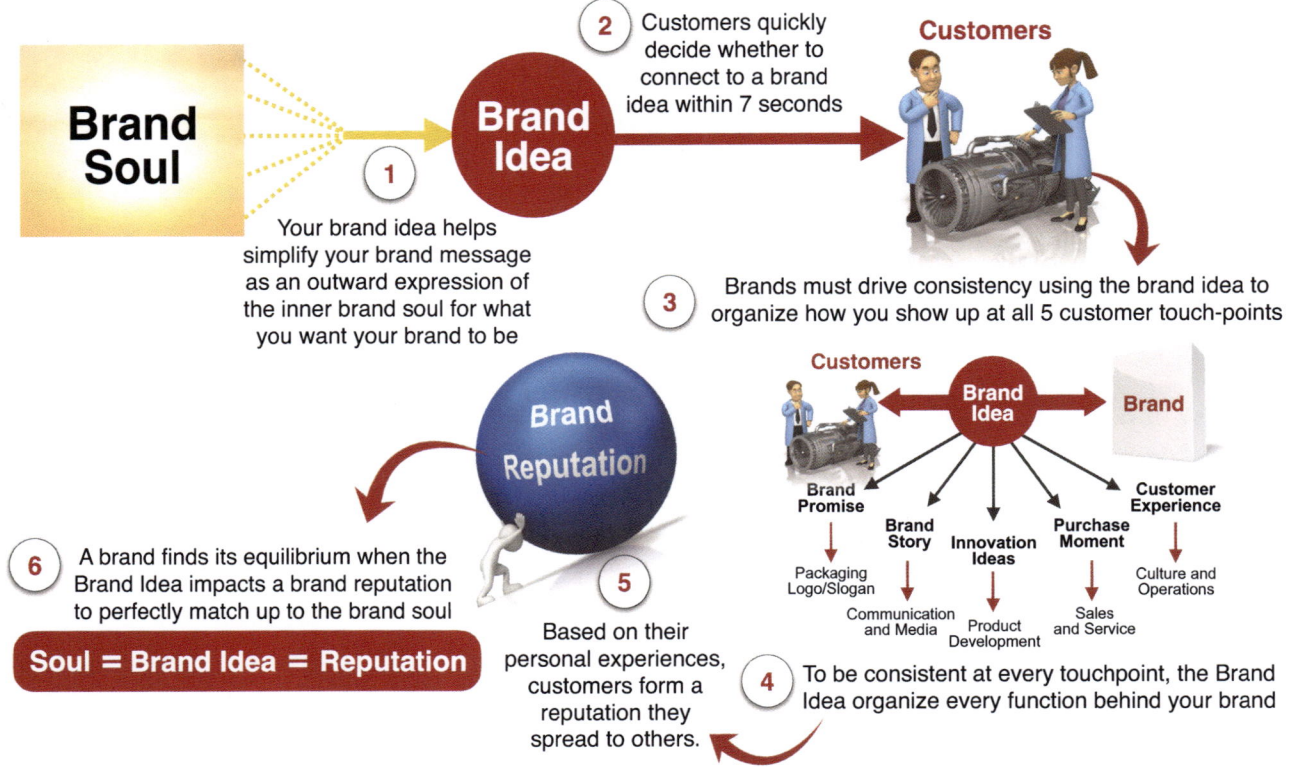

Everyone in your organization must be able to describe the brand in the same way, whether they're the most remote sales rep, technician in the lab, ad agency, or CEO.

When a brand is in trouble, the first thing I ask is, "Describe the brand in seven seconds for me." When I start to hear conflicting answers or confusion, I know the team lacks alignment. If you cannot consistently describe your brand within the walls of your organization, how could you ever expect customers to hold a consistent reputation in their minds?

When the brand does something in conflict with the brand soul, a healthy organization should resist and possibly even reject that action as outside of the cultural norms and beliefs of the brand. To accept something that goes against the brand's soul would put the culture at risk.

I have met brand leaders who would sooner fail than give up on their principles and beliefs. They say, "I don't want to sell out just to be successful." I respect their conviction because they understand themselves. A brand should be extremely personal to trigger the passion of everyone who works on the brand.

The brand idea must manage your brand reputation

The brand reputation lives within the minds of your customers, out in the crazy, unstructured, unorganized, and cluttered real world. While a brand tries to project itself out to the market, a brand reputation meanders and adjusts to the constant changes and complexities of the marketplace.

There are customer challenges to the brand reputation, including continually changing customer need states, conflicting voices from competitors, key influencers, or from your own partners.

The role of the brand idea works in the middle, between the brand and the customer, acting as a stabilizer between the internal passion at the heart of the brand soul and the outward opinions of the brand reputation.

A slogan is not a brand idea

While a brand idea must be short and pithy, please do not mix it up with an advertising tagline. From the world of consumer brands, while I love the "Just do it" campaign for Nike, it is an advertising slogan, not a strategic brand idea.

A slogan is not a robust enough idea to help guide the R&D team to design the next Nike shoe. It will not focus HR on who to hire for Nike's retail store and it will not help create the ideal consumer experience. The strategic brand idea for Nike should be, "Nike pushes your athletic boundaries beyond what you think is possible."

A slogan should never drive your brand strategy. A brand idea should drive your slogan.

Examples of B2B brand ideas

Here are **four examples** of brand ideas that gets the B2B brand down to the seven-second brand pitch. Grainger offers the "widest range of tools" while Intel owns making any computer "faster". Google organizes the world's information to make people more knowledgeable. Gore-Tex makes your product an "all-weather version."

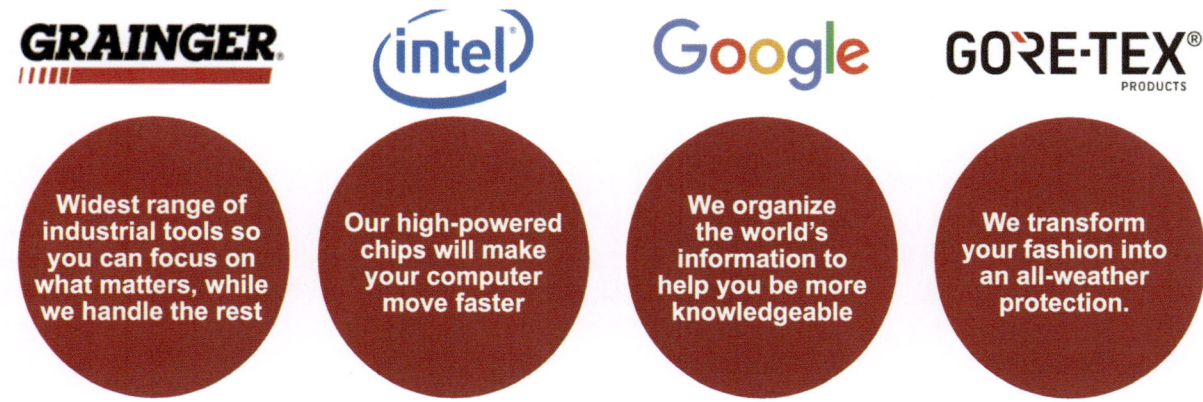

What is your one word to describe your brand?

There is power in narrowing your focus down to one or two word brand pitch. Once you figure out that one word, you will never do anything that jeopardizes or goes against that one word.

Grainger can never be out of stock on a tool. Intel can never come second place to another computer chip option. Google always has to find the solution. And Gore-Tex always protects.

Brand idea checklist

The brand idea must be **interesting** enough to engage and entice customers on a first encounter to want to know more. Keep it **simple** enough to gain entry into the customer's mind. Your idea must be **easily layered** to organize everything you do to match up with the five customer touchpoints, including the brand promise, brand story, innovation, purchase moment, and customer experience.

Brand idea checklist
- ✓ Interesting enough to entice customer on a first encounter
- ✓ Simple enough to gain entry into the customer's mind
- ✓ Unique enough to build a reputation
- ✓ Able to motivate customers to think, feel, and act
- ✓ inspiring employees to deliver the brand promise
- ✓ Easily layered to organize everything you do
- ✓ Ownable, so no other competitor can infringe on your space
- ✓ Confidently build your brand reputation over time

Your idea must be **unique** enough to build a reputation so customers will perceive the brand as better, different, or cheaper. Your idea must be able to **motivate** customers to think, feel, and act in ways that benefit your brand.

The idea must represent the inner brand soul of everyone who works on the brand, **inspiring** employees to deliver the brand promise and amazing experiences. Finally, the brand idea must be **ownable** so no other competitor can infringe on your space, and you can confidently build your brand **reputation** over time.

The brand idea blueprint

I created a brand idea blueprint, which has five areas that surround the brand idea.

On the internal brand soul side, describe the products and services, as well as the cultural inspiration, which is the internal rallying cry to everyone who works on the brand.

On the external brand reputation side, define the ideal customer reputation and the reputation among necessary influencers or partners.

The brand role acts as a bridge between the internal and external sides.

- **Products and services:** What is the focused point of difference your products or services can win on because they meet the customer's needs and separate your brand from competitors?

- **Customer reputation:** What is the desired reputation of your brand, which attracts, excites, engages, and motivates customers to think, feel, and purchase your brand?

- **Cultural inspiration:** What is the internal rallying cry that reflects your brand's purpose, values and motivations that will inspire, challenge, and guide your culture?

- **Influencer reputation:** Who are the key industry influencers and potential partners who impact the brand? What is their view of the brand, which would make them recommend or partner with your brand?

- **Brand role (archetype):** What is the link between the internal soul and the external reputation?

Using archetypes to determine the brand role

Borrowing from the world of psychology, where they use personality archetypes to describe people, we can use brand archetypes to help you figure out the role of your brand, which adds to your brand idea. When a brand offers spiritual, freedom or knowledge, they fit with the explorer, sage, or innocent archetypes.

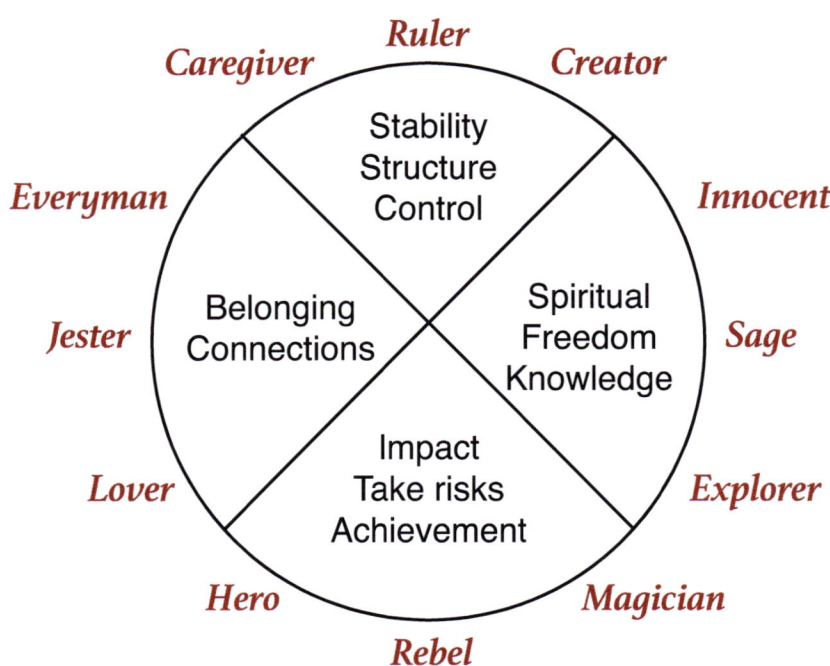

Brands delivering stability, structure, and control fit with the ruler, creator, or caregiver. Brands that take risks create an impact or reach for achievement; they fit with the hero, rebel, or magician. Then, brands that focus on belonging or connections, they may look to the everyman, lover, or jester.

- **Creator:** The artist and dreamers, who are imaginative, expressive, and innovative. They believe they can see a better future.
- **Ruler:** The industry leader, who are confident, responsible, and authoritative. They promise power, control, and stability to their customers.
- **Caregiver:** The helping hand, who is selfless, empathetic and nurturing. They offer protection, safety, and support.
- **Everyman:** The approachable brand who is down-to-earth, dependable, and honest. They offer a sense of belonging and comfort.
- **Jester:** The carefree brand who is joyful, carefree, and unusual. They give customers permission to have fun and be happy.
- **Lover:** The idealistic dreamer who is passionate, magnetic and committed. They exude passion and create desire with their customers.
- **Innocent:** The romantic dreamer brands who are optimistic, wholesome, and pure. They want a safer and more beautiful world.
- **Sage:** Trusted advisor and teacher, which is wise, articulate, and open-minded. They promise wisdom, wanting to help their followers.
- **Explorer:** The self-discovery brand, which is worldly, independent, and purpose-driven. They promise freedom, innovation, and experiences.
- **Magician:** The visionary brand which is unrelenting, driven, and charismatic. They offer transformative knowledge and new experiences.
- **Rebel:** The anti-establishment brand, which is unconventional, defiant, and free-spirited. The promise of a disruptive revolution.
- **Hero:** The winner brand, which is determined, skillful, and selfless. They fight off the enemy with the promise of triumph and success.

How to find your brand idea

Step 1: Keywords brainstorm for each of the five areas

With a cross-functional team working on the brand, start with a brainstorm of keywords for each of the five areas around the brand idea. Expose the team to the work you have done on the brand positioning statement, including details on the target profile, customer benefits ladder work, and the customer benefits sort. Ask participants to bring their knowledge, wisdom, and opinions from where they sit within the organization. The first step is generating 15-20 words that describe each of the five areas.

Products and services
Gray's Hex Lighting is the highest quality lighting, bringing brightness and shadows to faces.

Cultural inspiration
Our lighting innovation has as much of an impact on a Broadway play as anyone.

Customer reputation
Our stage lighting brings the actor's faces and emotional performances to life.

Brand role
Our lighting creates magic when it brings out the emotions of the actors and transforms the emotions of the actors for the audience.

Influencer reputation
World's best directors are inspired to deliver the greatest performances from their actors.

Step 2: Turn keywords into key phrases for each of the five areas

Next, get the team to vote to narrow down the list to the best 3-5 words for each section. You will begin to see specific themes and keywords. Take those selected words and build phrases to summarize each section.

Step 3: Summarize it all to create a brand idea

Once you have phrases for all five areas, the team should feel inspired to use their creative energy to come up with the brand idea.

Products and services
Gray's Hex Lighting is the highest quality lighting, bringing brightness and shadows to faces.

Customer reputation
Our stage lighting brings the actor's faces and emotional performances to life.

Cultural inspiration
Our lighting innovation has as much of an impact on a Broadway play as anyone.

Added touch of lighting magic to an already magical theatrical experience.

Influencer reputation
World's best directors are inspired to deliver the greatest performances from their actors.

Brand role
Our lighting creates magic when it brings out the emotions of the actors and transforms the emotions of the actors for the audience.

Find a summary statement that captures everything around the circle. Try to get a few different options for the brand idea you can test with both customers and employees.

How to write a brand concept

With all the homework you have done on the brand positioning and brand idea, you have everything you need to write a brand concept. Write your concept in as realistic a manner as possible, narrowing it down to one main benefit and two support points. It should be realistic enough to fit on your website, new product innovation, content copy, or your sales message.

Too many brand leaders try to write concepts that include everything, with a long list of claims and reasons to believe. There is no value in writing a concept just to pass a test only to find yourself unable to execute the concept in the market.

- **Headline:** The main headline should capture the brand idea. The headline is the first thing customers will see, and it will influence how they engage with the rest of the concept.

- **Insights:** Start every concept with a customer insight (connection point) or customer enemy (pain point) to captivate the customer enough to make them stop and think, "That's exactly how I feel." By sharing messages that resonate, you help your customers feel more engaged with your concept. The enemy or insight must also set up the brand promise.

- **Promise:** The promise statement must bring the main customer benefit to life with a balance of emotional and functional benefits. For Gray's Lighting, I combined the "brings actor's faces to life" functional benefit and "inspiration" emotional benefit into a main brand promise statement.

- **Support points:** The support points should close off any gaps that customers may have after reading the main benefit. An emotional benefit may require functional support to cover off any doubt lingering in the customer's mind.

- **Call-to-action:** Complete the concept with a motivating call-to-action to prompt the customer's purchase intent, which is a significant part of concept testing. Adding a supporting visual is recommended.

Our concept process helps test new product or services

At the early stages of your innovation process, I recommend turning the best ideas into product concepts that you can use to get feedback from customers. Below, you will find an example for a new service offering for Gray's Industrial Tools that promises same day delivery.

Our B2B brand positioning presentation template

Looking at all the brand positioning tools we have introduced throughout our book, below is an ideal process for how to lay out the slides to create your ideal presentation, whether to sell-in your positioning ideas to management, or setup for your brand book.

Our B2B brand positioning templates are available at beloved-brands.com

Work exercise

Using the brand that you are working on, build out your brand idea. Take the words with the most votes for each of the five areas, and write phrase for each one.

Once you have that done, try to see if you can find something in the middle. Come back with 2-3 options for the brand idea in the middle.

Products and Services:

Customer Reputation:

Cultural Inspiration:

Influencer Reputation:

Brand Role:

Once you have each area complete, try to figure out the brand idea

Chapter Eleven
How to use your brand idea to organize everything you do

A brand idea should be used to steer everyone who works behind the scenes of the brand.

B2B brands have an added layer of complexity compared to a consumer brand because the user, buyer, decision maker, and influencer within your customer each play a vital yet disconnected role in the path to purchase. I call it the "business development dance." While you may get one of them interested, it will require a bit of a dance to ensure everyone gets on board. As hard as it is to gain alignment within a company, it is even harder when you sit outside the company. Moreover, you might not even meet face-to-face with those people in these other roles.

Brand leaders must manage the consistent delivery of the brand idea over every customer touchpoint. Whether people are in management, customer service, sales, HR, operations, or an outside agency, everyone should look to the brand idea to guide and focus their decisions.

B2B brands should spend as much effort marketing internally, so everyone at your company understands and shares the idea behind your brand, as your people will be the ones who deliver your brand's promise to your customers.

We normally think of marketing as messages directed only to the customers. For a B2B brand, I recommend equal effort in the marketing to your own employees, as they are the front-line face of your brand, and their behaviors will establish your brand's reputation.

The internal marketing should build out the values and expected behaviors that will define the culture, innovation, and service delivery of your brand.

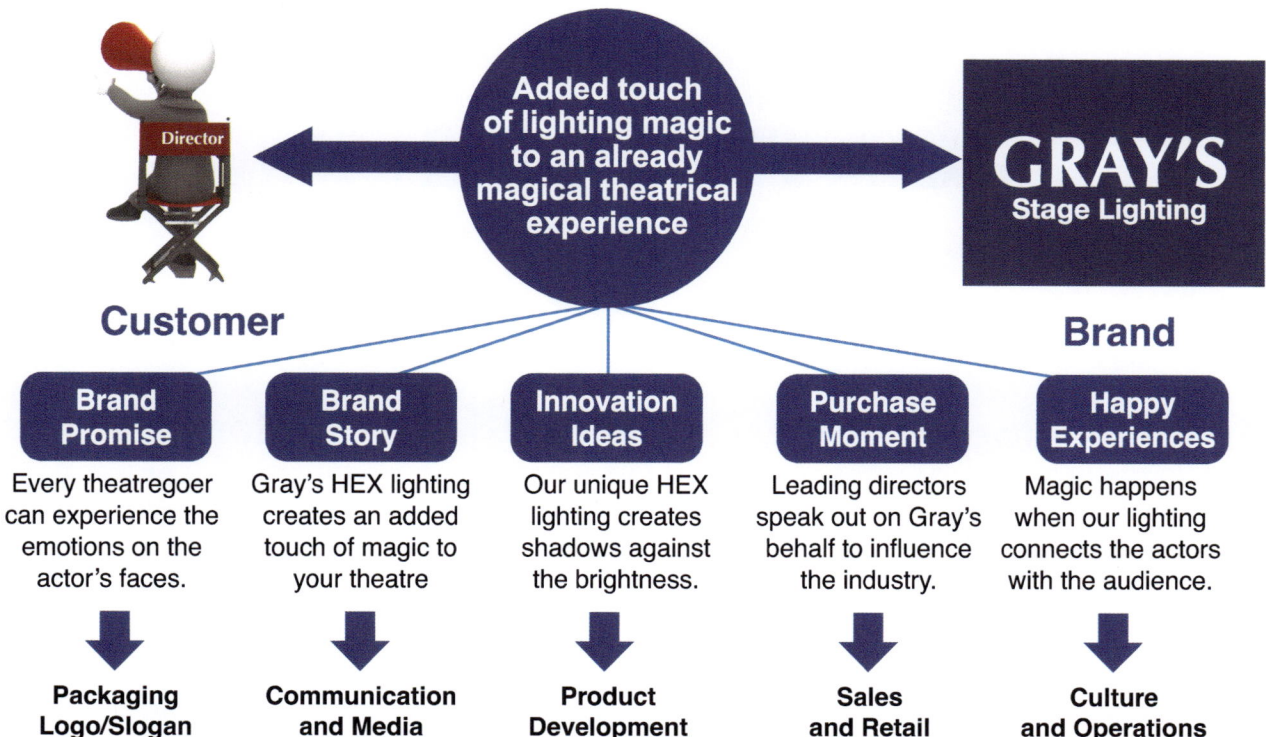

How to work the brand idea

The brand idea connects with your busy customers, then aligns around five customer touchpoints including the brand promise, brand story, innovation, purchase moment, and customer experience. Looking at the infographic on the next page, you can see how each of these touchoints help manage everyone who works on the brand.

- **Brand promise:** Use the brand idea to inspire a simple brand promise that separates your brand from competitors, and projects your brand as better, different, or cheaper based on your brand positioning. The promise sets up how you will communicate the logo, slogan, and sales material.

- **Brand story:** The brand story must come to life to motivate customers to think, feel, or act while establishing the ideal brand reputation to be held in the minds and hearts of the customer. The brand story should align all marketing communications across all media options.

- **Innovation:** Build a fundamentally sound product, staying at the forefront of trends and technology to deliver innovation. Steer the product development teams to ensure they remain true to the brand idea.

- **Purchase moment:** Move customers along their purchase journey with the brand idea helping to steer the sales team to close the sale and help the service team to manage the ongoing needs of the customers.

- **Customer experience:** Turn usage into a customer experience that becomes a ritual and favorite part of the customer's workday. The brand idea guides everyone who works on the brand to deliver great experiences, including operations delivery, as well as the overall culture of your company. This sets up the internal marketing to your employees, a shared venture between HR and marketing.

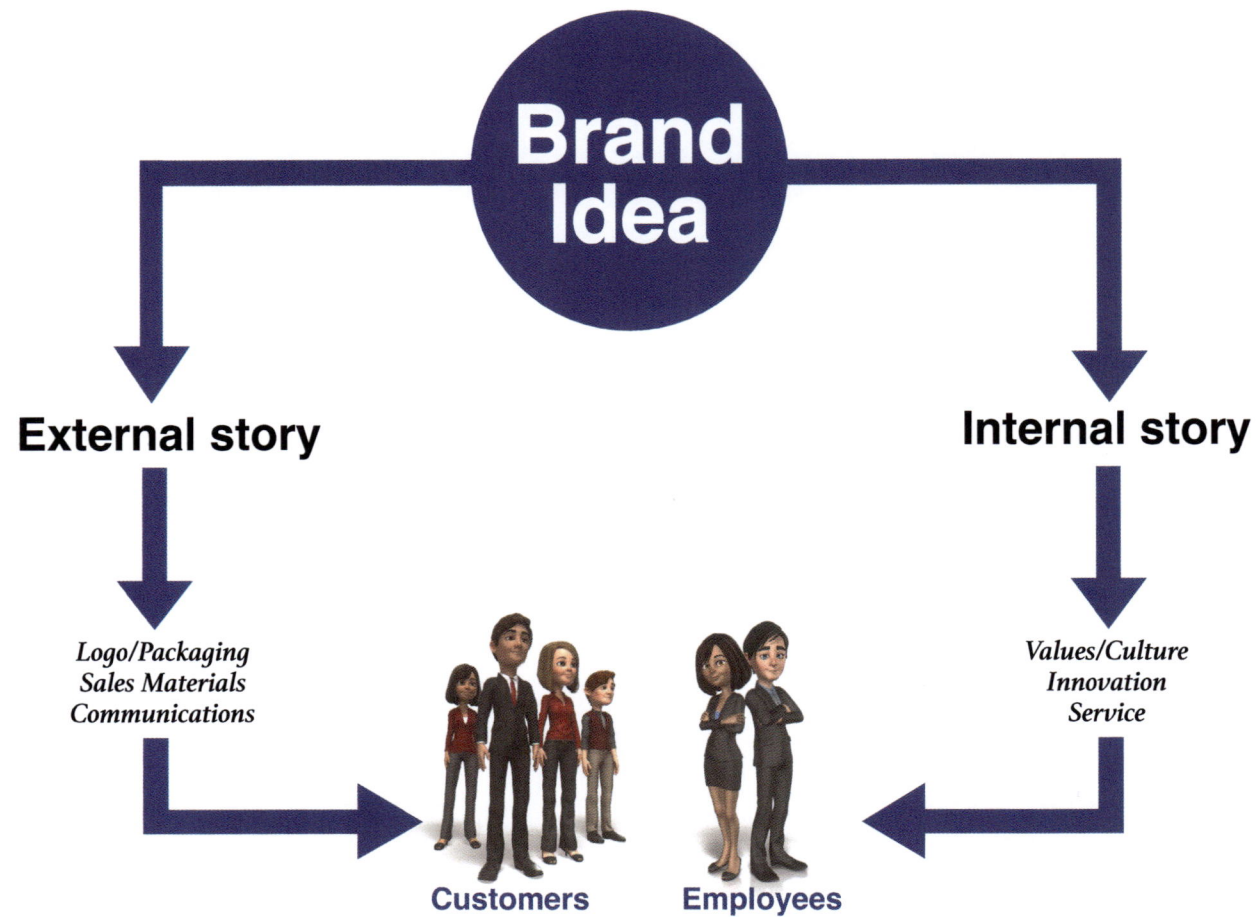

Marketing your brand to employees inside your own company

The best brands consistently deliver. When you build your brand idea, I recommend you use a cross-functional team, including salespeople, R&D, human resources, finance, and operations.

Use your internal brand communications tools to drive a shared definition of the brand idea, as well as getting everyone to articulate how their role delivers that brand idea. Give the external and internal brand story equal importance to the customer experience you create for your brand.

Everyone who works on the brand should use the brand idea as inspiration to guide consistent decisions and activities across every function of your organization. It is the people within the brand organization who will deliver the brand idea to the customer. Everyone needs a shared understanding of and talking points for the brand.

When you work on a brand that leads to the customer experience, your operations people will be responsible for the face-to-face delivery of your brand to the customer. Develop a list of service values, behaviors, and processes to deliver the brand idea throughout your organization.

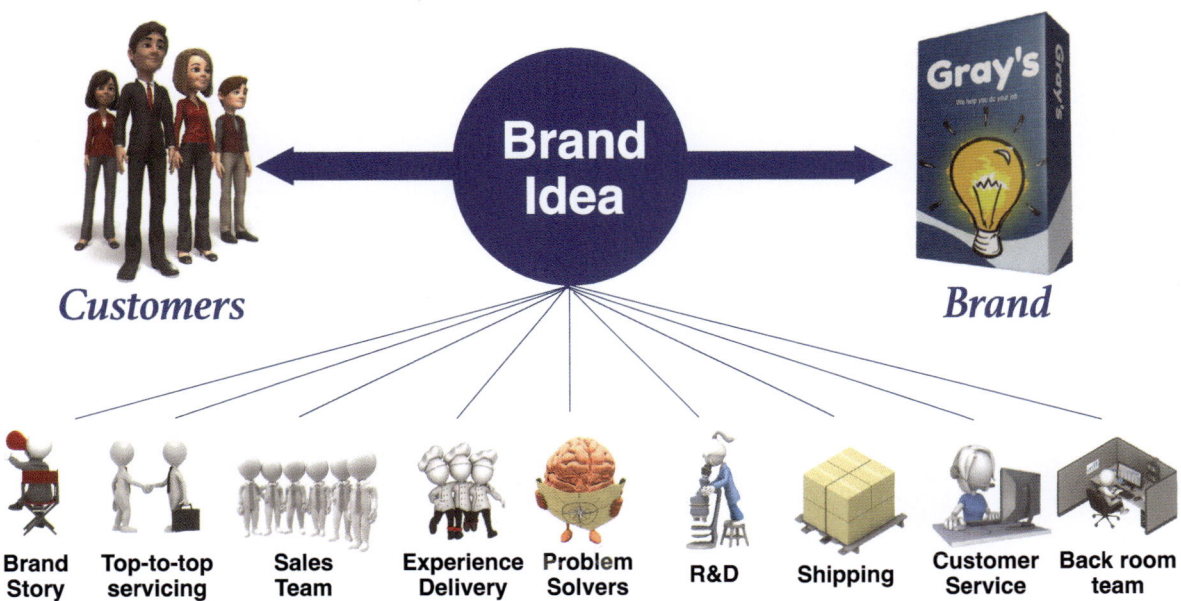

Using your brand idea to build a brand credo document

Having spent time at Johnson & Johnson, I was lucky to see how their credo document has become an essential part of the culture of the organization. Not only does it permeate throughout the company but you will also likely hear it quoted in meetings daily. It is a beautifully written document and ahead of its time.

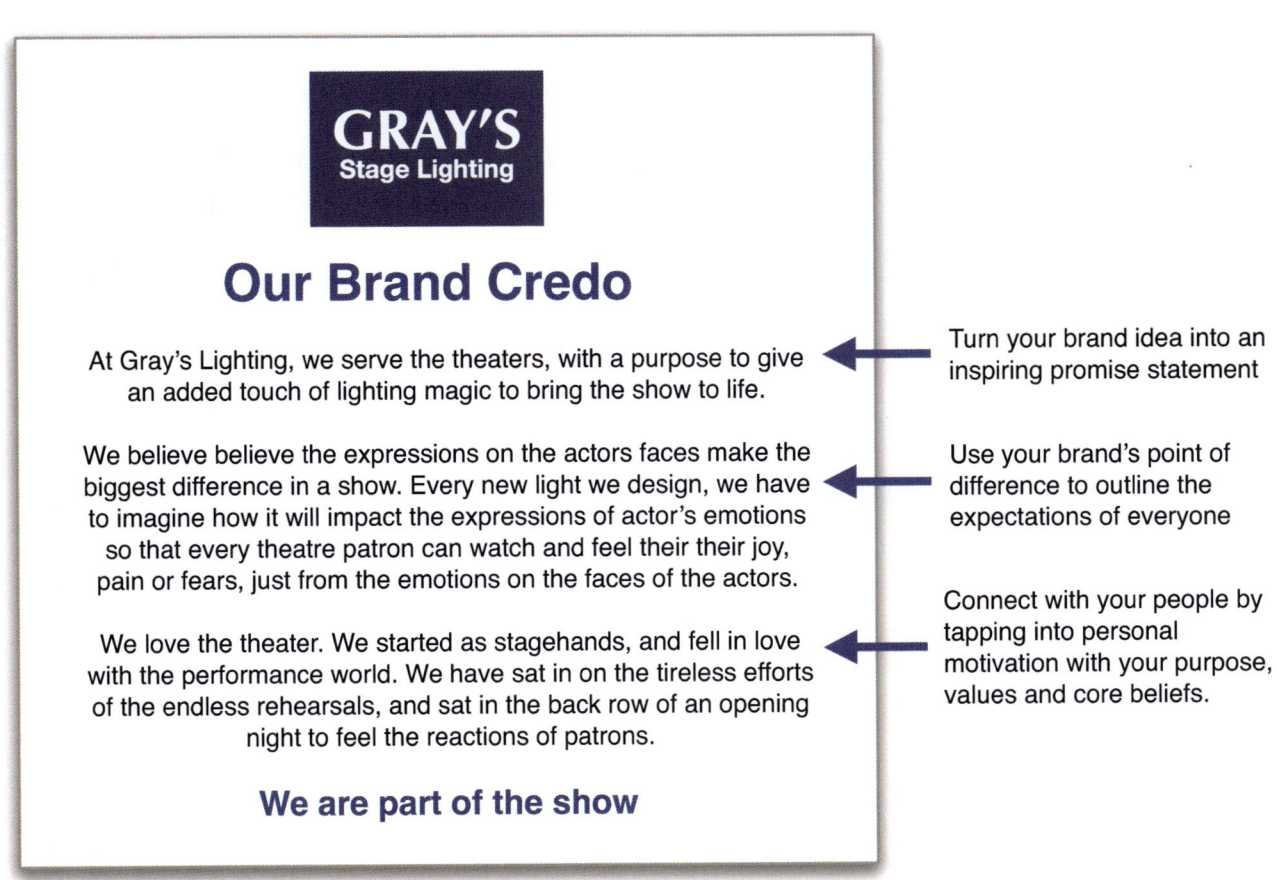

- Start with your **brand idea** and turn it into an inspiring **promise statement**, which explains to your people how they can positively impact your customers.
- Use your brand's core point of difference to outline the **expectations** of how everyone can support and deliver the point of difference. A great exercise is to get every department to articulate its role in delivering the brand idea.
- Connect with your people by tapping into the **personal motivation** for what they can do to support your brand purpose, brand values, and core beliefs. Make it very personal.

Translate your brand idea into a brand story

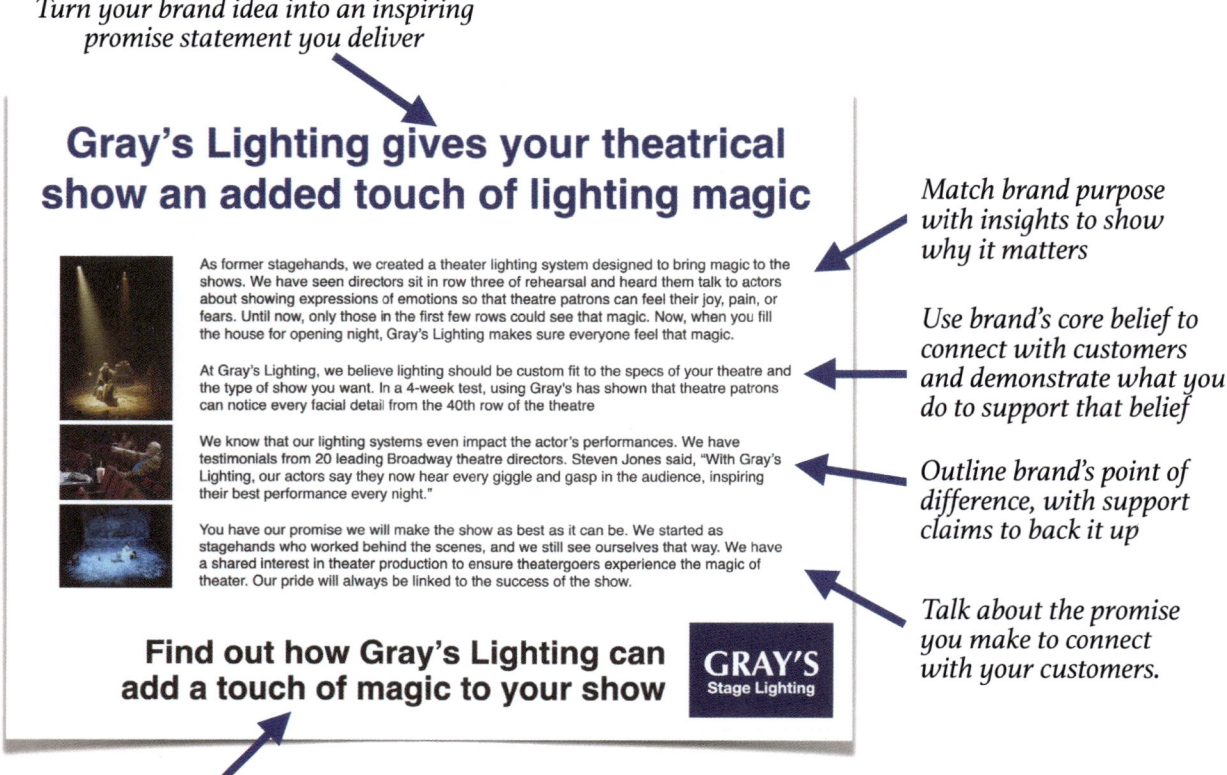

You can extrapolate all the work you have done so far into a brand story, which explains, "who you are." Use this brand story for your "who are we" your website, or as a summary description on LinkedIn, hiring websites, and your content marketing.

- Turn brand idea into an inspiring promise statement you will deliver.
- Match the brand purpose to customer insights showing why it matters. This thinking makes it highly personal, explains the story behind why you do what you do. This part of the story connects with customers.
- Use your brand's core belief to connect with customers and demonstrate what you do to support that belief.
- Talk about what makes your brand different and what claims you have to support your difference.
- Outline ways you connect with your customer and the promise you deliver.

You can even use this methodology to draft a customer email

Even for the simplest of communications, you can use the brand idea, customer insights, promise statement, reason to believe, and call to action, and build out a very simple email to your customer. This process will make it very easy for your sales team to engage with customers. It is a good structure to start with and then add in your own specifics to make it highly personal and impactful.

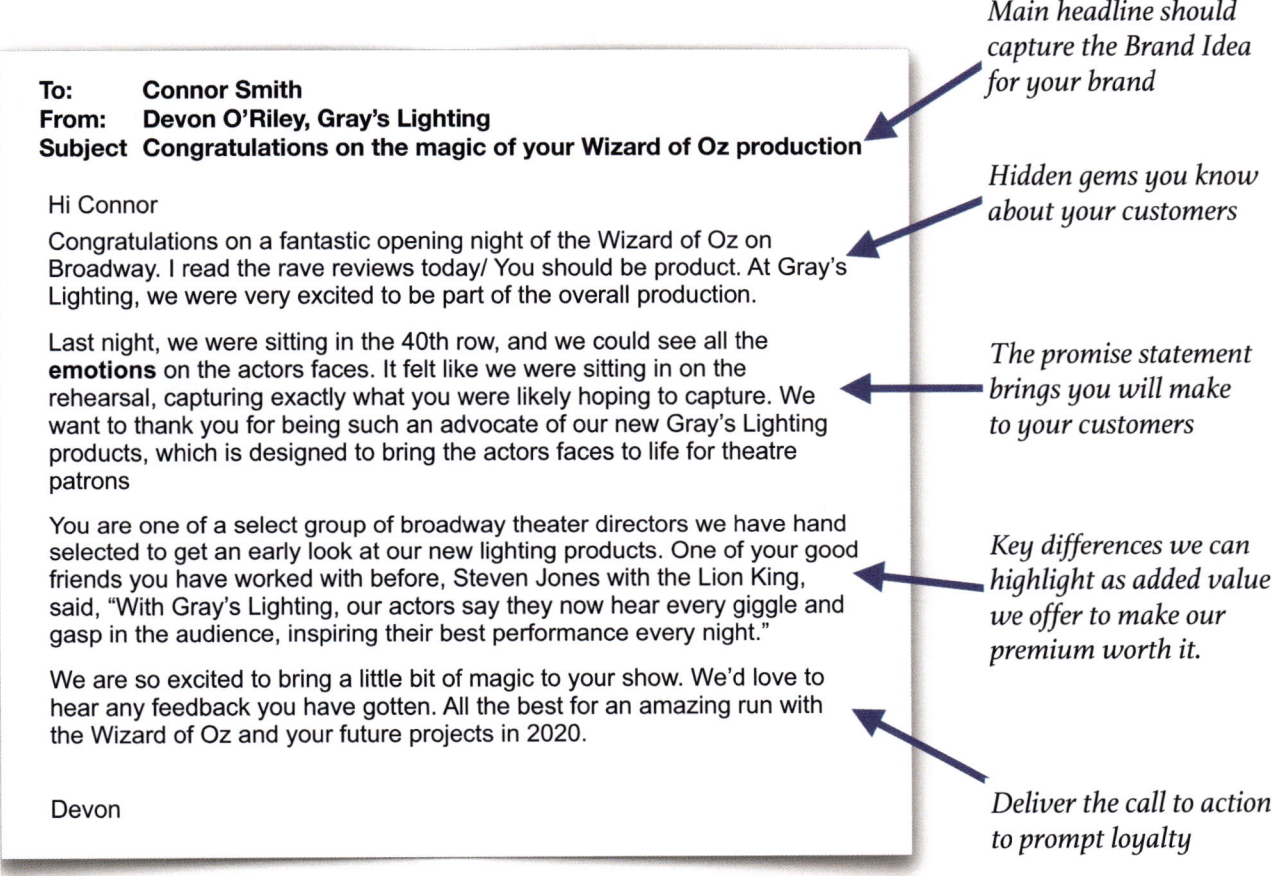

T-Mobile case study: It is about the culture behind the brand

When T-Mobile's so-called crazy CEO says, "I'm all about customers and employees" that doesn't sound so crazy at all. That crazy CEO takes the opposite approach to everything AT&T and Verizon do, backed up by an exceptional customer service idea that lays beneath the surface.

If you think marketing is just about logos and advertising, think again. Customer service is the secret sauce for T-Mobile, and the culture they have created allows them to deliver exceptional service.

They are now using a team approach focused on four questions in assessing the transformation over time:

1. Are our customers happier?
2. Are they staying with us longer?
3. And, are we deepening our relationship with them?
4. Then are we making their service experience low-effort?

How the brand idea stretches across the customer touchpoints

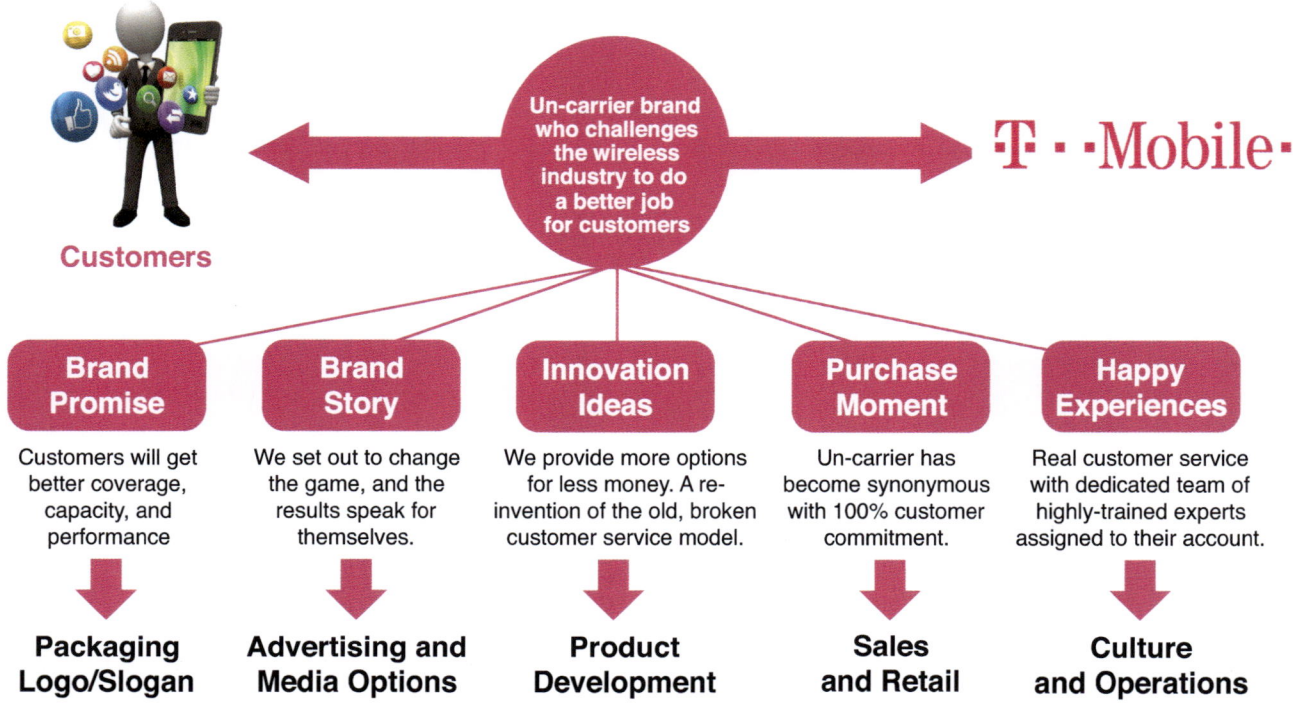

- **Brand promise:** Use the brand idea to inspire a simple brand promise that separates your brand from competitors, and projects your brand as better, different, or cheaper, based on your brand positioning. While the brand idea challenges the category to be better for customers, T-Mobile promises to deliver better coverage, capacity, and performance. This "un-carrier" idea allows them to deliver what they know their competitors cannot deliver.

- **Brand story:** The brand story must come to life to motivate customers to think, feel, or act while establishing the ideal brand's reputation to be held in the minds and hearts of the customer. The brand story should align all brand communications across all media options. T-Mobile takes a super aggressive stance with competitors, going head to head. The CEO refers to AT&T and Verizon as "dumb and dumber" every chance he gets. T-Mobile' TV ads are highly engaging among boring competitor ads and are as equally challenging as the CEO's voice.

- **Innovation:** Build a fundamentally sound product, staying at the forefront of trends and technology to deliver innovation. Steer the product development teams to ensure they remain true to the brand idea. When you look up T-Mobile's Un-carrier plans 1.0 to 13.0, you see it's a constant form of innovation that is customer-centric and 10 steps ahead of the competition.

- **Purchase moment:** The brand idea must move customers along the purchase journey to the final purchase decision. The brand idea helps steer the sales team and sets up retail channels to close the sale. T-Mobile has made it easier to switch, whether it's the free trial week, paying the competitor cancellation fees, or offering no contract.

- **Customer experience:** The brand idea guides everyone who works on the brand to deliver great experiences. It seems T-Mobile is the only brand that understands customer experience means loyalty, greater influence on inspiring friends to switch over, and the temptation of new customers to join up.

Once you have your idea, begin matching up brand values to deliver that idea.

T-Mobile stresses that great customer service has to start with a great culture. Here are their brand values:

- Frontline first, customers are first.
- Play to win and have fun.
- Results matter. Count on me to deliver.
- Be bold. Think big. Make a difference.
- Do it the right way.

New structure leads to a new type of teamwork

T-Mobile figured out customers were opting to use the self-serve options for the easy customer service issues, which meant those who reached the customer service reps had difficult issues to solve.

T-Mobile restructured its teams, moving from a one-on-one customer service approach to a team approach. Each rep was now part of a team, and they could access peers or tech specialists to solve these difficult challenges. They also had access to coaches, who were super reps who could join in and provide solutions.

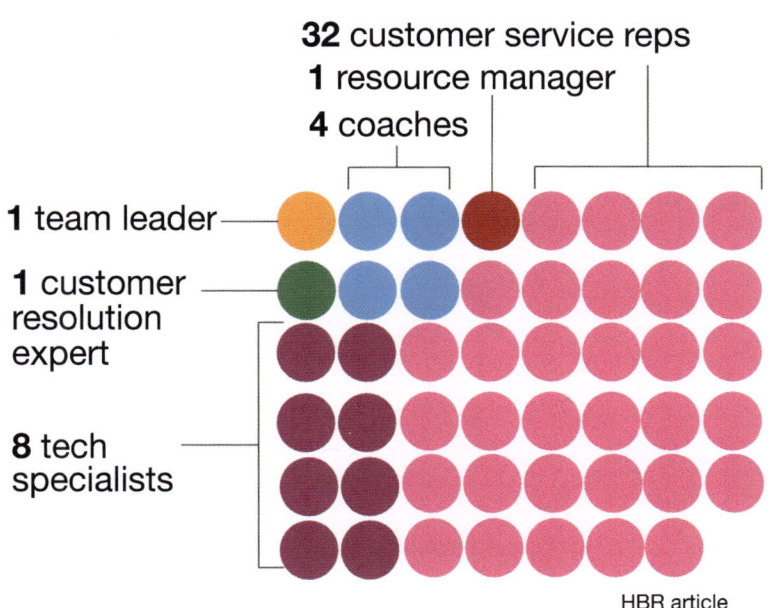

HBR article

T-Mobile saw a positive impact after this shift. As they solved issues as a team, there were 71% fewer transferred calls and 31% fewer escalated calls to a superior. As a result, the apology credits went down 31% and the number of lost customers went down 25%.

These results impact the bottom line because all the effort to get customers into the sales funnel is wasted if you can't retain them. The big result is happier employees and happier customers. The net promoter scores went up 56%, reflecting customers' willingness to recommend T-Mobile, feel satisfied, and stay loyal to the brand.

From all the sales growth T-Mobile has generated, they have doubled their share price in the past five years, while AT&T has not seen any growth, even with the tremendous stock market growth the past 2 years.

Writing a customer strategic objective statement with the a + b + c + d model

a. Deploy resources against building your brand capabilities helping solidify any one of the customer touchpoints: whether it is the brand positioning, brand communications, product innovation, purchase moment, or the customer experience.

b. Find a focused opportunity to connect with your focused target market, to tighten the bond and move them along the brand love curve from unknown to indifferent to like it to love it and onto the beloved stage.

c. Achieve a market impact that moves customers along their journey, moving them from aware to consider to search to buy to satisfied to repeat to loyal and finally to the brand fan stage.

d. Achieve a performance result that strengthens your brand's relationship with customers, either driving one of the eight power drivers or one of the eight profit drivers.

For T-Mobile, here's how to write that strategic objective statement:

Engage a process fix **(a)** to the T-Mobile customer service department **(b)** and improve the customer experience **(c)** to reduce customer churn and increase share **(d)**

The hub-and-spoke brand management system

Brand management was built on a hub-and-spoke system, with the brand manager expected to sit right in the middle of the organization, helping drive everything and everyone around the brand. However, it is the brand idea that lies at the center with everyone connected to the brand expected to understand and deliver the idea.

Work exercise #1

Using the brand that you are working on, describe how your brand idea stretches across each of the five touchpoints

- Brand Promise:

- Brand Story:

- Innovation Ideas:

- Purchase Moments:

- Happy Experiences:

Work exercise #2

Build out your ideal brand concept

- What is the customer insight or enemy?

- What is the main benefit?

- List out two Reasons to Believe

- Call to action

Chapter Twelve
How to build a brand plan everyone can follow

Have you noticed people who say, "We need to get everyone on the same page" rarely have anything written down on one page?

The same people who use the term "fewer bigger bets" are fans of little projects that deplete resources.

People say they are good decision-makers, yet struggle when faced with two distinct choices, so they creatively find a way to justify doing both options.

A brand plan is an opportunity to make decisions on how to allocate your brand's limited resources to the smartest ideas that will drive the highest return.

Think of the plan as a decision-making tool to align your team with the best financial investment choices and the best decisions on how to deploy your people. The plan should then align and focus everyone who works on the brand, including the leader who writes the plan.

In this chapter, I will show you how to get your **annual brand plan** and your **five-year brand strategy roadmap** down to one page each!

Start with the five questions worksheet

While it is easy to get writer's block, it can be worse when you sit at your computer staring at a blank screen with the word "Vision" staring back at you.

Here are **five simple questions** to help you kickstart your first thoughts about your brand plan and decide on the big picture elements of your plan before fine-tuning and perfecting the writing.

1. Where could we be?
2. Where are we?
3. Why are we here?
4. How can we get there?
5. What do we need to do?

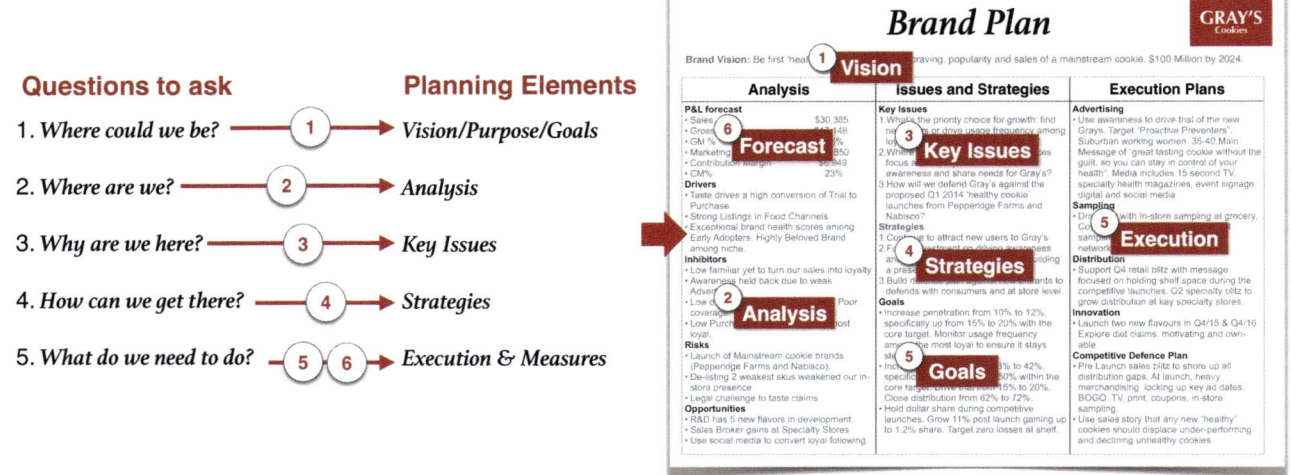

Your written answers will start to reveal a rough draft outline of your brand vision, analysis, key issues, strategies, and some thinking on your execution and measurement, which form the entirety of your brand plan.

When you start your brand plan, the worst thing you can do is open up a PowerPoint document and begin to type away on a blank page. You will get writer's block, or you will assemble a complete mess.

Remember back to when you wrote a term paper in college. The essay was always easier to write and a much better end product when you took the time to write out a rough draft outline before you started the final document.

To start your rough outline, force yourself to write out **three bullet points** for each of the five simple questions. Make it challenging to narrow down your list to the top three points, as the extra effort now will help focus your mind on the most significant points.

It is very easy to get lost in the planning process. Many brand leaders will spend a few weeks writing a plan. As you solicit conflicting input from across the organization, it will add a layer of confusion to the plan you must sort through. It is easy to get lost in a mess.

I recommend you **start with the five questions** then keep coming back to this document a few times throughout the process to make sure you stay on track. These five questions keep you grounded and focused throughout the planning process.

Brand plan rough draft

1) Where could we be?
- To be bring our real life lighting magic to the stage, one show at a time.
- Make Gray's $100 Million by 2022.
- Double digit growth rate

2) Where are we?
- Successful launch to the Broadway market, but time to transition Gray's from a product-led brand into an idea-led brand
- Need to connect with customers by owning idea of "Touch of Magic" lighting, rather than just selling quality lighting.
- Begin to dominate and lead the "stage lighting" theatre segment

3) Why are we here?
- We have not figured out the priority choice for growth: find new directors or drive usage frequency among loyalists.
- We need to drive our awareness and share needs for Gray's.
- There is a high risk of energy efficient launches from SST and LGI?

4) How can we get there?
- Continue to attract new directors to Gray's
- Focus investment on driving awareness and trial with new directors and building a presence with production houses.
- Build a defence plan against new entrants that defends our strength with directors.

5) What do we need to do?
- Use awareness to drive trial of the new Grays HEX Lighting as "Touch of Magic" brand positioning.
- Launch "Bright Ideas" blog and white papers to capture attention of production houses.
- Leverage "Ten best designs" award for industry PR, to gain attention with directors and production houses.

Also, as I will mention later, the flow of the plan mirrors the complexity of an orchestra, so it is important to use these five questions to see the entire plan simultaneously to ensure you keep everything flowing together.

Avoid misfits within your brand plan

When you write a plan, think of it like conducting an orchestra. There are a lot of moving parts and, if you do not stay organized, the plan may begin to look like many scattered thoughts.

When your plan is disjointed or looks like a collection of disconnected ideas, it will confuse and meet resistance, which are counterproductive to the reason why you create a plan. A smart brand plan should have a consistent flow in the writing as you move from the vision through to execution. Like an orchestra playing in perfect harmony, everyone is playing the same song.

When you write something that does not fit, it tends to stand out like, "a tuba player playing their own song." When I managed a marketing team, I came up with this analogy and started to call plan misfits "tubas."

From my experience, senior leaders are skilled at finding "tubas," which can derail your presentation, as the debate becomes more about why the "tuba" is there and less about the bigger aspects of your plan. Go "tuba hunting" by reading through your brand plan and eliminating the "tubas" before your management finds them.

The worst "tubas" are those elements of the plan that seems to 'die a quick death' in the document or they 'come from out of nowhere' with no analytical setup.

The two worst types of "tubas"

1. **A reasonable idea is presented early on and dies a quick death never to be seen again in the plan.**

   - If, early on in your plan, you say part of your brand vision or purpose is "to be the disruptive leader in innovation," then why is there no innovation strategy, innovation process or new products for the next four years? Sure, your vision sounds catchy. However, it appears to be a misfit "tuba" with very little to do with the rest of your plan.

2. **A creative tactical idea presented late in the plan seems to come out of nowhere.**

   - If the focus of your plan for a new product launch is to drive early trial, then why is there a significant investment in your tactical execution plan to create a VIP club for high-frequency users? If there is no analytical set-up of an opportunity or strategic set-up, then a tactic that comes out of nowhere late in the plan is a "tuba." It risks causing conflict or confusion.

The 5-year brand strategic roadmap

The first one-page format is for your **long-range brand plan**. Every brand should have a five-year plan to lay out the big picture elements, including brand vision, purpose, and values.

It then layers in the brand idea to guide everyone on how to deliver a consistent brand across the five customer touchpoints.

The key issues lay out which obstacles lie in the way of achieving your vision and the strategies then answer those key issue questions. Keep tactics within the long-range plan as broad guideposts rather than specific programs with detailed execution.

Brand Strategy Roadmap

Vision: Be the lighting brand Broadway directors see as essential to their show. Make Gray's a $100 Million brand by 2022.

Purpose: At Gray's, our purpose is to help directors put on the most magical Broadway shows they could ever imagine.

Values: Passion for the theater, we think like directors, family-run, pride matters, and we do our homework

Brand Idea: Gray's provides an added touch of magic to an already magical theater experience.

Brand Promise	Brand Story	Innovation	Purchase Moment	Customer Experience
Every theatregoer can experience the emotions on the actor's faces.	Gray's HEX lighting creates an added touch of magic to your theatre	Our unique HEX lighting creates shadows against the brightness.	Leading directors speak out on Gray's behalf to influence the industry.	Magic happens when our lighting connects the actors with the audience.

Goals: Increase awareness, in-theater trial demos, hold share, increase the off-broadway penetration.

Issues:
1. How do we shift Gray's from a product-led launch into an idea-led brand to own "magic"?
2. How do we use loyal advocates to establish Gray's in the production house buyer's mind?
3. How do we defend against entry of mainstream lighting (GE, Philips) into the high-end stage lighting segment?
4. How do we keep growth momentum by closing the identified gaps in distribution?

Strategies:

Content marketing to trade up directors	Influencer program to drive trial demos	Claims to defend against new entrants	Use social media to reach off-broadway

Tactics:
- White Papers
- Video Story telling
- Video interviews of patrons

- Influential directors
- Social media
- Film one of the demos

- Blitz current customers
- Claims data vs competitors
- Industry advisory panel

- Social Media program
- East coast sales blitz
- Direct mailer nationally

The annual brand plan

As you transition to the annual brand plan, the vision stays the same, but the key issues and strategies become more specific to line up to the particular current situation.

- **Analysis:** The analysis section lays out the summary from the deep-dive business review with an overview of the top three points, which envelop what is driving your brand's growth, what is inhibiting your brand's growth, which threats could hurt your brand, and what opportunities your brand faces.
- **Key issues and strategies:** The key issues and strategies section focuses on the top three issues getting in the way of achieving your vision, which you should put in question format. Moreover, the strategic solutions are the answers that match up to each of those questions. Set goals to measure your brand's performance against each strategy.
- **Execution:** The execution section maps out the specific plans for each of the chosen execution areas that align with the most essential customer touchpoints.

Brand Plan

Brand Vision: : Be the lighting brand Broadway directors see as essential to the show. Make Gray's a $100 Million by 2030.

Analysis	Issues and Strategies	Executional Plans
P&L forecast • Sales $30,385 • Gross Margin $17,148 • GM % 56% • Marketing Budget $8,850 • Contribution Margin $6,949 • CM% 23% **Drivers** • In theater tests and director's brand satisfaction converts trial to purchase. • Strong support from the Broadway directors—creates key influencers to go to new markets. • Exceptional brand health among Early Adopters. Highly Beloved Brand among niche. **Inhibitors** • Awareness weak—especially with production houses—who are more focused on price. • Low distribution at product houses segment due to poor sales coverage. • Low repeat frequency, even among loyal. Directors need to re-sell each new order. **Risks** • Mainstream lighting brands (GE, Philips). • De-listing 2 weakest skus in contractor segment weakens overall presence • Legal Challenge to competitive claims **Opportunities** • R&D has 5 new designs in development. • Sales Broker create gains at contractors • Social media to convert loyal following.	**Key Issues** 1. How do we shift Gray's from a product-led launch into an idea-led brand to own "magic"? 2. How do we use loyal advocates to establish Gray's in production house buyer's mind? 3. How do we defend against entry of mainstream lighting (GE, Philips) into the high-end stage lighting segment ? **Strategies** 1. Content marketing to get Broadway directors to book a demo program and trade up 2. Use demo program to sign up highly motivated theater directors and drive share 3. Use high performance claims to defend against new entrants with most loyal high volume directors to hold onto key customers **Goals** • Increase penetration from 10% to 12%, specifically up from 15% to 20% with the core target. Monitor usage frequency among the most loyal to ensure it stays steady. • Increase awareness from 33% to 42%, specifically up from 45% to 50% within the core target. Drive trial from 15% to 20%. Focus for sales is to close contractor gaps going from 62% to 72%. • Hold dollar share during competitive launches and continue to grow 11% post launch gaining up to 1.2% share. Target zero losses at distribution	**Content Marketing** White Papers on the impact of lighting. Video story telling of our case studies, using our loyal directors to tell the story. Video interviews of patrons to highlight the impact of the lighting. **Influencer program** Use key influential directors. Tell story through social media. Film one of the demos . **Distribution** Support Q4 sales blitz with message focused on holding shelf space during the competitive launches. Q2 contractor blitz to grow distribution at key contractor. **Social Media** Social Media program. East coast sales blitz. Direct mailer nationally **Competitive Attack Plan** Pre Launch sales blitz to shore up all distribution gaps. At launch, heavy merchandising, locking up key buyer dates, BOGO. In-theater demo. Claims data vs competitors. Industry advisory panel **Innovation** Building new product pipeline. Explore lighting options for social media. New face recognition claims.

I first came up with this **"brand plan on a page"** format when I led a team with 15 brands. It helped me see the big picture quickly, rather than having to hunt through a big thick binder. Also, the sales team appreciated the ability to see the entire plan on one page quickly. Most salespeople also had 15 brands to manage with each of their customers. Everyone who works on the brand should receive the one-page plan and keep it close by to steer their day-to-day decisions.

Writing the plan with the power of threes

I believe in **"the power of threes."** As I said earlier, your brand plan should help you make decisions on where to focus and allocate your limited resources. As a guideline, for an annual plan, I recommend you focus on the **top three strategies**, then focus on the **top three tactics for each strategy**.

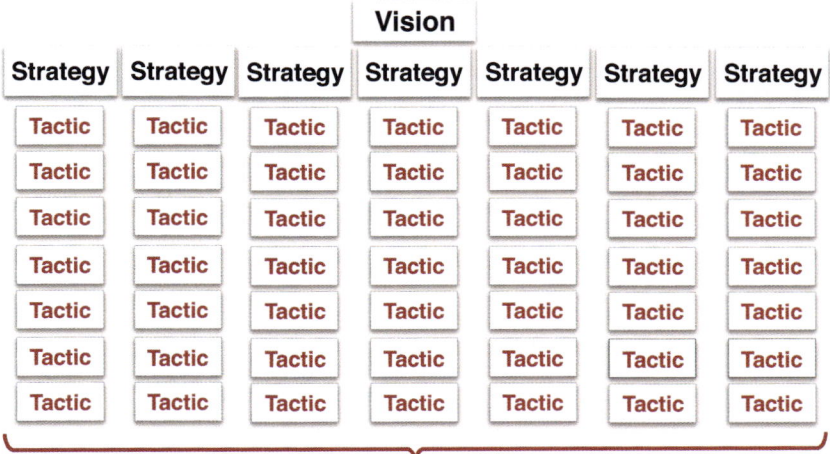

That means nine significant projects for your brand to focus your limited resources against during the year. Compare the subtle difference with what happens when you try to do five strategies with five tactics: the plan quickly explodes into 25 projects, and seven by seven leads to 49 projects. That would cripple your brand's limited resources. What if you never get to the forty-ninth project but it was the most important project? With fewer projects, you will be able to execute everything with full passion and brilliance.

I see too many marketers with a long list of things they need to do. They are so busy; they have no time to think about what matters to their brand. They have very little passion for any one particular project; they are trying to get everything done. This thinking is not the ideal behavior a brand needs to become a beloved brand.

Brand vision

A well-written brand vision should be the ultimate end-in-mind achievement, which answers, **"Where could we be?"** Think about significant accomplishments that would make you feel completely fulfilled. Put a stake in the ground to describe an ideal state for your future.

Every smart brand plan must start with a brand vision statement. When I see brand teams who struggle, they usually lack a brand vision.

> "If you don't know where you are going, you might not get there."
>
> — Yogi Berra

Some organizations get so fixated on achieving short-term goals they chase every tactic in front of them just to make their numbers. Your vision should steer your entire brand plan. Choose the language and phrases within your vision that will inspire, lead, and steer your team.

Examples of best-in-class vision statements for B2B brands

Princess Margaret Hospital
To conquer cancer in our lifetime.

LinkedIn
Create economic opportunity for every member of the global workforce.

Go Daddy
Radically shift the global economy toward small business ventures

Amazon
Be the earth's most customer-centric company.

John F. Kennedy
"I believe that this nation should commit itself to achieving a goal, before this decade is out, of landing a man on the moon and returning him safely to earth."

GE
Become #1 or #2 in every market we serve and revolutionize this company to have the speed and agility of a small enterprise.

Smithsonian
Shape the future by preserving our heritage, discovering new knowledge, and sharing our resources with the world.

Intel
If it is smart and connected, it is best with Intel.

Cisco
To change the way we work, live, play, and learn.

TED
The power of ideas to change attitudes, lives and, ultimately, the world.

WWF
To reconcile the needs of human beings and the needs of others that share the Earth.

Use these statements to inspire you as you write your own vision statement. Maybe you will see something that feels familiar to what is in your mind or at least a structure for how you would write your own vision statement.

Your vision should scare you a little and excite you a lot. You should wonder if you can achieve it and then think of how it would feel if you did. While we do not always accomplish every vision, we rarely achieve more than we thought was possible.

Once you establish your vision, it sets up the key issues of your plan, including obstacles in the way of achieving your vision, which then sets up the strategies for how to reach the vision. As mentioned earlier, a brand plan has to flow like an orchestra, with each element directly related to the others.

Imagine the perfect picture

To be a visionary, you must be able to visualize your future. You should be able to imagine the perfect picture of your brand in the future, to helps answer, "Where could we be?" Imagine it is five or ten years from now.

Brainstorming your vision

1. What is your future revenue or market share? — *$100 M in sales by by 2024*
2. What customers do you need to do to grow? — *Need to get younger dentists*
3. Describe the future culture of your company. — *Customer Centric*
4. What do you want people to say about your brand?
5. What do your own people find motivating about working on your brand?
6. How do you want a customer to describe their experience with your brand? — *Most popular. High net promoter*
7. Name some of the future accomplishments that would make you proud.
8. What do you do better than anyone else on the planet? — *High Quality Comfortable*
9. Name something out-of-the-box that would make people talk about your brand. — *Older audience, need everyone*
10. Biggest brand fans who love you the most?

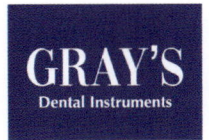

Brand Vision:
Be the most popular dental tools among all generations of dental professionals generating $100 Million by 2024.

You wake up in the most fantastic mood. Think about where you are in your personal life and your business life. Start to imagine an ideal state of what you want. Visualize a perfect future of what has you in such a good mood and write down the most important things you want to achieve.

1. What is your future revenue or market share?

2. What customers do you need to do to grow?

3. Describe the future culture of your company.

4. What do you want people to say about your brand?

5. What do your own people find motivating about working on your brand?

6. How do you want a customers to describe their experience with your brand?

7. Name some of the future accomplishments that would make you proud.

8. What do you do better than anyone else on the planet?

9. Name something out-of-the-box that would make people talk about your brand.

10. Who are your biggest brand fans who love you the most?

Checklist for what makes a vision great:

- ✓ Your vision should last **5-10 years**.
- ✓ It should help you imagine the **ideal** picture of "where could we be."
- ✓ Describe your **dream**, describing what you see, feel, hear, think, say, and wish for your brand.
- ✓ It should be **emotional** to motivate all employees and partners to rally behind it.
- ✓ It must be **easy** to understand, in plain words, which may already be a familiar phrase within the company.
- ✓ A great vision is a balance between **aspiration** (stretch) and **reality** (achievement).
- ✓ Consider adding a **financial** (sales or profit) or share **leadership position** (#1) number.

Cautions and caveats when writing your brand vision statements:

1. A vision should not be a positioning statement.
2. Make sure you have not already achieved it.
3. Do not make strategic statements. It is not the "how."
4. Try to be single-minded. Keep tightening it. Do not include everything!
5. Focus on how to build a purpose-driven beloved brand

How to build a purpose-driven brand

Finding your brand purpose answers the big question of **"Why does your brand exist?"** It should force you to explore the underlying personal and honest motivation for why you do what you do.

Ikigai (生き甲斐) is a Japanese concept that means "a reason for being."

It is an intersection of what you are good at, what you love, what the world needs, and what you can be paid for.

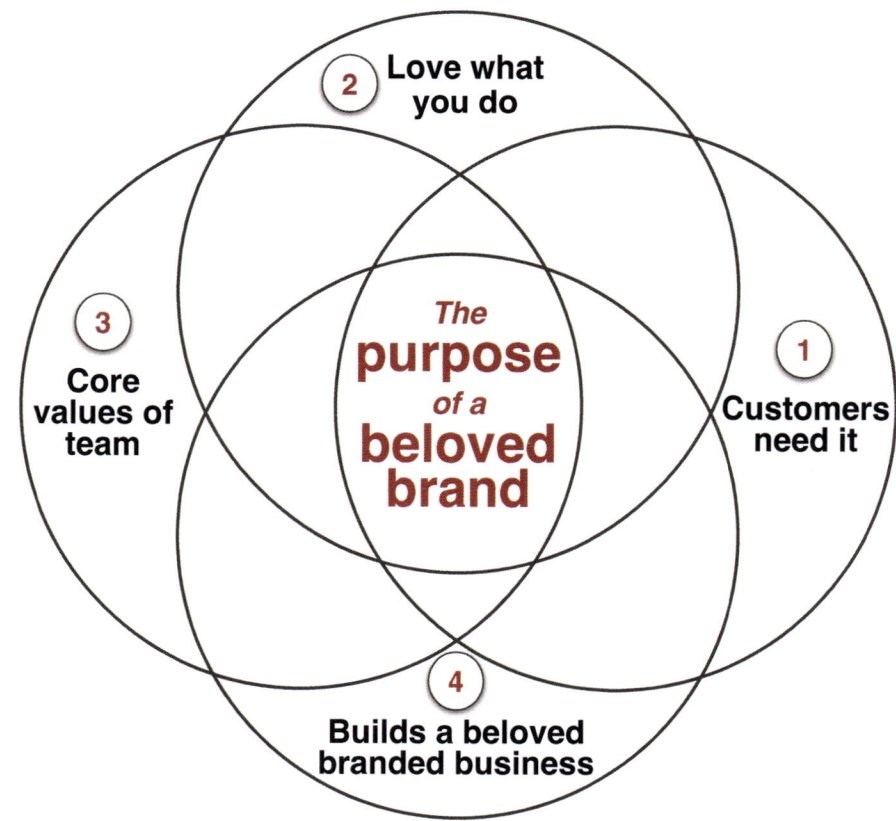

Brand purpose can be a powerful way to connect with both employees and customers, helping define your brand soul. While this Venn diagram looks somewhat crazy at first, trust me, it works as an excellent tool for building your brand's purpose.

This Venn diagram has four significant factors, which match up:

1. Does it fit with what **customers** need or want?
2. Does it deliver your **passion** in loving what you do?
3. Does it fit the **core values** of your team?
4. Can you build a beloved and successful branded **business**.

Your brand purpose will come to life at the intersection that meets the customer needs, fulfills your passion, stands behind your values, and yet still builds a successful branded business.

The how-to model helps find your brand purpose

While the Venn diagram creates the purpose with the intersection of all four circles, you can find your own brand purpose by defining each combination of circles, one at a time, which expresses the four pillars that will deliver your brand purpose

A. Focus your passion on building a tight emotional bond with your most cherished customers

- Combines customer needs **(1)** with loving what you do **(2)**. All the passion you put into your work should focus on becoming a favorite brand of your customers. You should love what you do and love what it does for your customers. How your customers react should drive your inner motivations.

B. Build your branded business around a unique, ownable, and motivating brand idea

- Combines customer needs **(1)** with building a successful branded business **(4)**. Build a brand idea to organize everything you do to deliver a consistent brand that will move customers through their customer journey and become a beloved, high-growth, powerful, and profitable branded business. A sincere desire to build a tight bond with customers will drive your business success.

C. Inspire a values-driven culture to provide happy customer experiences

- Combines living the values of the team **(3)** with creating a successful branded business **(4)**. Your people are the "difference-makers" in delivering an incredible brand. They create a brand worthy of being loved to drive higher prices, lower costs, enter new markets, and create new uses. Link your people to driving the power and profits of your brand.

D. Inspirational work makes it a favorite place to work

- Combines loving what you do **(2)** with the values of the team **(3)**. Your values provide the backbone of your company, a set of beliefs and motivations linked with how people want to work. The values encourage your people to demonstrate their passion and create a culture where your people will never settle for OK when greatness is attainable. Allow them to inject passion into the brand, knowing they can share in the pride of the team when the brand is successful.

Example of brand purpose for Gray's Lighting

Take the work within the four pillars to build the brand purpose. The final purpose statement is, **"Our purpose is to help theater directors put on the most magical Broadway shows they could ever imagine."**

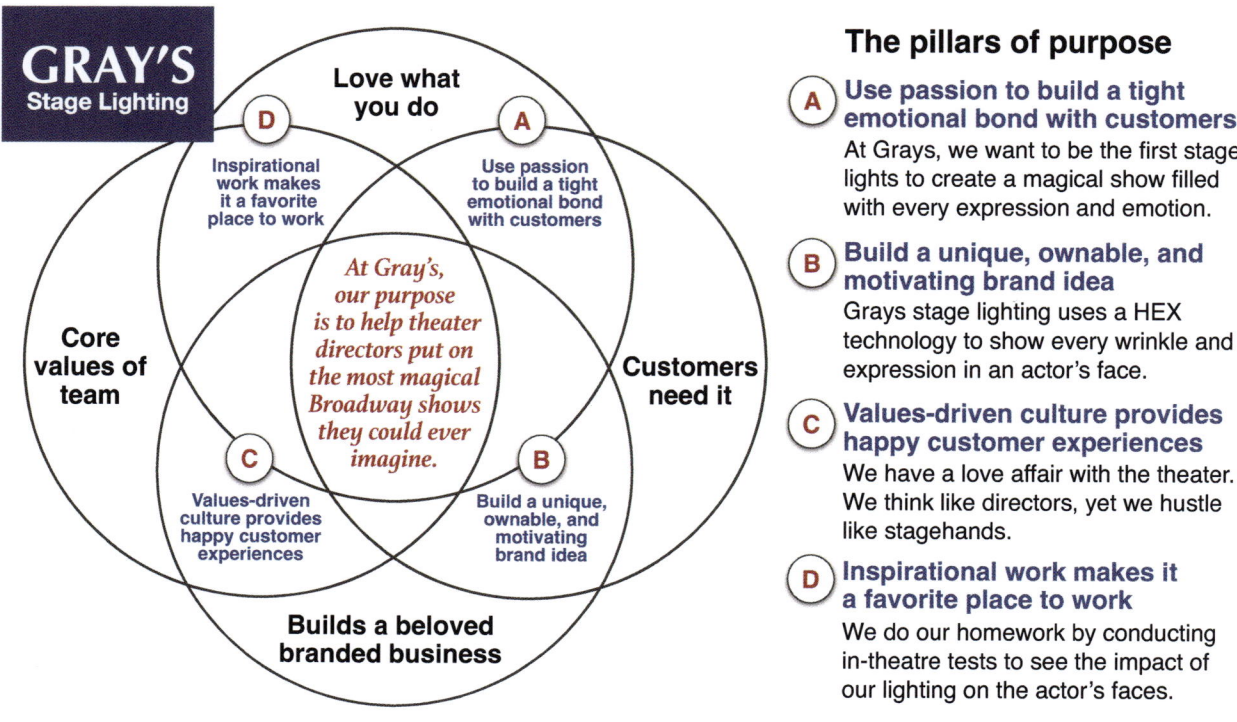

Brand values

Brand values form the backbone of your organization. They may come from your **background**, how you grew up, rules you identify with or how you see your priorities in life.

Your **beliefs** come from your experience, helping explain why and how you choose to do business, how you treat your people, and how you conduct yourself as a leader and as a person in the community. These beliefs should be personal, ethical, or rooted in frustration for how you see things happening in the world.

Your **inspirations** should excite team members who work behind the scenes of the brand. Inspirations should stimulate your people to go beyond the norms of effort or passion.

For organizations, I believe it works best when your people have input into creating and building your values because they will feel included, heard, and invested in your brand's success.

Maybe that is one of my own core values in a bottom-up approach to building brands. However, the closer your values reflect the realities of what your people believe in, the more successful you will be in using those values to inspire greatness.

Brand values for Gray's Lighting

Brand values

Passion for the theatre	Before we were in the lighting business, the Gray's family worked as stagehands in theater production jobs. We share your passion for the stage, and we know the pressures of the business side.
We think like theatre directors	We believe the best lighting starts with the needs of our directors. We source technology, our labs work tirelessly to ensure our stage lighting is amazing enough to become our director's favorite.
Our people make the difference	We are always listening to our directors as our creative inspiration. Then we push ourselves to deliver beyond what you expected.
Passion matters in everyone	We love the stage and we hope that it shows. Everyone on our team shows up every day with a passion to help make a difference and contribute to building Gray's Lighting into a brand that directors love.
We do our homework	For every innovation, we conduct in-theater tests to see if patrons will notice the richer shadows that helped bring every facial detail and emotion to life from the 40th row of the theatre.

Situation analysis

Before you plan where to go next, you need to understand, **"Where are we?"** A deep-dive business review should look take a 360-degree view to dig into the issues related to the marketplace, customers, competitors, channels, and the brand. Later in the book, I will go deeper into how to conduct a deep-dive business review.

For the brand plan, provide a summary of the factors driving the brand's growth, the factors inhibiting the brand's growth, the untapped opportunities, and the potential threats you see.

The **drivers** are the factors of strength or inertia, which are currently accelerating your brand's growth. These are brand assets, successful programs, and favorable customer, technology, or channel trends. Drivers also include new products, successful marketing communications, or performance with channel partners.

The **inhibitors** are the factors of weaknesses or friction that slow down your brand's growth. These are the "Achilles heel" of the brand, which could include unfavorable customer trends, changes in the way people shop, competitive pressures, or even gaps compared to your competitors.

The **opportunities** are specific untapped areas in the market that could fuel future brand growth. They include unfulfilled customer needs, new technologies on the horizon, regulation changes, competitive openings, new distribution channels, or the removal of trade barriers.

The **threats** are identifiable activities that could impact your brand's growth in the future. These include significant competitive activity, competitive technology gains, changing customer dynamics, unfavorable distribution changes, or future potential trade barriers, which would impact your brand's growth.

Summary of Analysis

Drivers	Inhibitors
• In theater tests and director's brand satisfaction converts trial to purchase. • Strong support from the Broadway directors—creates key influencers to go to new markets. • Exceptional brand health support among early adopters, already highly loved brand among niche of directors.	• Awareness weak—especially with production houses—who are more focused on price. • Low distribution at production houses segment due to our low sales coverage. • Low repeat frequency, even among loyal, as directors need to re-sell each production house on using Gray's lighting.
Opportunities	**Risks**
• R&D has 15 new designs in development focused on energy efficiency, longer lasting, and lower cost options. • Sales Broker to create gains with contractors for new theater builds. • Explore social media as a tool to convert and engaged their loyal following.	• Launch of mainstream lighting brands (Philips, GE) into the energy efficient space • De-listing of the weakest skus in contractor channel would weaken overall presence • Legal challenge to our competitive claims.

While you brainstorm a long list, **narrow your focus** to the top three points for each of the four areas. As you move from the analysis to the issues, ensure you find a way to continue or enhance the drivers, while you minimize or reverse the inhibitors. You also want to build specific plans to take advantage of the opportunities and reduce or eliminate the most severe threats.

Strategies

The strategies in the brand plan answer, **"How can we get there?"** Each strategy must provide a clear, definitive answer to each of your key issues. When I was in business school, I had a marketing professor who would say 15 times per class, "It is all about choices. It is all about choices."

The brand plan is a great tool to force you to make **tough decisions**, as you apply your brand's limited resources of dollars, time, people, and partnerships against an unlimited number of choices. It is easy to get distracted by more and more options.

However, brand leaders must use the brand plan process to limit their choices down to those that move your brand along the pathway towards your stated brand vision. Choose the strategic options that provide the highest return on effort (ROE) or the highest return on investment (ROI).

Frame your brand's key issue in question format.

How do we shift Gray's from a product-led launch into an idea-led brand to own "magic"?

The answer to that question becomes your strategy

Content marketing to competitive customers **(a)**, using key influencer directors **(b)** to trigger theater production houses to book a demo program with Gray's Lighting **(c)** which will help close the deal **(d)**.

We showed how to come up with the right key issue questions in Chapter 2 as we used our Strategic ThinkBox to look at your brand's core strength, customer bond, competitive dynamic and business situation. Once you have the best key issue questions, now is the time to answer them with our strategy statements.

Start with Strategy Statements

As a reminder, you should start off by writing your strategic objective statement using the four components of the **a + b + c + d model** outlined in Chapter 2 on strategic thinking:

a. **Build capabilities to deliver the vision:** The investment in a capabilities to deliver the strategy whether building the brand promise, brand story, purchase moment, product innovation and customer experience. These crystal clear marching orders to the team leave no room for doubt, confusion, or hesitation. In the example above, Gray's will invest in the purchase moment by *"Content marketing to competitive customers."*

b. **Focused opportunity:** The breakthrough point where the brand will exert pressure to create a market impact. In the example, the identified opportunity to take advantage of is the *"using influencer directors."*

c. **Market impact:** Achieves a specific desired market impact with a stakeholder you will attempt to move, whether it is customers, sales channels, competitors, or influencers. In this example, the desired impact is to *"trigger theater production houses to book a demo program with Gray's Lighting."*

d. **Performance result:** Drive a specific performance result linked to the market impact, either making the brand more powerful or more profitable. In this example, "which will help close the deal."

Pick your resources and apply against a capability. Look for opportunity that is happening in the marketplace that can supercharge your investment. Choose a market impact that moves customers along their journey, tighten the bond with customers, or solidify the brand positioning. The performance result harnesses more power or profit.

Refer back to our strategy statement cheatsheet in Chapter 2.

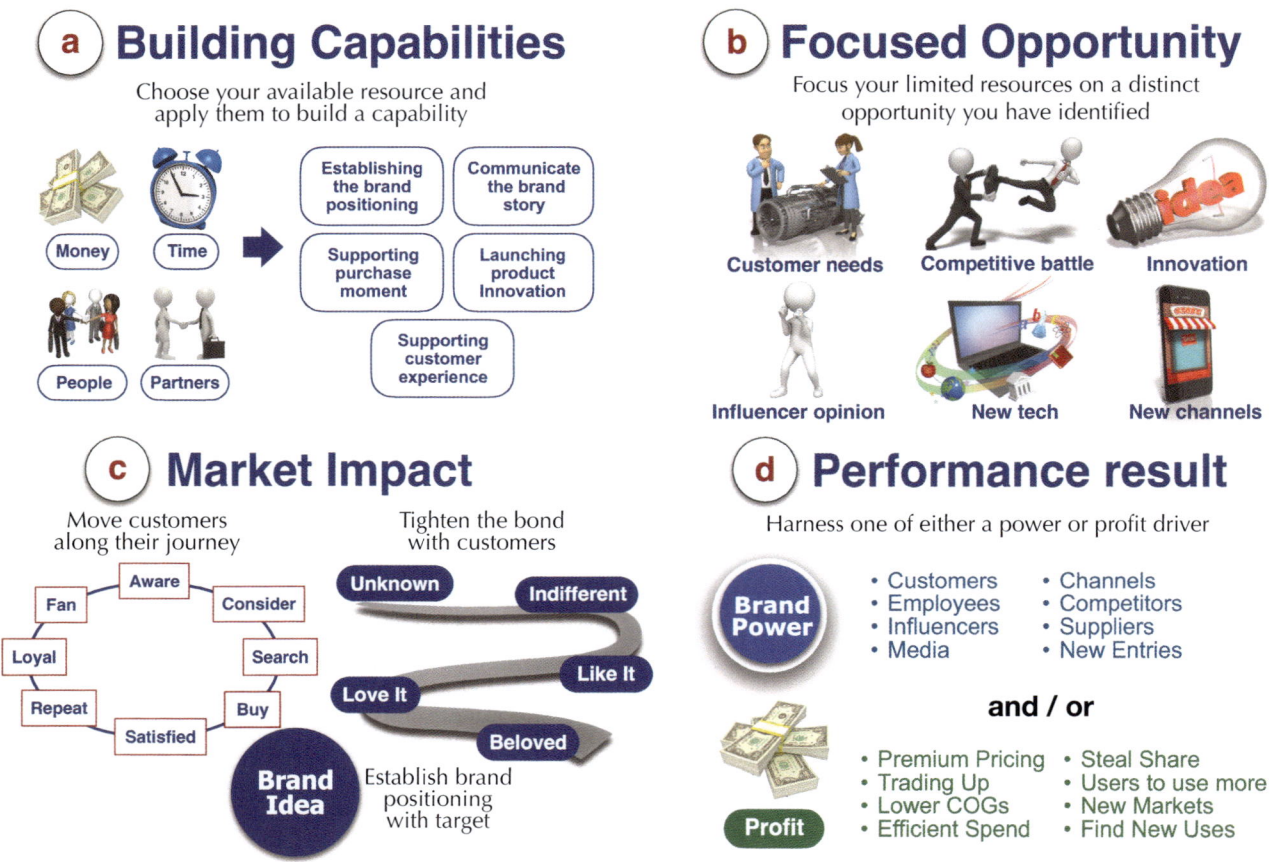

Our A + B + C + D strategy statements can run your brand

With these chunky strategy statements, you can decide on your team's budget and structure based on the skills you need and select the right execution partner. The strategy helps determine how to build on your core strength, bond with customers, or win competitive battles.

You will have the desired response on your creative brief, you can align with your sales team, and you will know how to judge the work you see. It will help you set your sales forecast, impact your profit margins and set your market share goals.

While it takes much work to get to this strategy statement, it will pay off for you. This strategy statement will show up on each strategy page of your plan, it will be at the top of your creative brief, and it should be what you use to see if your execution delivers on the strategy.

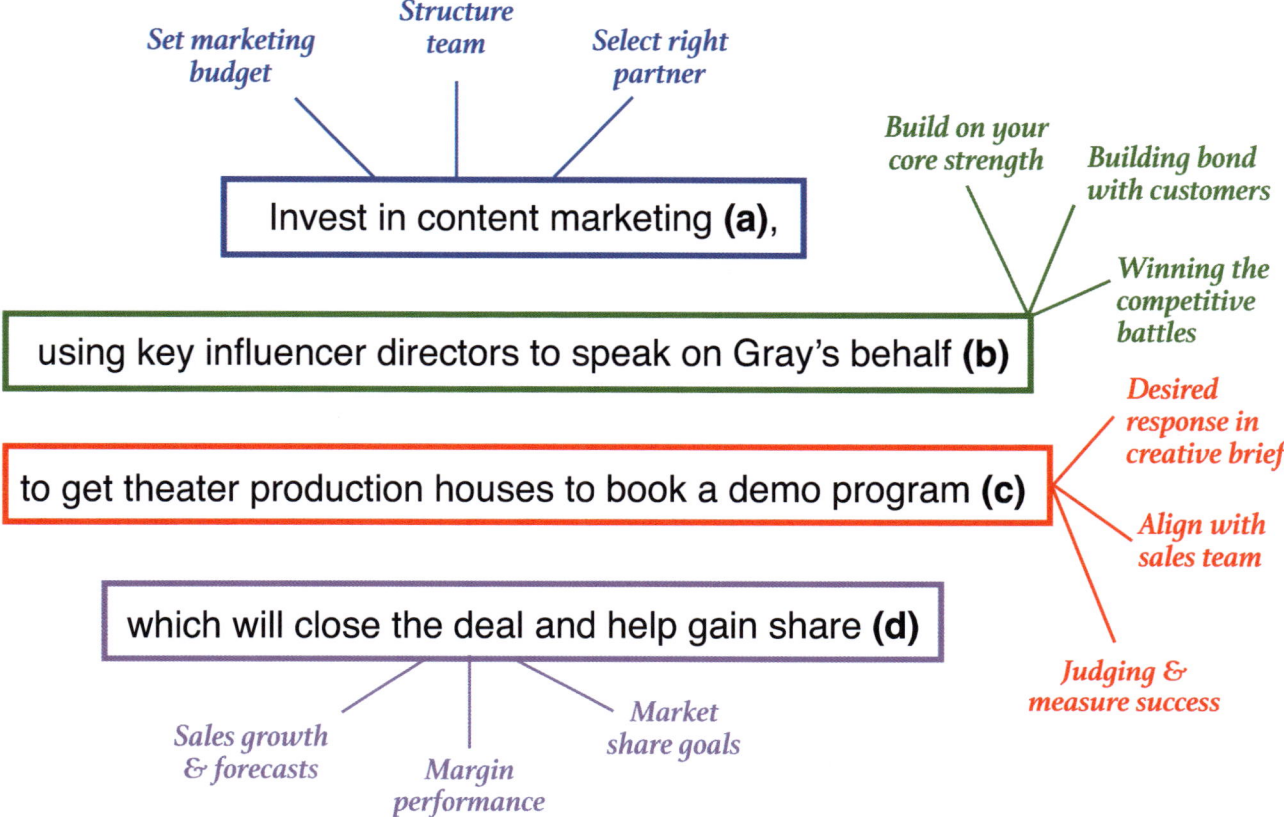

Turn your chunky strategic statements and into tighter strategy statements

The method I use creates a very long strategic statement first, before writing a pithier version of the strategic statement. You will notice the wording feels quite chunky and far too long. Once you have three steadfast strategy statements, you can narrow them down to a headline.

Chunky strategy statements

Invest in content marketing **(a)**, using key influencer directors to speak on Gray's behalf **(b)** to get theater production houses to book a demo program **(c)** which will close the deal and help gain share **(d)**.

Strategy headlines

Content marketing using "magic" to trade up directors up to our premium lighting.

How to lay out each strategy

Your effort in writing these clunky statements will not go to waste. Once you have decided on your top three strategies, you can lay out a specific slide to explain each strategy within your presentation.

- Include headline and the clunky strategic statement (told you it would not go to waste).
- The goals measure the ideal result of this strategy.
- Then list three tactical programs, where you will invest your resources.
- I also insert a "watch out statement" to show I am proactively addressing any issue I feel could derail my presentation.

Here is an example for Gray's Lighting, of a strategy slide format you can follow:

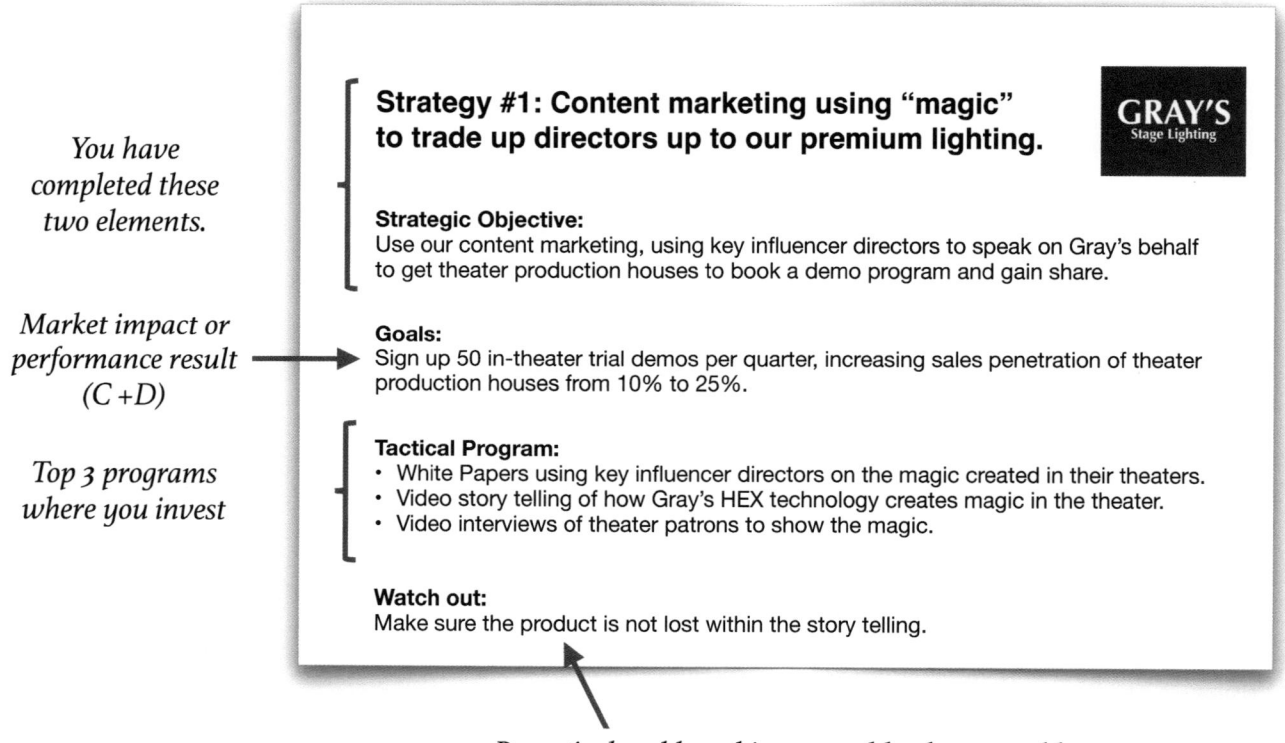

You have completed these two elements.

Market impact or performance result (C +D)

Top 3 programs where you invest

Strategy #1: Content marketing using "magic" to trade up directors up to our premium lighting.

GRAY'S Stage Lighting

Strategic Objective:
Use our content marketing, using key influencer directors to speak on Gray's behalf to get theater production houses to book a demo program and gain share.

Goals:
Sign up 50 in-theater trial demos per quarter, increasing sales penetration of theater production houses from 10% to 25%.

Tactical Program:
- White Papers using key influencer directors on the magic created in their theaters.
- Video story telling of how Gray's HEX technology creates magic in the theater.
- Video interviews of theater patrons to show the magic.

Watch out:
Make sure the product is not lost within the story telling.

Proactively address biggest pushback you could receive and answer it before being asked.

Plans for Gray's Industrial Products

Brand Strategy Roadmap

Vision: We create an easier work-life for the hardest-working people. Revenue to $100 Million, with 20% profit by 2030

Purpose: We work hard so you can work smarter, faster, and easier

Values: Service before self, speed matters to our customers, listen to solve, encourage teamwork, push for new ideas

Brand Idea: The fastest delivery backed by the smartest advice in the tool business				
Brand Promise	**Brand Story**	**Innovation**	**Purchase Moment**	**Experience**
We hire the smartest tradespeople who can respond to your most challenging issues	The widest range of industrial tools with a reputation for high-touch service	Innovative tools to make make you work-life smarter, faster, and easier	We are ready to serve, whether in the field with you or through our new DTC platform	Experienced tradespeople who are ready to help solve any problems

Goals: By 2030, $200 Million in sales with 20% profit, 30% of revenue coming from DTC

Issues:
1. How do we build bond with our most loyal customers, while reaching new younger customers?
2. How to launch a DTC platform around next day delivery?
3. What is the strongest grow investment payback to turn the business results round? New products? Acquisitons? DTC launch? Geographic expansion?

Strategies

Service our best customers	Direct to Customer platform launch	Explore product & service innovation	Acquisition to enter new markets
Tactics • Account management and service levels • Invest in sales analytics • Loyalty program	• DTC website, and future app • Logistics including ordering, warehousing, delivery • Drive new account sign-ups	• Product improvement across all product lines • Environment: energy efficient, recycled materials, carbon neutral	• Safety, security, marine • Acquire infrastructure to help DTC growth • Enter Asia market

---

Brand Plan

Brand Vision: We create an easier work life for the hardest-working people. Revenue to $100 Million, with 20% profit by 2030

Analysis	Issues and Strategies	Executional Plans
P&L forecast • Sales $90,385 • Gross Margin $51,148 • GM % 56% • Marketing Budget $8,850 • Contribution Margin $9,949 • CM% 13% **Drivers** • One-stop shop for construction, manufacturing, trades • Outstanding service levels • #1 tool supplier in North America **Inhibitors** • Direct shipments of Amazon, Wilson tools cut sales by 20%, and price by 10% • Gray's has fallen from #2 to #7 on plumbing due to lack of innovation **Risks** • Continued loss of DTC sales, mostly with trades • Government contracts in 2023 require meeting new environmental standards **Opportunities** • Innovation in plumbing, construction, fire • Highlight our peer-to-peer advice • Explore entering new categories including security, marine, and HVAC • Explore acquisition in Asia	**Key Issues** 1. How to launch a DTC platform around next day delivery? 2. How do we maintain bond with our most loyal customers, while reaching new younger customers? 3. How to position Gray's DTC platform against Amazon or other smaller players? **Strategies** 1. Build a DTC platform to reach younger customers 2. Use loyalty program to hold onto biggest customers during DTC launch 3. Advertise the launch of Gray's Direct **Goals** • 5,000 account registrations of the new DTC site, with 50% first orders, 10% third orders, 50 online reviews • 70% aided awareness of DTC, Marketing Communications has 50% brand link, $10 million sales • Maintain sales volume from top 1,000 accounts, and maintain 10% price premium	**Build the DTC Platform** • Create the Gray's Direct brand including logo/design, concept, strategy • Logistics including website, ordering, service, warehousing, transportation • Set up Account management team, outreach, working with sales team • Manage forecasted growth to ensure logistics keeps up with delivery expectations **New Marketing Communications for DTC** • Email campaign supported with social media and a launch contest • New Marketing Communications creative, with digital, print and OOH media. Ensure Gray's Direct Marketing Communications fits the Gray's brand standards. • Inside sales blitz following up on email. **Loyalty program for the base** • Build customer profiles for the top 1,000 accounts by volume • Set up loyalty points program to earn travel, sports tickets, sports equipment • Sales blitz to call to on top accounts, with in-person meeting, explain loyalty program **Support sales team** • New look/feel of brochure, posters, trade shows, truck demo programs. • Super Bowl contest / March Madness sweepstakes

Work exercise #1

Using the brand that you are working on, use our five questions with three bullet points to do a rough draft of your brand plan.

1. In an ideal state, where could your brand be in five to ten years
2. How would you describe where the brand is today?
3. Explain the reasons why are we where we are today?
4. What 3 strategies would help your get where you need it to be?
5. What are the activities we need to do to deliver those strategies?

Work exercise #2: Brand Vision

1. Using the same brand from the previous exercise, use 2-3 of brand vision questions to help paint the perfect picture for five years from now.
2. Use those answers to narrow down to a brand vision statement

Work exercise #3: Brand Purpose

1. When it comes to your brand, what aspect is it that you are most passionate about?
2. What is the most unique, ownable and motivating part of your brand?
3. What is the core belief or behaviour that provides your customers with the best experience possible?
4. What do you do that will make your brand one of your customer's favorite brands?
5. Use those answers to narrow down to a brand purpose statement

Work exercise #4: Strategic ThinkBox

Using the brand that you are working on, use our Strategic ThinkBox and assess what you think is going on relative to the core strength, customer bond, competitive battles and business situation.

- Core Strength
- Customer
- Competitive
- Situation

Translate that thinking into your best Key Issue questions

Work exercise #5: Strategic objective statement

As you look to answer your key issue questions, try writing out a strategic objective statement using our a + b + c + d method.

a: Capabilities

B: Focused opportunity

c: Market impact

D: Performance result

Work exercise #6: Laying out the strategy

Now that you have the key issue questions, let's lay out the overall strategy page that answers each issue.

Headline

Strategic Objective

Goals

Tactical Program

Watch Out

You can find our brand plan templates on *beloved-brands.com*

Summary definitions of the brand plan

Vision:
- The vision should answer the question, "Where could we be?" Put a stake in the ground that describes an ideal state for your future. It should be able to last for five to 10 years. The vision gives everyone a clear direction. It should motivate the team, written in a way that scares you a little and excites you a lot.

Brand purpose:
- The purpose has to answer the question, "Why does your brand exist?" It's the underlying personal motivation for why you do what you do. The purpose is a powerful way to connect with employees and customers, giving your brand a soul.

Values:
- The values you choose should answer, "What do you stand for?" Your values should guide you and shape the organization's standards, beliefs, behaviors, expectations, and motivations. A brand must consistently deliver each value.

Goals:
- Your goals should answer, "What will you achieve?" The specific measures can include customer behavioral changes, metrics of crucial programs, in-market performance targets, financial results, or milestones on the pathway to the vision. You can use these goals to set up a brand dashboard or scoreboard.

Situation analysis:
- Use your deep-dive business review to answer, "Where are we?" Your analysis must summarize the drivers and inhibitors currently facing the brand, and the future threats and untapped opportunities.

Key issues:
- The key issues answer the question, "Why are we here?" Look at what is getting in your way of achieving your brand vision. Ask the issues as questions to set up the strategies as the answer to each issue.

Strategies:
- Your strategy decisions must answer, "How can we get there?" Your choices depend on market opportunities you see with customers, competitors, or situations. Strategies must provide clear marching orders that define the strategic program you are investing in, the focused opportunity, the desired market impact, and the payback in a performance result that benefits the branded business.

Tactics:
- The tactics answer, "What do we need to do?" Framed entirely by strategy, tactics turn into action plans with clear marching orders to your teams. Decide on which activities to invest in to stay on track with your vision while delivering the highest ROI and the highest ROE for your branded business.

Chapter Thirteen
How to build your brand's execution plans

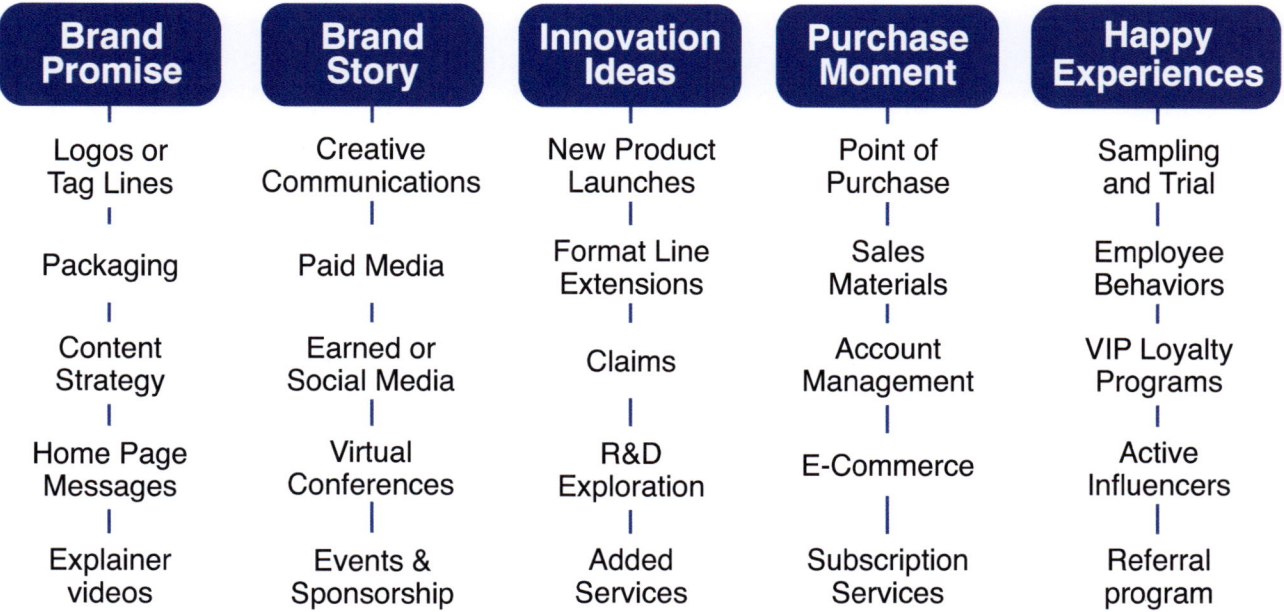

Align your execution plans

For each execution investment, write a separate execution plan as an organizing tool to ensure everyone has specific marching orders on the particular strategy related to their function, leaving no room for misinterpretation.

Every strategic investment you make deserves an execution plan. Use the five customer touchpoints to guide your execution choices for the development of a specific execution plan:

- **Brand promise:** Create an execution plan related to the development of a brand book, logos, slogans, look and feel, packaging, content strategy, sponsorships, and the homepage.

- **Brand story:** To communicate your brand's story, look at creative communication options, and paid, earned, shared, and owned media choices. Align communication, social media, search, PR, and content management.

- **Innovation:** Use execution plans to steer the product development team on new product launches, line extensions, claims, acquisitions, partnerships, market research, and product exploration.

147

- **Purchase moment:** Develop execution plans with your sales team, related to specific channels, customer promotions, deals, pricing, trade spend, sales materials, account management, sales force deployment, customer marketing, and e-commerce.
- **Customer experience:** Possible execution plans include the creation of service values, service behaviors, employee training, sampling, loyalty programs, events, websites, and influencer programs.

B2B brand communications plan

The brand communications plan answers seven questions. These questions steer and inspire the creation of the brand story work, so the brand communications work will establish your brand positioning, and motivate customers to see, think, feel, do, or influence. The plan must answer the following questions:

1. What do we need our communications to do? (Brand strategic objective statement)
2. Who is in our desired customer target? (Most motivated people to buy what we do)
3. What are we selling? (Our main customer benefit we stand behind)
4. Why should they believe us? (Support points to back up the main benefit)
5. What is our organizing brand idea? (Brand soul, essence or DNA for the brand)
6. What do we want people to see, think, feel, do, or influence? (Desired response)
7. Where will our customer be most receptive to see and act upon our message? (Media plan)

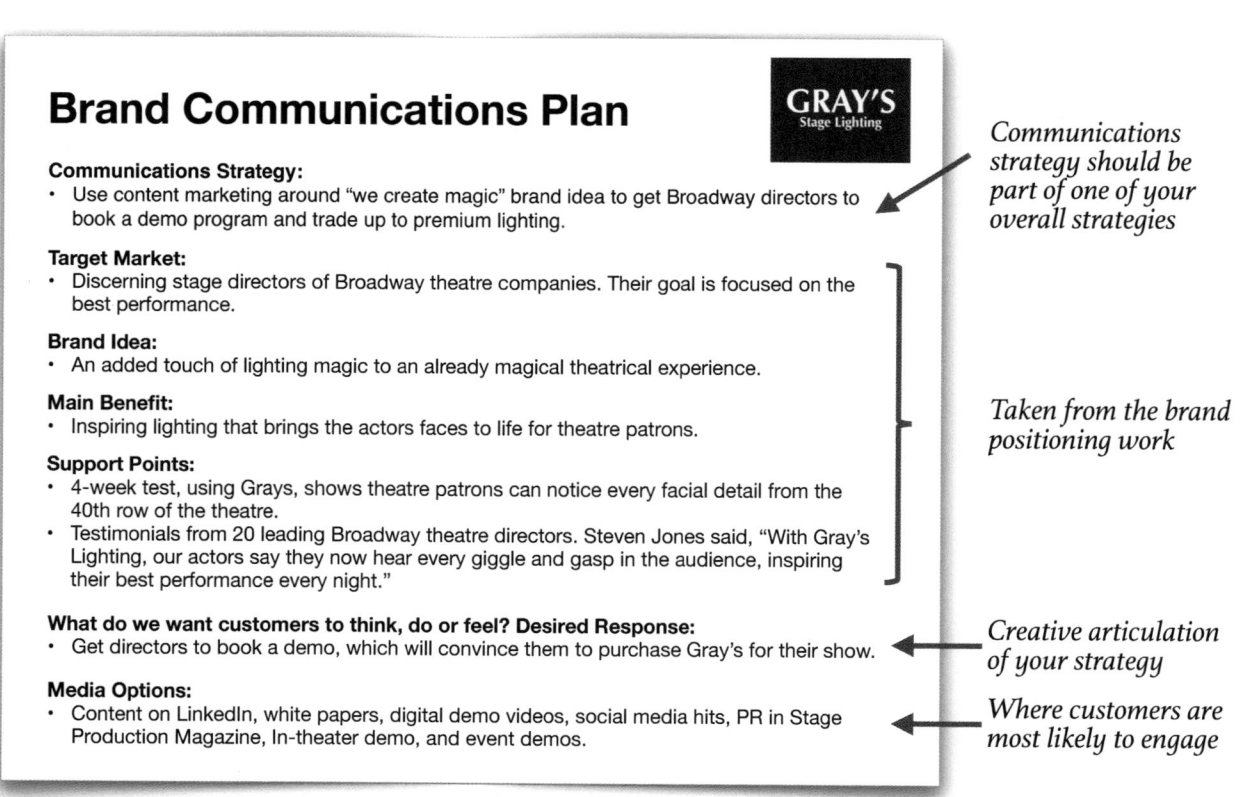

Innovation plan

Use your brand idea to guide the product development team to manage innovation ideas at the exploratory stage, (beyond five years), pipeline ideas (two to five years) and go-to-market launch plans (within the next two years). As the brand leader, you need to influence, manage, and even direct your product development team to ensure they focus on the brand strategy.

Innovation Plan

Innovation Strategy:
- Use high performance claims to defend against new entrants with most loyal high-volume directors to hold onto key customers. Build out Gray's line up around energy efficiency trends.

Customer Needs:
- **Target Market:** Discerning stage directors of theatre companies. Their goal is focused on the best performance. **Customer Insights:** "Of course, directors are crazy perfectionists. We have to be to keep up with the crazy perfectionist down the street. We rely heavily on experts to do their part." Customer needs: Experts not paying attention to details, noticeable flaws, flat performance.

Brand Strengths
- **Market Reputation:** Gray's is the market leader of speciality theater lighting, known for great servicing.
- **Manufacturing & Skills:** Have patents on key lighting product technology.
- **Sales & Distribution:** We know the theater business better than competitor, offering direct selling and servicing.

Brand Idea and Brand Positioning
- **Brand Idea:** Gray's provides an added touch of magic to an already magical theater experience. **Brand Positioning Statement:** Inspiring lighting that brings the actors faces to life for theatre patrons. A 4-week test, using Grays, has shown that theatre patrons can notice every facial detail from the 40th row of the theatre. We have testimonials from 20 leading Broadway theatre directors.

Internal beacon to inspire the team
- Our lighting innovation has as much of an impact on a Broadway play as anyone.

Project status:
- Launch Project "Stage Door" in 2024, Project "Wild" in 2025. Explore natural colours and extended shadows claims that will motivate customer target and be ownable for Gray's.

Sales plan

Brand leaders work side by side with the sales team to manage the consumer through the purchase moment. The brand plan should guide the sales team on specific strategy and goals. Given that your sales team owns the selling execution and the customer relationship, work to gain the sales team's alignment and buy-in on the best ways to execute your brand's strategy through direct selling, channel management, and e-commerce options. The collaborative decisions include pricing, distribution focus, shelf management, promotional spending, customer marketing, customer analytics, and specific promotional tools.

Sales Plan

Sales Strategy:
- Sales blitz to drive trial with off-Broadway directors, to solidify our presence beyond Broadway and gain new users.

Customer Target
- **Target Market:** Discerning stage directors of theatre companies. Their goal is focused on the best performance. With each customer, map out the user, influencer, buyer and decision-maker. **Insights:** "Of course directors are crazy perfectionists. We have to be to keep up with the crazy perfectionist down the street. We rely heavily on experts to do their part." **Customer Needs:** Standing out, being loved with positive reviews, intimate theater experience.

Customer Decision-makers
- **Users:** Directors focused on getting the best, will need to influence the production company. **Decision-maker:** Producers who want to drive early gate receipts and overall profit. **Buyers:** Will always compare details of brands and push for low price. **Influencers:** Mentors and peers who constantly push each other to make production better.

Brand Idea and Brand Positioning
- **Brand Idea:** Gray's provides an added touch of magic to an already magical theater experience. **Brand Positioning Statement:** Inspiring lighting that brings the actors faces to life for theatre patrons. Theatre patrons can notice every facial detail from the 40th row of the theatre. We have testimonials from 20 leading Broadway theatre directors.

What do we want customers to think, do or feel?:
- Get directors to book a demo, which will convince them to purchase Gray's for their show.

Execution tactics
- The use of event and in-theater demos, sales blitz to broadway directors and off-broadway directors, and singing up key directors to be used for case studies and testimonials as part of our influencer program.

Specific sales programs in place
- Q1: Off-Broadway sales blitz to grow distribution at key specialty theater.
- Q3: Broadway sales blitz with message focused on holding key cheaters during the competitive launches.
- Q4: Use event demos to convince directors to book in-theater demos

Partnering with sales using our 3-6-9-12 approach

Work collaboratively with your sales team. The worst marketers try to ram their ideas through sales, expecting them to follow your orders. Come up with ideas together. I recommend having quarterly meetings between sales and marketing with a collaborative look at the next 3 months, next 6 months, next 9 months and next 12 months, focused on specific tasks.

Next 3 months	Next 6 months	Next 9 months	Next 12 months
Focus on **execution of the details** for those ideas about to go into the marketplace. Logistics, final sales message, forecasts, ship dates, instructions to execution teams.	Make **final decisions** on best program. Details include forecasts, final art, messaging, sales presentation, and any data support.	Based on the brand/customer issues, **brainstorm possible solutions** such as promotions. Narrow to top ideas to explore logistics and costs.	Discuss **strategic issues** related to brand and customer. New products, pricing, major investment changes. Get results and feedback on prior executions.

Making tactical decisions

The principles of focus mean you have to limit the execution ideas to those that will best match your brand's limited resources.

Here is a tool that will allow you to assess the potential return on effort (ROE) for possible marketing activities. I call it the "big easy" execution decision-making grid.

Take each execution plan and hold a creative brainstorm. Put each tactical idea on a Post-It note. Then plot the ideas onto the grid as to whether the idea will have a big impact versus a small impact on your business results, and whether the tactical idea will be easy to execute versus difficult to execute.

JUST DO IT — Brainstorm ways to make these ideas even bigger

BIG EASY — Big Wins Easy to do

AVOID — Bad ROE, drain on resources

MAKE EASIER — Brainstorm easier ways to get it done

The top ideas rise to the big easy quadrant in the top-right corner. The goal of this tool is to narrow down your focus to the best three activities for each plan while eliminating those ideas that are potential resource drains. While you may not always have access to the data to find the ROI before launching a program, you should be able to use your instincts and judgment to assess ROE.

Project plans

A brand plan is not complete without project plans. For every chosen marketing activity, your project plan should list specifics around the project owner, support team, project budget, goals, milestones, and hurdles.

When you have a team running your brand, these project plans are a very

Project	Direct Sampling
Strategy	Sampling moms to drive trial and convert to sales.
Owner	Ryan Jones
Team	Ryan, Stephanie, Stuart
Sponsor	Steve Smith
Goals	Drive awareness/trial for new product, $1.5 million in sales for Q2, re-enforce brand message in store.
Deadline	In market March 20th
Milestones	• Retail calls Oct 5 • Select sampling vendor Oct 15 • Develop store list Dec 1st • Sample production and shipping to stores
Hurdles	• Gaining retail acceptance • Achieving added display • Lining up sampling with advertising
Budget	$500,000

efficient way to manage your people and ensure the specific projects remain on track.

If everyone on your team is using the same one-page format, it will make it so much easier for you to run your team. You can use this format to set up regular check-in meetings with your staff to keep every project moving towards completion.

Planning calendar

Your brand plan should include an **activity calendar** to guide everyone who will execute the plan, so everyone can see how the execution elements fit. It allows you to manage the finances of the organization and the people who will deliver the work.

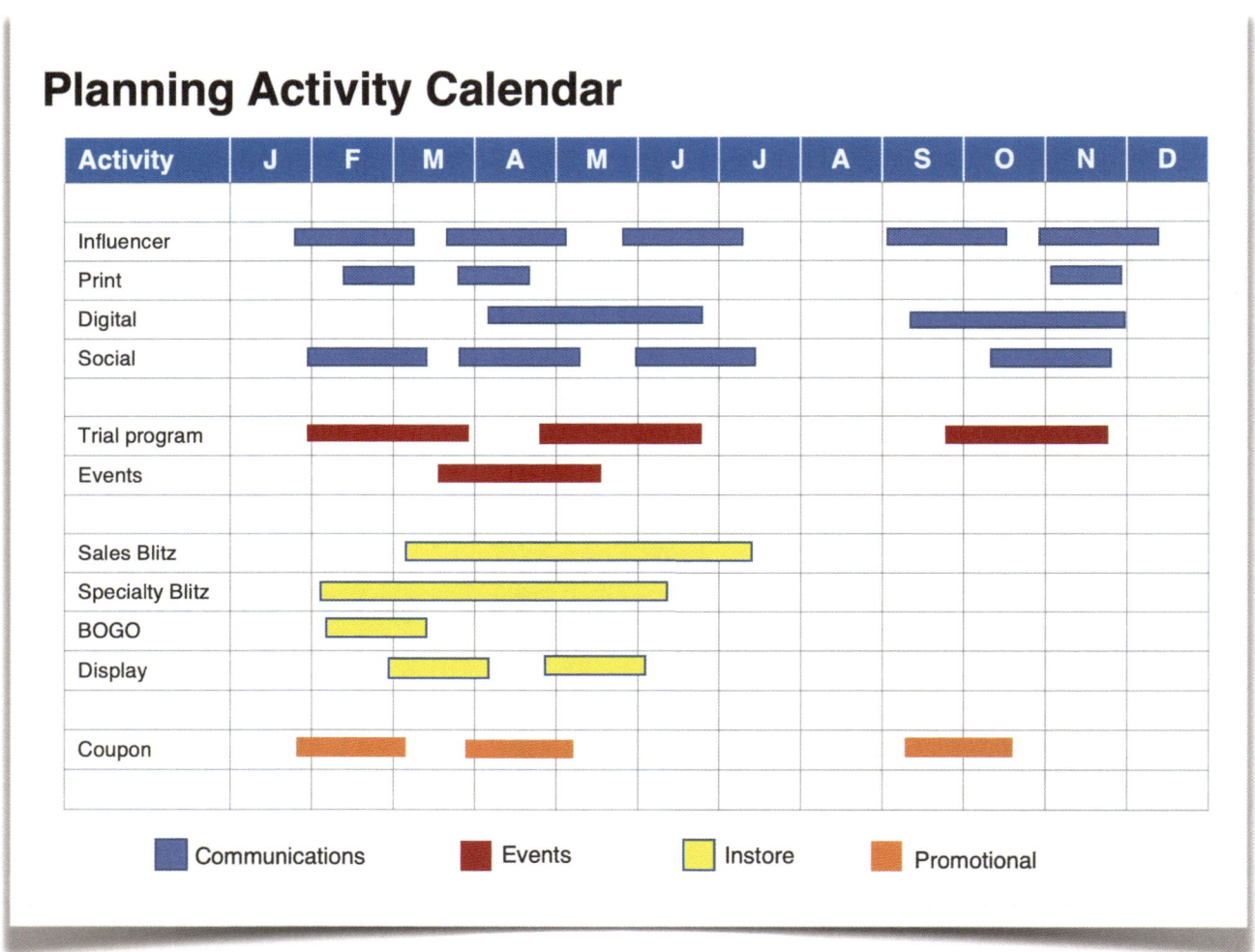

Brand measurement

You have to measure what matters. A good brand plan lays out key measurements and controls, including a marketing budget, sales forecast, and a profit statement for the brand.

Your brand plan should also include a brand dashboard with goals linked to financial performance (sales, margins, profit), brand health measures (market share, awareness, trial, repeat, loyalty) and execution performance tracking (marketing communications or innovation).

S. M. A. R. T. goals are specific, measurable, achievable, relevant, and time-bound

- **Specific:** State exactly what you want to accomplish, including who, what, where, when, and why. Focus on distinct market impact results (market share, program tracking, brand funnel data, retail performance metrics, voice of customer, and product rating scores) and financial business results (sales, margin, spend ratios, and profit), as well as significant milestones that move the brand towards your stated brand vision.
- **Measurable:** How will you demonstrate and evaluate the extent to which you have met the goal? The goal is usually tracked compared to last year, competitors, category norms, or milestones towards the end goal.
- **Achievable:** Set stretch goals with the ability to achieve the outcome. Use action-oriented verbs.
- **Relevant:** Link each strategy to a specific goal, as well as a five to ten year goal tied to your vision, which can have an annual milestone.
- **Time-bound:** Set target "by when" dates linked to significant milestones or deadlines. Break them out quarterly, annually, and over a five-year time horizon. A brand needs specific deadlines for major spend projects, all marketing communications, production schedules, in market timing, as well as all launch dates.

Goal	2021	2022	Comment
Sales	$25MM	$30MM	Continue 20% growth rate
Share	0.8%	1.2%	New premium line has 7.5% share
Distribution	62%	72%	Increase coming mainly from fixing specialty.
Awareness	33%	42%	Below norm, 80% among niche, < 20% overall
Trial	34%	37%	New format helped drive trial
Repeat	4%	5%	High quality taste converts high repeat
Gross Margin %	55%	57%	Launching new premium line up.
Profit %	19%	15%	Increased marketing spend in year 1 of launch
Ad Brand Link	62%	70%	Building on current brand equity in TV ad
Purchase Intent	70%	70%	Should hold strong as we trade up.
Customer Satisfaction	58%	60%	Halo impact from new premium line up.
Freshness Index	12%	20%	Increasing % sales from new launches.

Our B2B brand plan presentation template

It is easy for a brand plan presentation to get out of control, with too many slides and a lack of flow. This makes it difficult for your senior management to follow along and buy into your brand plan. Based on what we have shown throughout our book, we have created an ideal process for how to lay out the slides in an ideal presentation. This includes the tools you have seen throughout the book.

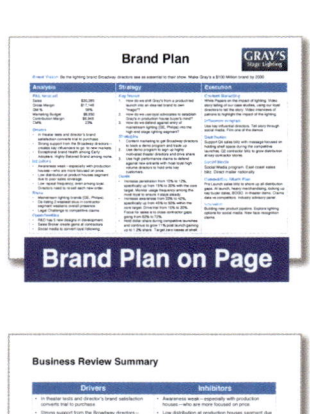
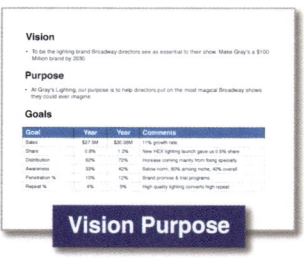
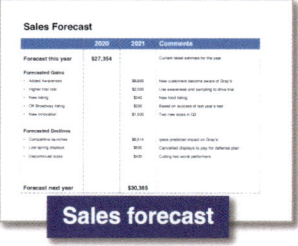
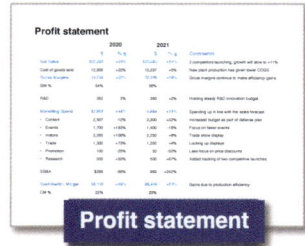
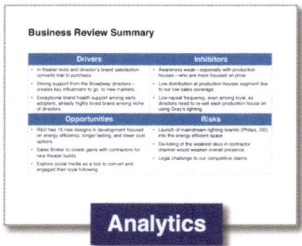
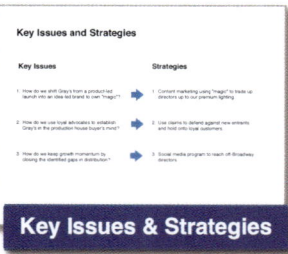
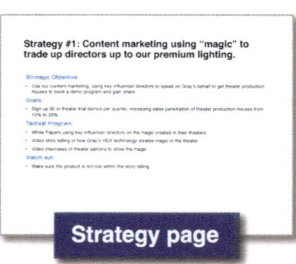

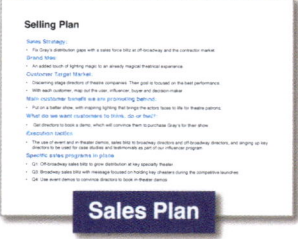

Our B2B brand plan templates are available for purchase at **beloved-brands.com**

Work assignment #1

Using the brand that you are working on, use our process to complete your brand communications plan

Communications Strategy:
-

Target Market:

Brand Idea:

Main Benefit:
-

Support Points:
-
-

What do we want customers to think, do or feel? Desired Response:
-

Media Options:
-

Work assignment #2

Using the brand that you are working on, look at everything you have created so far, complete a rough draft of the overall brand plan.

Vision:

-

Purpose:

-

Values:

Goals:

Key Issues:

1.
2.
3.

Strategies

1.
2.
3.

Tactics:

Chapter Fourteen
How to write a creative brief to set up brilliant execution

Before writing a creative brief, make sure you have done your homework on developing a winning brand communications strategy that combines the work of your brand positioning, brand idea, and the brand plan.

The briefing stage plays a crucial role as the bridge between your smart strategy and your brilliant execution.

> **As a B2B brand, your role is to make your customer successful**

I believe brand leaders should control the strategy yet give more freedom on execution. Too many marketers have this backward. They give up too much freedom on strategy then try to control the creative outcome of the execution.

Make the **tough decisions** to narrow the brief down to:

- One strategic objective
- One tightly defined customer target
- One desired customer response
- One main message
- Two reasons to believe.

I meet resistance when I show people that list. You should see the resistance that your eight-page brief will meet.

Our Marketing PlayBox steers the best "in the box" thinking.

The best creative marketing ideas come through in-the-box creativity using problem solving where the box is your brand strategy. Save your blue sky out-of-the-box thinking for random inventions or a new brand launch. We build on the Strategic ThinkBox we showed in the strategic thinking section, and now look at a Marketing PlayBox to ensure that our marketing execution work to be focused on our target, fit with the brand, deliver the message, and execute the strategy. While we will show how our Creative Brief sets up the Marketing PlayBox, we will introduce our Creative Checklist in the next chapter to see if the ideas are staying in the box.

Our Marketing PlayBox that marketing ideas need to play in has four dimensions.

1. First, we want marketing execution that is focused on the brand's desired target market.
2. Second, we need to make sure our marketing execution fits with the brand.
3. Third, we want the marketing execution to deliver the brand's main message.
4. Finally, we need to use the brand strategy to move customers in ways that benefit our brand.

A creative brief defines the Marketing PlayBox that the creative must play within.

1. We want marketing execution that is focused on the brand's desired target market.

You will notice that half of our creative brief template is about the customer. The best marketers do a ton of work to provide detail knowledge of the customer.

To start, define the target with combination of demographics, behaviors, and attitudes, and links how a brand could fit into other parts of their healthy lifestyle. Most importantly, focus on the dimensions that matter to the target.

Do not spread your limited resources against a target so broad that it leaves everyone thinking your message is for someone else.

Target the people who are the most motivated by what your brand does best, and make your brand feel personal so your target customer feels special. A brand must make customers think, "This brand is for me."

Next, add customer insights that provides little secrets hidden beneath the surface. Indeed, your communications experts will love working with customer insights. These insights help explain the underlying behaviors, motivations, pain points and emotions of the customers.

In addition, we lay out the pain point of the customer using the customer enemy that we know torments our target market every day.

2. We need to make sure our marketing execution fits with the brand.

A smart creative brief uses a brand idea that organizes everything we do. Add Brand Assets that includes past work that has worked including visuals, slogans, copy points, logos, fonts, and colors.

Don't cross the line by telling what type of creative you want. Stay confident that you have written such a great brief, that you do not need to control the creative outcome. Give the expert enough freedom for them to come up with great ideas.

3. The marketing execution must deliver the brand's main message.

Highlight the main message you know will work based on the brand positioning work that leverages the functional and emotional benefits that are most motivating to customers and ownable for the brand.

Explore using our brand positioning template. Build marketing communications that gets customers to do only one thing at a time, whether it's something you want them to see, think, do, or feel, or influence their friends. Force yourself to make a decision that links the marketing communications objective with your brand strategy.

Do not put so many messages into your ad; customers will see and hear a cluttered mess. They will shut down their minds and reject your ad. They will not know what you stand for, and you will never build a reputation for anything. Start a conversation that shows what the customers get or how they will feel. Do not just yell features at the customer. Use your brand idea to simplify and organize your brand messaging.

4. We need to use the brand strategy to move customers in ways that benefit our brand.

Make sure everyone is clear on the brand strategy, by having one very clear objective in the creative brief. Importantly, try to get customers to do one thing. Not everything. As well, provide media choices to explore, but be willing to maneuver based on the creative ideas that come back.

Biggest mistakes I see with the Creative Briefs

When I see marketers writing a **big, wide brief** with too many objectives, a vague target, and cluttered messaging, I wonder if you have unknowingly created too much strategic freedom.

While you might think writing a big, wide creative brief provides room for creativity, it does not. Your agency will see you as confused, and will likely just peel the brief apart, rewrite the brief how they want, then provide you with strategic options, instead of creative options. The problem is that you will be choosing your strategy based on which ad you like.

When I see marketers write a **big, long laundry list of mandatories**, everyone knows you are just trying to control the creative output. Do not create a tangled web of mandatories that almost write the ad itself, or you will trap the creative team into taking various elements in the mandatory list and build a Frankenstein-type ad. If you want great work – and I know you do – give your agency the creative freedom they need.

How to transform your strategy into a creative brief

Let's look at the seven questions of the brand communications plan I outlined in the brand plan chapter:

1. Who is in our customer target?
2. What are we are selling?
3. Why should they believe us?
4. What is our organizing brand idea?
5. What do we need our marketing communications to do?
6. What do we want people to think, feel or do?
7. Where will our customer be most receptive to see and act upon our brand message?

Do the strategic homework you developed through the brand communications plan, and begin to populate the **13 questions** of your creative brief.

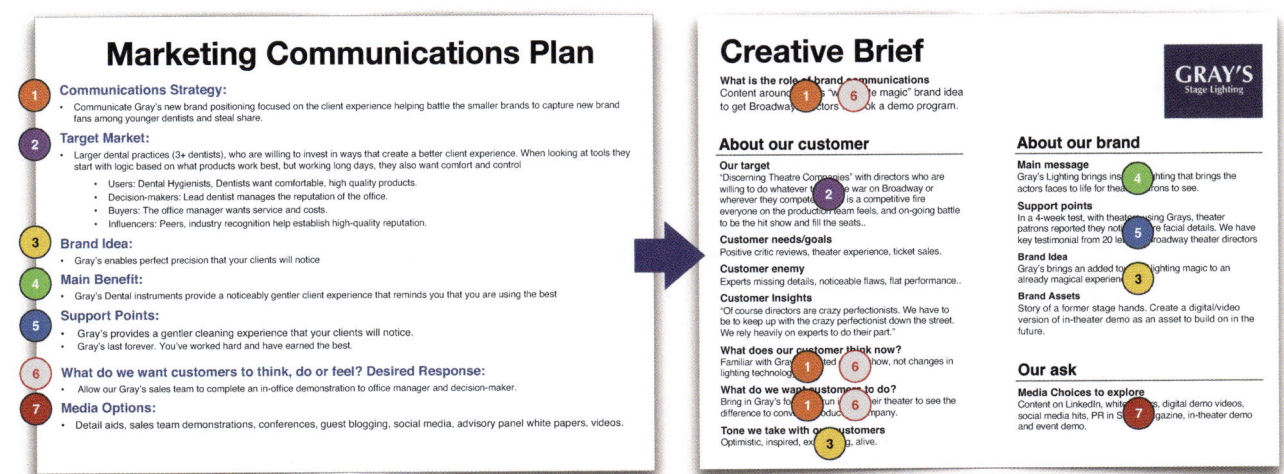

Dissecting the creative brief, line by line

I will dissect the Gray's Industrial Tools creative brief, with a line-by-line review to demonstrate examples of smart and bad creative briefs. This brief is to support the launch of same day service. I have seen many of the bad brief examples over the years to show you what not to do. I will use some of our principles I have talked about to show you a smarter brief. While each line in the brief has a role to play, the brief should have a natural flow, similar to the flow I talked about in the brand plan chapter.

Creative brief

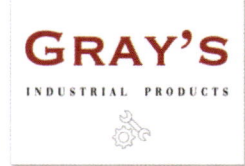

1 What is the role of communication?
Advertise Gray's Direct 'same day delivery' positioning to meet the fast delivery needs of younger contractors to drive trial and get early sales for the launch into the direct shipping marketplace

About our target

2 Our target
Hard working people who carry tools to help them do their jobs. They know time is money, speed is good, and despise any delays. Younger contractors / tradespeople are more open to using technology to keep track of projects and their business.

3 Moment of accelerated needs
Looking at their crew sitting around doing nothing waiting for tools to be delivered

4 Their enemy
Delays, missed deadlines, work projects backing up, crew sitting around not working.

5 Their Insights
Our consumers know that time is money. "If I hire people, there is nothing worse when they end up sitting around all day because we don't have the right tools to do the job. There goes the budget and deadline."

6 What does our target think now?
Gray's has always been known for their great service, but younger contractors are starting to see them as slightly slower than more modern options like Amazon.

7 What do we want our target to do?
Get younger industrial contractors or tradespeople to sign up for Gray's Direct.

About our brand

8 Main message
Sign up for Gray's Direct so you can get our same day delivery of tools to your job site

9 Support points
No one is faster than Gray's Direct. Order on our website and we will get you the tools you need the same day, right to your job site. Sign up for our Uber delivery within hours.

No one knows tools more. You still get access to Gray's knowledgeable advice. We hire tradespeople to be ready to take your call, who can help you out in real time, and then get you the right tools when you need it.

10 Brand Idea
The same day delivery backed by the smartest advice in the tool business

11 Brand Assets
Well known to hire retired tradespeople to provide real world advice, Gray's is a 100 year old brand, #1 in the industry

12 Tone we take with our target
In control, reliable, calm, street smart, informed

Our ask

13 Media Choices to explore
Digital and social media, trade magazine, email list, out-of-home billboards near job sites

Dissecting the creative brief, line by line

I will dissect the Gray's Industrial Tools creative brief, with a line-by-line review to demonstrate examples of smart and bad creative briefs. This brief is to support the launch of same day service. I have seen many of the bad brief examples over the years to show you what not to do. I will use some of our principles I have talked about to show you a smarter brief. While each line in the brief has a role to play, the brief should have a natural flow, similar to the flow I talked about in the brand plan chapter.

1. What is the role of brand communication to the market?

A bad brief has an unfocused objective:
- Drive awareness of Gray's Direct, steal market share from Amazon, get loyal contractors to recommend to peers, and get current users to stay loyal to Gray's Industrial during transition.

A smart brief has a focused objective:
- Advertise Gray's Direct 'same day delivery' positioning to meet the fast delivery needs of younger contractors to drive trial and get early sales for the launch into the direct shipping marketplace

Smart briefs start with one very clear objective, while bad briefs try to accomplish too many things at once. If you get this line wrong, it can destroy the entire brief. With the example above, the smart brief narrows the decision to one objective (book a trial demo). A clear objective helps steer the direction for the rest of the brief. The bad brief makes the mistake of trying to do two things at once.

I see too many brands put "drive penetration and usage frequency" at the top of the brief. It is the sign of a lazy mind. Do you realize how different these two strategies are? Can you see how much you will drain your resources when you try to do both with the same ad?

These two strategies have two separate targets, two different brand messages, and potentially two different media plans. Your agency will divide the brief in half, and come back with one ad to drive penetration and another to drive usage frequency. As a result, you will pick your brand strategy based on which ad you like best.

> **Penetration vs. frequency**
> - A **penetration strategy** gets someone new with minimal experience with your brand to consider dropping their current brand to try you once and see if they will like your brand. That will take a lot of hard work.
> - A **usage frequency strategy** involves someone already familiar with your brand, and your job is to convince them to change their behavior about your brand. They will either have to change their current life routine or substitute your brand into a higher share of occasions.
>
> **Pick one strategy, not two**

If your brand has an issue with both penetration and usage, I recommend you write two separate creative briefs, with two independent projects, budgets, and media plans.

From a brand plan viewpoint, I would also recommend you stagger these two strategies into different fiscal years to ensure you are not just dividing your limited resources and doing a poor job with both strategies. Do you want to get more people to use you or the same amount of people to use more? Pick one.

2. Who are we talking to?

A bad brief has an unfocused target:
- Current customers, new customers, employees, or distributors. Anyone who uses tools including contractors, government, or DIY customers. They may use distributors, or shop at Home Depot, Walmart or use Amazon. They buy 4.6 to 33.9 tools per year.

A smart brief has a focused and well-defined target bulls-eye:
- Hard working people who carry tools to help them do their jobs. They know time is money, speed is good, and despise any delays. Younger contractors / tradespeople are more open to using technology to keep track of projects and their business.

One of the most significant correlations with brand success is to resonate so well with customers that they feel, "This brand is for me." You can only achieve that by speaking directly with a precise, tight bullseye B2B customer target.

A good brief uses a combination of demographics, behaviors, and attitudes, and, in Gray's Industrial Tools case, links how lighting could fit into their goals to be successful. These details paint a full picture of who we are talking to. In the bad, unfocused creative brief above, the target is pretty much everyone, so it will be hard for anyone to feel the communication will be speaking directly to them.

3. What's the customer's needs and goals?

A bad brief focuses on tactical goals:
- Quality product, responsive service at a reasonable price.

A smart brief aligns with the highly personal needs and goals of your customer:
- Looking at their crew sitting around doing nothing waiting for tools to be delivered

With a B2B brand, one of your main roles is to make your customer successful. You have to listen to understand their goals, so you can align your brand with the achievement of those goals.

4. What's the customer enemy we are fighting?

A bad brief has the business problem as the lead:
- Gray's is the dominant industrial tool supplier, is losing sales to Amazon and other DTC options. Gray's is unknown among customers, but is an opportunity to capture.

A smart brief has a clearly stated customer problem:
- Delays, missed deadlines, work projects backing up, crew sitting around not working.

The brief should reflect your customer's problem, not a business problem related to how customers buy your brand. Think back to the target market chapter and use your customers' pain point or enemy, which torments them every day. Think of how your brand will battle that enemy on behalf of your customers.

In the example of a smart brief, the customer's enemies are delays, missed deadlines, work projects backing up and the crew sitting around not working. This shows you understand the customer. When you put an emotional enemy in your brief, it allows the creative process to get into the emotional space right away. That is much more powerful than a functional problem such as losing weight or reducing calories.

In the bad brief example above, focusing on business problem rather than customer emotion is a classic flaw of leading with a business-driven problem that talks about a brand's problem with customers.

5. Customer insights

A bad brief has data over insights:
- Gray's product quality drives high trial (50%) compared to other launches (32%). Contractors order 3.4x per month compared to customers who shop the category when they buy a new house.

A smart brief has deep, rich insights:
- Our customers know that time is money. "If I hire people, there is nothing worse when they end up sitting around all day because we don't have the right tools to do the job. There goes the budget and deadline."

Tell a story about the customer, using insights to connect and show "We get you." As discussed in the Target Market chapter, customer insights come to life when you start them with the word "I" to force yourself to get in the customer's shoes and then put them in quotes to begin to use the customer's voice. Express the insight in such a captivating way in your content communication that will make customers stop and say, "Hmmm, that's exactly how I feel. I thought I was the only one who felt like that."

> **The best way to express customer insights is to start with the word "I" that gets in the customer's shoes and then put the insight into quotes, to speak with the customer's voice.**

The smart brief above really goes deep to gain an understanding and build a story through the voice of the customer. It captures their inner thoughts, uses their own word choices, and expresses their feelings. In the bad brief, there are no real insights. It is just a bunch of data points, without any depth of explanation or story. It will be hard for the creative team to write an engaging story with stats.

6. What does our customer think now?

A bad brief provides data only, without a well-drawn conclusion:
- Gray's has always been known for their great service with industrial customers, but DIY customers have never heard of Gray's.

A smart brief defines where customers currently are with the brand:
- Gray's has always been known for their great service, but younger contractors are starting to see them as slightly slower than more modern options like Amazon.

You can use the **brand love curve** from the customer strategy chapter to capture how customer feel about your brand. Use the analytics from brand funnel analysis, the voice of customer (VOC), market share data, loyalty data, and net promoter scores to determine where your brand sits on the curve.

The bad brief above just throws out random statistics; it fails to turn the data into stories that form a meaningful analysis. The smart brief draws an honest conclusion that your brand is at the indifferent stage for most customers. Lighting is a low involvement category for directors.

7. What do we want customers to do?

A bad brief tries to trigger too many responses:
- We want to get industrial contractors to THINK Gray's Direct is unique, FEEL loyal because they can stay in control, and TRY Gray's to see if they like them. Then, once they LOVE the new delivery, INFLUENCE friends (DIY customers) to try.

A smart brief focuses on the desired response that comes from the strategic objective:
- Get younger industrial contractors or tradespeople to sign up for Gray's Direct.

The best brand communication can only get the customer to do one thing at a time, so you should focus your desired response to get customers to see, think, do, feel, or influence others. Make the choice. Decide on what you want the desired response to be before you decide on the stimulus, which is the next question of the brief.

2 — Only once you decide on what you want from customers can you answer "What should we tell customers?"

1 — Start with the ideal desired outcome for what you want your customer to see, think, do, feel or influence.

The bad brief above sets up an unrealistic attempt to get customers to think, feel, and try – and all in one piece of brand communication.

Conversely, the smart brief narrows the focus to prompting younger industrial contractors to sign up for Gray's Direct which aligns with the strategic objective of the brand plan. The belief within the purchase journey is that signing up for Gray's will help close the sale more than any one piece of brand communication.

Too many marketers already know what they want to say before they even know the response they want from their customers. Turn that around and start with the desired response, which comes from your brand plan. Only then can you decide what to say to achieve that response.

8. Tone we will take with our customers

A bad brief uses clichés that are all over the emotional map:
- Optimistic, smart, down-to-earth, trusted, popular yet friendly.

A smart brief focuses on the emotional zones your brand is trying to win:
- In control, reliable, calm, street smart, informed

With Gray's Industrial, the two emotional zones the brand positioning focuses on "in control" and "knowledge." The related support words, in the emotional benefit clusters includes reliable, calm, inspired, informed, control, and street smart, which can help define the ideal emotional tone and manner of your brand.

The bad brief is all over the map with emotions. It seems half the briefs I see contain "smart, trusted, reliable and friendly." They have almost become clichés without thought. Using our emotional zones from the brand positioning chapter, you will see those words fall into five distinct emotional zones. These words would make your brand appear schizophrenic in tone.

9. What should we tell customers? (Main message)

A bad brief tries to communicate too many things at once:
- Gray's Direct is the modern DTC option so you can get same day delivery of tools to your job site, but it's also the traditional industrial tools you've trusted for 100 years

A smart brief focuses on one main message, bringing the customer benefit to life:
- Sign up for Gray's Direct so you can get our same day delivery of tools to your job site

The smart brief above narrows down to one thing the simple message of "same day delivery." The bad brief has a laundry list of several unrelated messages. Most are just product features, instead of a primary customer benefit. It is a marketing myth to believe that if you tell the customers a lot of things, at least they will hear something. The truth is that when you tell customers too many messages, they will just shut you out and not listen to anything you say.

10. Why should customers believe us?

A bad brief lists random claims about your brand:
- Gray's have been in business for 100+ years, satisfying generations of tradespeople. We know what you need more than modern options. Give us a call to set up an appointment to come into meet our experts. If you need tools quickly, explore our Gray's Direct option, which is as good as Amazon

A smart brief uses the support points to close off lingering gaps:
- No one is faster than Gray's Direct. Order on our website and we will get you the tools you need the same day, right to your job site. Sign up for our Uber delivery within hours.
- No one knows tools more. You still get access to Gray's knowledgeable advice. We hire tradespeople to be ready to take your call, who can help you out in real time, and then get you the right tools when you need it.

Only use support points to close off any potential gaps in your logic. Listen to customers for possible doubts they may have relative to your main message. Based on Logic 101, you can win any argument using two premise points to conclude. The same should hold true for a brand. Force yourself to use a maximum of two support points.

The smart brief above focuses on two support points, which back up your main message. The bad brief throws out random claims that have nothing to do with the main message.

11. Brand idea

A bad brief throws out random features to anyone:
- Everyone loves Gray's. Premium tools with great service. Most preferred, highest quality, carpenters recommend. Now on Amazon.

A smart brief uses the brand idea that organizes everything we do:
- The same day delivery backed by the smartest advice in the tool business

A smart brief uses the brand idea that drives everything we do. The bad brief example above targets everyone and lists random features and claims. However, it does not contain any customer benefits. If you only tell customers what you do, and not what customers get, you risk leaving it up to their interpretation.

> **Tell customers what they get, not what you do.**

12. Brand Assets

A bad brief throws out random features and ideas to control the creative:
- Avoid humor as a sarcastic tone will not work with target/subject. Preference is for real testimonials, supported by before and after, using our celebrity DIY TV host. Must show 90-day guarantee. Show brand name in first five seconds. Use celebrity spokesperson. Set in a house or high rise. Add 2007 best new product seal for authority.

A smart brief uses distinctive creative and strategic assets to build behind:
- Well known to hire retired tradespeople to provide real world advice, Gray's is a 100 year old brand, #1 in the industry

The smart brief builds creative and strategic assets. Stay confident that you have written such a great brief, that you do not need to control the creative outcome. The bad brief starts to try and control the creative outcome.

13. Media choices

A bad brief uses too many media choices, especially early in the process:
- Detail aids, conference demos for reps, website to access, targeted direct mail and emails, customer support tools. Videos, Need to use Facebook, Twitter, and Instagram. Must be able to use video on YouTube.

A smart brief provides a range to see what the creative looks like first:
- Digital and social media, trade magazine, email list, out-of-home billboards near job sites

At the briefing stage, you might have ideas around what type of media you want to use, but it is difficult to know the ideal media until you see the creative idea. At this point, provide a potential media guideline with a lead media option and possible media choices to support. The unfocused bad brief above offers a laundry list of media choices, which will only spread your limited resources so thin that nothing will have the desired impact you hope for. When you try to be everywhere, you might end up nowhere.

Mandatories

A good brief gives freedom to the creative team to explore:
- 25% of the print must carry the Devon's Hammers logo as part of our agreement. Include our legal disclaimer on the demo test and 12-week study.

A smart brief has very few mandatories with none of them steering the creative outcome. Stay confident that you have written such a great brief, that you do not need to control the creative outcome. Give some creative freedom to allow your agency the opportunity to look at the best way to express and deliver your strategy.

The bad brief would use a list of mandatories to steer the creative outcome with a prescriptive list that backs the agency into a creative corner. The agency is expected to tick off each mandatory, so they will create messy, ugly "Frankenstein" content to try to piece everything together.

Creative brief

What is the role of communication?
Communicate Gray's new brand positioning focused on the client experience helping battle the smaller brands to capture new purchases among younger dentists and steal share.

About our target

Our target
Larger dental practices (3+ dentists), who are willing to invest in ways that create a better client experience. When looking at tools they start with logic based on what products work best, but working long days, they want comfort and control

Moment of accelerated needs
When dental professionals deliver a rough experience, they know they risk losing a client.

Their enemy
Poor client experience means losing clients.

Their Insights
"I'm always looking to improve the experience of our clients. We work so hard to get new clients, that we fear doing anything wrong that will jeopardize the client's experience."

What do they think now?
Gray's have the best tools in the industry, but they are really expensive. I wish we could afford them.

What do we want them to do?
Talk to their office manager or decision-maker and request a product demonstration to showcase what a difference Gray's makes.

Tone we take with our target
A comfortable choice, reliable and in control.

About our brand

Main message
Gray's Dental instruments provide a noticeably gentler client experience that reminds you that you are using the best

Support points
Gray's last forever. Backed by the highest grade of Yamato steel plus our free annual sharpening program keep your tools feeling as sharp as the day you bought them. When you feel the sturdiness and weight of our premium dental tools, you are experiencing the Gray's quality that will give you the confidence to clean the most difficult stains on the teeth and reach the most difficult places in the mouth

Brand Idea
Gray's enables perfect precision that your clients will notice

Brand Assets
Distinctive Blue handle, 100 year old, #1 brand, brand of desire for older dentists.

Our ask

Media Choices to explore
Detail aids, sales team demonstrations, conferences, guest blogging, advisory panel white papers, videos.

The mini brief

Going too fast sometimes takes too long. With the explosion of media options, timing is everything. Unfortunately, there are too many "phone call briefs" happening. Even worse, no brief at all.

Without a brief, too many things could go wrong. When you see the creative options, you have to rely on your memory and instincts. When you try to present it to your boss, there is nothing to guide them through their decision-making.

One round of rejection by your boss, and you will be wondering why you did not just take the 15-30 minutes to organize your thoughts and **write a mini brief.** If your brand has a solid brand communications plan, you should be able to create a mini brief with a clear objective, customer target and insight, the desired response, and the main message

Mini brief

What is the role of communication?
Highlight Gray's new brand positioning focused on the client experience through a creation of an advisory panel with quarterly white papers.

About our HCP

Our target
Larger dental practices (3+ dentists), who are willing to invest in ways that create a better client experience. When looking at tools they start with logic based on what products work best, but working long days, they want comfort and control

HCP Insights
"I'm always looking to improve the experience of our clients. We work so hard to get new clients, that we fear doing anything wrong that will jeopardize the client's experience."

About our brand

Main message
Gray's Dental instruments provide a noticeably gentler client experience that reminds you that you are using the best

Support points
Gray's last forever. Backed by the highest grade of Yamato steel plus our free annual sharpening program keep your tools feeling as sharp as the day you bought them. When you feel the sturdiness and weight of our premium dental tools, you are experiencing the Gray's quality that will give you the confidence to clean the most difficult stains on the teeth and reach the most difficult places in the mouth

Creative Brief for Gray's Lighting

Creative brief

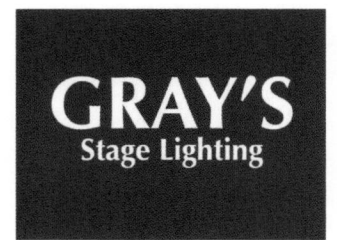

What is the role of communication?
Content around Gray's "we create magic" brand idea to get Broadway directors to book a demo program.

About our target

Our target
"Discerning Theatre Companies" with directors who are willing to do whatever to win the war on Broadway or wherever they compete. There is a competitive fire everyone on the production team feels, and on-going battle to be the hit show and fill the seats..

Customer needs/goals
Positive critic reviews, theater experience, ticket sales.

Customer enemy
Experts missing details, noticeable flaws, flat performance..

Customer Insights
"Of course directors are crazy perfectionists. We have to be to keep up with the crazy perfectionist down the street. We rely heavily on experts to do their part."

What does our customer think now?
Familiar with Gray's. Fixated on the show, not changes in lighting technology.

What do we want customers to do?
Bring in Gray's for a test run inside their theater to see the difference to convince production company.

Tone we take with our customers
Optimistic, inspired, exhilarating, alive.

About our brand

Main message
Gray's Lighting brings inspiring lighting that brings the actors faces to life for theater patrons to see.

Support points
In a 4-week test, with theaters using Grays, theater patrons reported they noticed more facial details. We have key testimonial from 20 leading Broadway theater directors

Brand Idea
Gray's brings an added touch of lighting magic to an already magical experience.

Brand Assets
Story of a former stage hands. Create a digital/video version of in-theater demo as an asset to build on in the future.

Our ask

Media Choices to explore
Content on LinkedIn, white papers, digital demo videos, social media hits, PR in Stage Magazine, in-theater demo and event demo.

The ugly creative brief

If we take all the examples of the bad brief from Gray's Industrial Products, below is a summary of everything that becomes the ugly creative brief.

Work exercise: Completing the Creative Brief

Using the brand that you are working on, come up with a creative brief for a new communications campaign.

What is the role of the communication?

Who is our target?

Who is the customer's enemy?

What are the insights we know about our customer?

What does our customer think now?

What do we want our customer to think, see, do, or feel?

What is the tone of voice?

What is our main message?

Support points?

What is the brand idea?

What are the brand's assets to build upon?

What media choices should we explore?

Chapter Fifteen
How to make communications decisions to break through the clutter

In the past, B2B leaders thought of marketing communication as a support for the sales team or the opportunity to announce a new product launch. With so many media options, today's B2B brand leaders recognize the opportunity to tell the brand's story in a way that can connect with specific customers and tighten the bond with customers.

In this chapter, I will go through creative communications, media, and new product innovation. Think of marketing execution as a business investment that showcases your brand story through creative execution to help connect your brand with customers where they are most willing to engage, listen, think, feel, and act in ways that pay back your brand.

I will revisit our Marketing PlayBox to ensure the work stays focused on the customer target, builds on the brand, communicates the main messages, and delivers the strategy.

Here are six questions to help build your communications plan:

1. What is the size of your brand's media budget?
2. What is your brand's core strength?
3. How tightly connected is your brand with your customers?
4. Where can you best impact the customer journey?
5. Where will your customers be most open to engage, listen, think, feel, and act?
6. What media choices will best deliver your brand's creative execution?

Summary of our six media planning questions

1. What is the brand's budget size?

Start with the size of your business and the related gross margins available to spend. Look at the past media ROI and creative communications results as a projection for success. Identify the brand or business impact from previous campaigns, and match up to potential strategy you are looking at this time.

2. What is your brand's core strength?

Explore the differences of whether your brand is a story-led, product-led, experience-led or price-led impacts and how it impacts your main message. Generally, story-led and product-led need significant budgets, to reach a large audience. Experience-led brands are a slower build and rely on word of mouth. Price-led brands needs efficient media choices to quickly trigger the transaction.

3. How tightly connected is your brand with your customers?

Where does your brand sit on the brand love curve? Where you sit impacts the communication focus getting customers to see, think, buy, feel or influence. You should filter based on the degree of competitive threats you face in the market. The higher the competitive battle, the higher the marketing spend.

4. Where can you best impact the customer journey?

Understand how your customer moves from awareness, consideration, search, buy, satisfy, repeat, loyal and to becoming a brand fan. Match up to the communication focus of the strategy to the stage where you can have the greatest impact, related to your overall brand strategy in the brand plan.

5. Where are customers most open to engage, think, listen, feel, and act?

Who is your target customer target, including users, buyers, decision-makers, or influencers? What part of the their life are they most willing to watch, listen, learn, engage, decide and act? How can you align with their day-in-the-life or moments during the week or year. For significant purchases, you can align to special life-changing moments. Are there adjacent or related products/services linked to your brand?

6. What media choices will best deliver the creative execution?

Your brand idea should drive the creative idea, which then drives your priority for gaining attention, brand link, communication or stickiness. Stay open on media during the creative development process to ensure your creative can fit with the best media choices. What is the size of your brand's communications budget? What is the size of your brand's communications budget?

       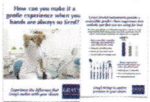 

Brand story | **Home Page** | **Explainer Videos** | **Search Engine** | **Social Media** | **Paid Media** | **Influencer Marketing** | **Sales Material** | **Trade Shows**

Balance the media choices by looking at media efficiency, quality, impact, and fit with the brand. The efficiency of media math starts with reach and frequency.

- **Reach** is the number or percentage of different people exposed to the message at least once over a specific period.
- **Frequency** is the number of times that a person will be exposed to the message within a particular period. Be careful to avoid relying on efficiency alone, as you need to balance it with the quality of the media choices.

I always set aside about 10 percent of my media budget to create a high impact to generate early attention to a new campaign or product innovation.

Use your **strategic thinking** to understand how much you can invest. You need to focus your limited resources on a distinct opportunity point you have identified based on a potential change in the market. The reasons you would strategically invest in media include:

- Discovery of a new brand message you know will motivate customers to buy your brand.
- Identified change in customer needs, motivations, or behaviors, which will benefit your brand.
- Shift the competitive dynamic with an opportunity to make gains or a necessity to defend.
- Continue to fuel brand growth with a window to drive brand profits.
- New distribution channel you can use to move customers through before competitors do.
- The launch of a breakthrough product innovation that offers a competitive advantage to your brand.

To make the media investment pay off, you need to be able to drive a performance result that pays back with an increase in brand power you can use in the future or an immediate increase in brand profit.

Six factors to help guide you on the size of your media investment:

1. Brand profit situation, looking at margin rates and the size of the business.
2. Past media ROI projected forward as a forecast of the potential.
3. Impact of your current creative communications tracking results
4. Future investment opportunities or future threats to battle.
5. Degree of competitive pressures in the marketplace and their levels of media spend.
6. Comparative opportunity cost for investing elsewhere.

What is your brand's core strength?

Decide whether your brand will be story-led, product-led, experience-led, or price-led impacts your brand message and related marketing communication choices.

If your brand is **product-led**, focus on standing out with trend influencers and early adopters. Use an interruptive and visual media choice to demonstrate and explain what makes your product better. You can share the video demonstrations on your brand's website or through social media. Invest in search to help prospects who may have questions and need more information. Mobilize expert influencers to trigger trend influencers and early adopters to make informed purchases.

Product
"What we make is better than everyone else."

For **story-led brands**, use media to create a movement behind your idea, purpose, core belief, or stance. Connect with like-minded customers who could become potential early brand lovers and influence their network to turn your brand into a movement. Bring your brand's concept, purpose, or story to life using emotional storytelling media, such as TV, long-copy print, and storytelling content built to share. This approach allows those early brand lovers to spread awareness with influence and gives your brand an active voice on social media.

Story
"Our story, idea or purpose makes us different."

Experience
"Our great people make the difference in our amazing experience."

When your brand's strength is the **customer experience**, building your brand awareness takes time. Be patient. The slower build will be well worth the time invested once you hit a

Price
"We are smarter and able to deliver the same at a much lower cost."

tipping point. Start by engaging key influencers and expert reviewers (industry critics) early on to reach the trend influencer customers who will build word-of-mouth within their network. Build and manage the online customer review sites to entice other users to try your brand's fantastic experience. Consider allowing your staff to share their personal, authentic "wow" stories to become part of the brand's communication. It is your great people who make the difference—you can use media to build that story.

When you are a **price-led brand**, you need high sales volumes to cover the lower margins. The most successful price brands invest in call-to-action, efficient media options, and point of sale media to trigger transactions.

How connected is your brand?

For **unknown** or **indifferent brands**, invest in the early part of the B2B customer journey with media focused on building awareness to establish the brand positioning in the mind of customers to separate your brand from the pack. You also need to get your brand into the customer's consideration set.

Brands at the **like it** stage must separate themselves from others to build momentum and create a following. Focus on closing the deal by motivating customers to buy. You can use search tools and deal-closing claims at the point of sale to resolve any remaining doubts.

Brands at the **love it** stage must turn your customer's repeat purchases into higher usage frequency and become a favorite part of your customer's day. The creative must instill emotional benefits, linked closely to the customer's life moments.

An excellent tool to use is to map out the "day-in-the-life" of your target customer and place messages where they are most likely to engage. Use customer insights to make the messages personal to make customers feel special and attached to your brand.

At the **beloved brand** stage, you should begin shifting to a maintenance media plan, enough to maintain your brand's leadership presence and perception. Stay aware of the competitive activity, which may force you to adjust your budget levels.

At this point, you can shift some of your media resources into enhancing the customer experience to retain your happy customers and to drive a deeper love to harness an army of brand lovers. You can begin creating shareable experiences for your brand lovers to share with their friends.

Use the brand love curve to focus your media objectives and strategy

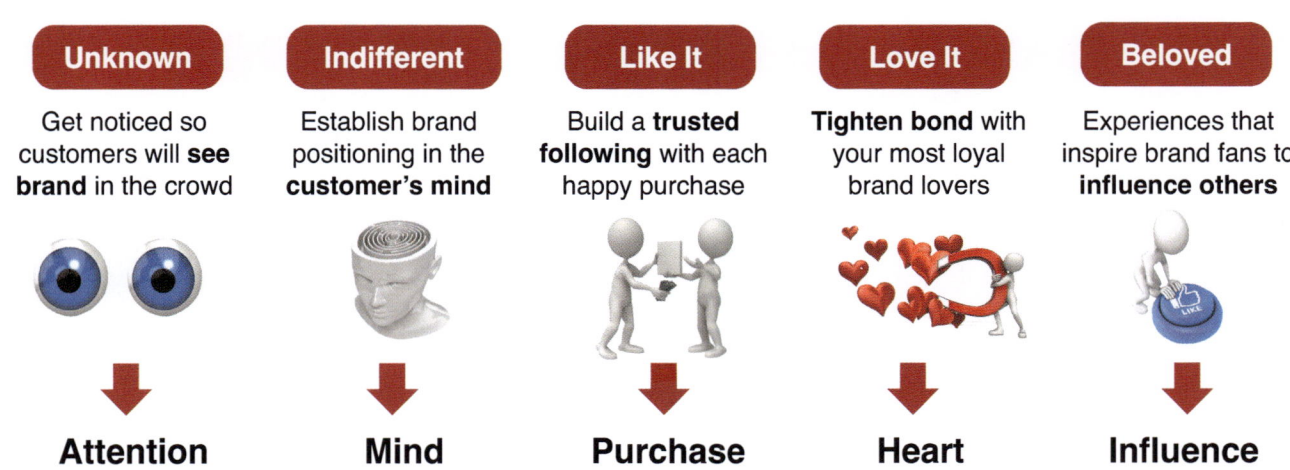

Where can you best impact the customer journey?

Old-school marketing used to yell their messages at every possible customer using trade shows or industry-specific publications, then move those customers naturally through the brand funnel from awareness to purchase and loyalty.

It was all about the interruption of customers with brands focused primarily on closing an early sale. Many times, the more annoying the ad, the better it would work.

New-school marketing whispers to the most loyal brand fans who sit within a customer company, hoping they drive awareness by influencing their peers.

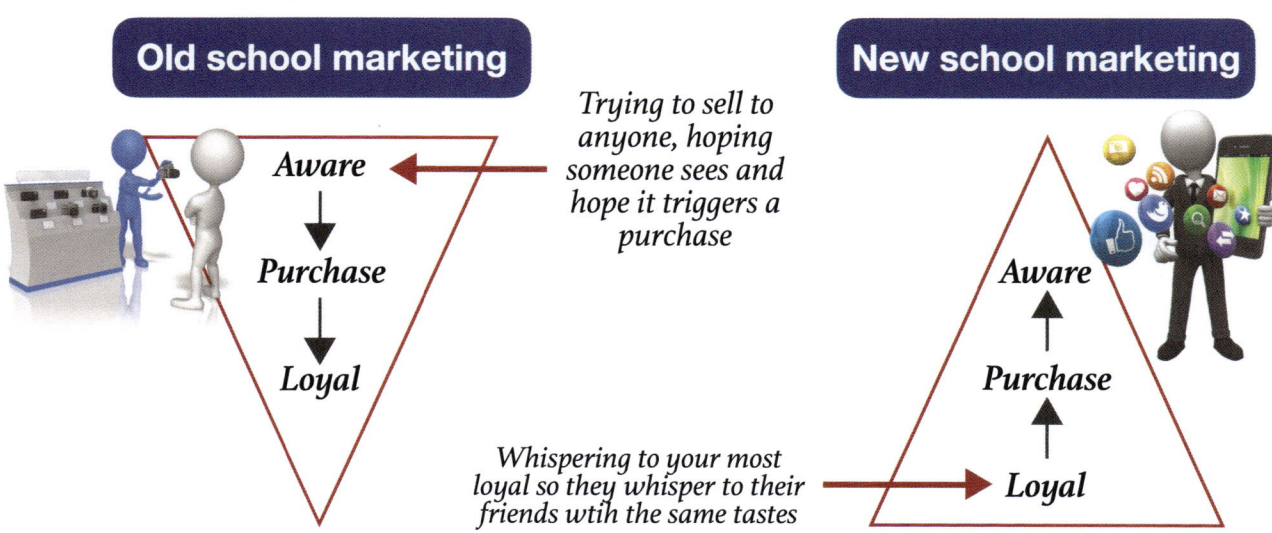

Word-of-mouth from a peer will bring more influence to their purchase decision than a random trade show encounter. They also look to the brand lovers, giving them evidence the brand does deliver what it promises.

In the **brand strategy section**, I showed you how brands evolve from a craft brand to a disruptor, to a challenger brand and finally to a power player.

One significant distinction is what type of customers they focus on. I introduced the idea of a customer adoption curve, which leverages four types of customers:

- Trend influencers
- Early adopters
- Early mass
- Late mass

I will use this thinking to show how brands can use influencers to trigger each type of customer, as the brand evolves from the entry-level craft brand to the power player mass brand.

The role of influencers on the customer adoption curve

The **trend influencer customers** always want leading-edge stuff and are first to try within their social set. They stay aware of what the wise experts are saying, whom they trust or rely upon for knowledge.

For brands competing in B2B markets such as technology, creative services, B2B, or food, there are leading expert reviewers or bloggers who have become the voice of the marketplace.

Marketers who offer a real revolutionary addition to the category should target and brief these wise experts to ensure they fully understand the brand story and point of difference. This information increases their willingness to recommend new products.

The **early adopter customers** rely on their trend influencer friends for the details of new brands. However, they will also look to industry icons as a secondary source for validation. If the industry icons are speaking out on the new product, it assures the early adopter the new brand is about to hit a tipping point. These customers always want to stay ahead of the curve, so they will adopt it now.

Early mass customers look for the advice of trusted peers whom they respect within their network. These are the people we go to for advice on a given subject.

The early mass also looks to early brand lovers for validation of proven success. This satisfaction level gives them evidence the brand does deliver what it promises, which increases brand trust.

The **late mass audience** is slow to adopt; they look to co-workers for recommendations on what everyone else is using but only when they feel comfortable enough to buy the brand.

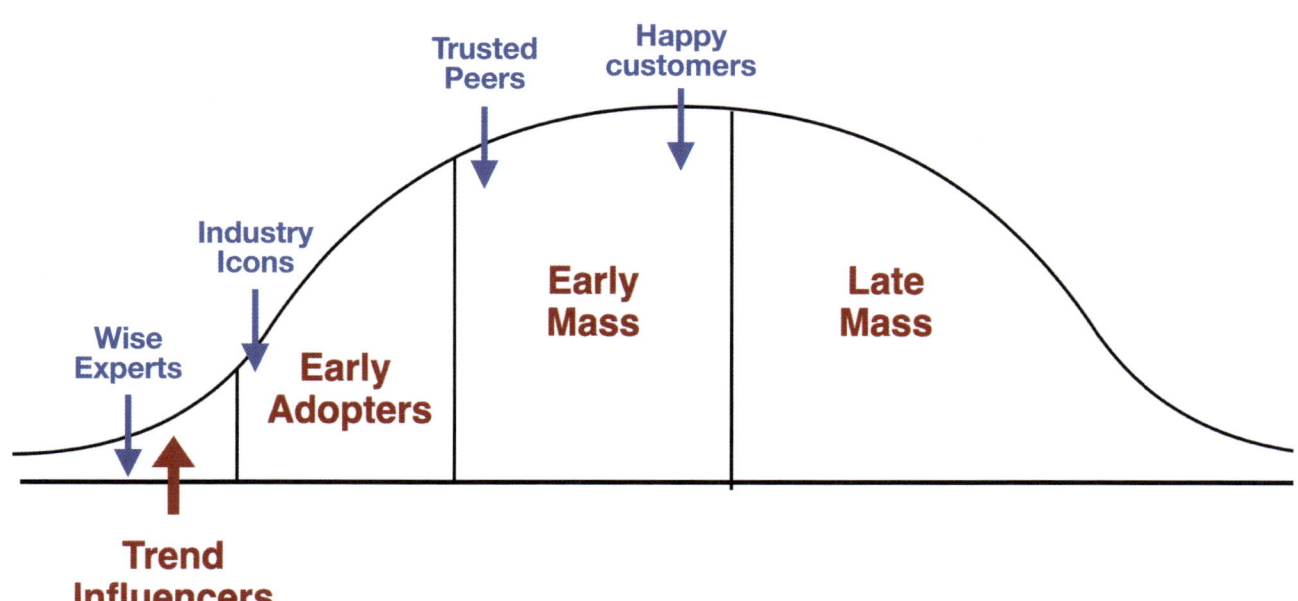

Manage your customers through their purchase journey

While we talk a lot about customer-based social media options, we are seeing bigger opportunities for B2B brands, whether you are trying to reach users, buyers, decision-makers or influencers. It allows us to find prospects and move them through their journey. We look at attract, inform, close, service and delight.

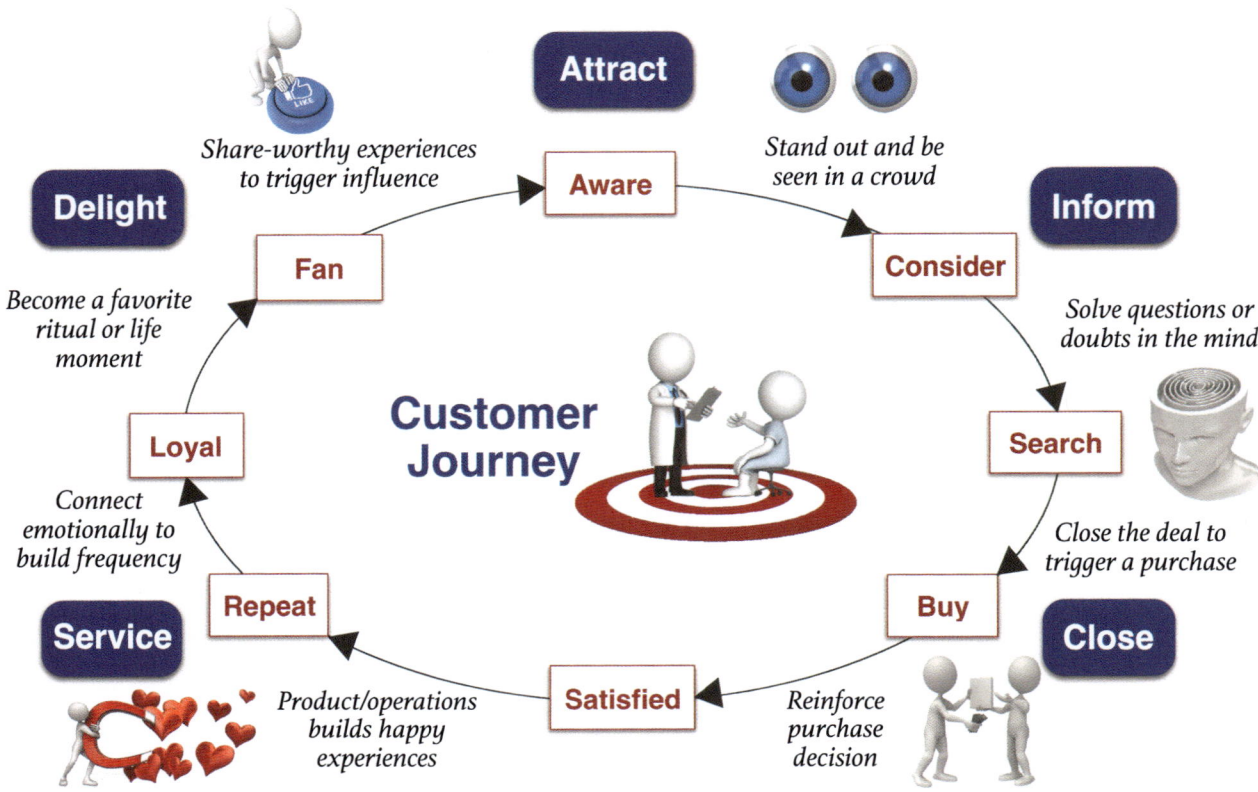

To **drive awareness**, you need your marketing communications to stand out and be seen in a crowd using messaging that balances being creatively different and strategically smart. When your messages are smart but not different, they get lost in the clutter. On the other hand, when your messages are different but not smart, they will entertain customers, but do nothing for your brand. Your communications must be smart enough to trigger the desired customer response to match your brand strategy.

To move B2B customers to the **consideration stage**, use influencers to teach those who seek to learn more. Use public relations to make the brand part of the industry news, whether through traditional, social, or blogger channels. Engage online user reviews or industry-specific review sites.

For more complex or higher risk purchase decisions, many B2B professionals will rely on **search** for almost everything, even if to confirm what makes sense. Marketers can use search sites, such as Google, expert review sites, and online content or long copy print media.

Over the last decade, I am see a shift where B2B professionals prefer to take the time to do their own research rather than a face-to-face call from a sales rep.

The **brand website** comes into play and should include the right information to close off gaps or doubts, then move customers towards the purchase decision.

Account-based marketing (ABM) can be used to move customers along their purchase journey to help trigger an initial purchase with displays, trial programs, or sales materials to prompt customers. Remarketing is a great tool to push customers who might feel stuck at the consideration stage to reconsider and buy.

After the purchase, use the account-based marketing to turn usage into an early purchase into a ritual among your most loyal users. Cultivate a collection of brand fans, using VIP programs and experiential events with exclusive deals — layer in emotional marketing communications to tighten the bond.

Once you have a strong base, you can mobilize your brand lovers by intentionally creating shareable experiences, which will trigger brand lovers to share your brand communications with their network through social media.

With social media tools, the smartest brands are getting their most engaged customers to drive awareness by sharing your message – and even enthusiastic user-generated content.

For B2B brands, always keep in mind the **four-headed monster** we talked about in the customer session, with the user, decision maker, buyer, and influencers. As you shift to engaging individuals, recognize the role each plays, and then match up your marketing communication to their specific needs.

> *Create valuable, relevant, and consistent content for each stage of the customer journey*
>
> 1. Create something that *attract* prospects to drive awareness and consideration.
>
> 2. Use insight to connect, listen to their needs, provide the *right information* to help them decide
>
> 3. Earn their trust, to give them the comfort they need to help *close the deal* to turn them into buyers.
>
> 4. Use high-touch *service* creates an exception experience turning them into a happy customers
>
> 5. *Delight* your most loyal customers so they influence their peers to become new prospects

Use your brand idea to align marketing communication choices

In today's cluttered media world, use your brand idea to help organize all types of marketing communication efforts, including your brand story, sales material, trade shows, homepage, search, social media, and any influencer marketing. When telling your brand story, you now have many media options available, including white papers, a regular blog, LinkedIn, trade shows, and face-to-face presentations.

The challenge is making sure you tell the same brand story, with consistent layers of brand messaging. There is nothing wrong with repetition, especially if you are using various media options to make it more engaging. You might get bored with your words long before any customer will.

Brand story — Tell company story in ownable, breakthrough, motivating way.

Home Page — Share knowledge to influence and close sale of products/services

Explainer Videos — Make your brand easier to use drives up purchases

Search Engine — Make customers smarter so they more informed decisions

Social Media — Enlist brand advocates to influence others customers.

Paid Media — Broad reach behind new message to drive new leads

Influencer Marketing — Leadership voice within industry and at conferences.

Sales Material — Manage customers through their purchase journey

Trade Shows — Bring brand to life and project ideal customer experience

Tell your brand story in an ownable, breakthrough, and motivating way across media options

Create a 'Who are we' story

Use our brand story structure to set up a 'who are we' summary. Start with the brand idea to create an inspiring promise statement that sums up what you deliver. Match your brand purpose with insights to show why your brand matters. Use your brand's core belief to connect with customers and demonstrate what you do to support your belief. Outline your brand's point of difference, with support claims to back it up. The 'who are we' can show up on your website, LinkedIn page, and sales material.

Home page

Think of your home page like the front door of your business. Start with a concise overview of what you do and who you are. Be welcoming, easy to navigate, and with a clear headline. Set up your website through the eyes of your customers. Showcase your products or services to help customers explore on their own. Use a blog to educate your customers. If you plan to sell, make it easy to convert visitors into leads or customers.

On-page optimization (easy to read)

You need to optimize your web pages to make it easy for Google to crawl and index. Ensure that your content, layout, and code are all up-to-date so that Google can understand what your website is about and how it fits with answering queries from their users.

- Many factors impact optimization including word count, title tags, H1 titles, meta descriptions, security of your site, site speed for desktop and mobile.

- Domain Authority (DA): score from 1-100 that predicts how well a website will rank on Google search results. Created by Moz.

- Search engine result pages (SERPs): ranking factors that determine order to rank web pages in their SERP.

Off-page optimization (easy to find)

Optimizing your brand content to rank higher in search engines. Use high quality backlinks, social media shares, social bookmarking, guest blogging and on-topic blogging.

Getting backlinks sends signals to the Google algorithms that your content is worthy. Social media shares will also help drive more backlinks.

Using opinion blogs / white papers

White papers and blogs work best when you take a stance on topics that are important to your customer. They enable you to project your belief as a way to connect with them.

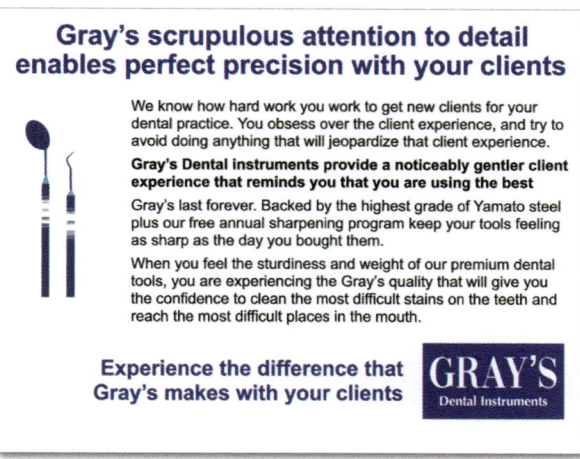

White papers inform or educate your customer, with your brand embedded as one of the solutions. They give your team members a voice and set them up as experts. You can pair with an advisory panel to bring expert voices in to support your brand messages. Share your white papers via social media, email, trade shows, or drop them off on an in-person sales call.

Paid Media

Add paid media to capture your customers where they are most willing to engage. Use a headline that captures their attention, integrate your brand into the creative to ensure strong brand link, focus on one main message and find creative ways to stick in the customer's mind.

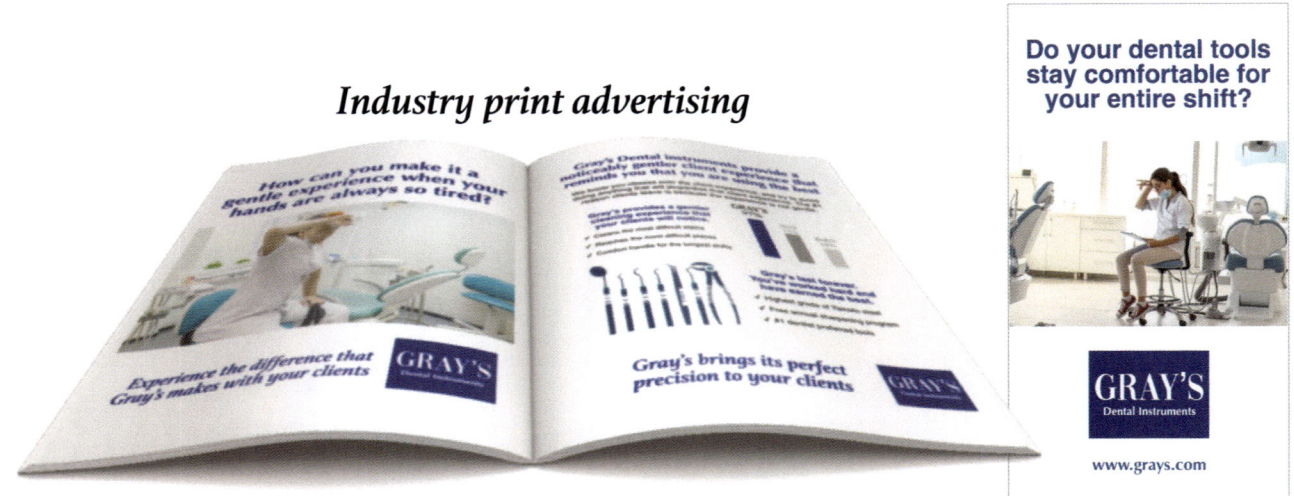

Industry print advertising

Digital ads

Explainer Videos

A well-executed explainer video should provide solutions and answers to most questions that might arise in the minds of potential customers before they even ask them. Explainer videos should generally be 30-90 seconds in length, which translates into a written script of around 200 words or less in most cases. It not only creates awareness for the brand but also builds trust by providing a level of transparency and sincerity that is difficult to replicate through other mediums. The best types for B2B are the whiteboard animation or motion graphics that fit the tone of what you are selling.

Use social media to project your brand voice

- Social media provides an opportunity to reach all levels of customers, including users, buyers, decision-makers and influencers.
- Get your employees involved using content your employees will be proud to share. Tell their stories and highlighting their accomplishments.
- Focus your social media on 5-6 topics using a balance of long-copy articles, videos, photos, or memes. Include PDF shares of white papers, links back to your website, and events you are promoting.

Pick a lead social media vehicle

- LinkedIn works best for long-copy content, focused on important issues to reach your customers. Use your company page to generate followers and engage your key executives to send out content.

- Use Twitter to project quick hot-take opinions or to provide quick customer service response through DMs. Be careful as it is the wild west.

- YouTube is a great platform for easy-to-follow explainer videos.

- Facebook provides a broad reach, complimented with paid media.

- Use a social media scheduler (Hootsuite, Edgar, Buffer etc) to create a balanced and full schedule.

Account based marketing (ABM)

Account based marketing (ABM) starts with the belief that every individual customer or prospect has different needs, behaviors, and desires. You gather customer data, transform it into insights about the customer, and tailor their messages to meet these individual needs by creating personalized messages and offers for each customer or prospect.

Customer relationship management (CRM) systems (Salesforce or Hubspot) are designed to find, attract, and nurture profitable customers by identifying key decision makers or influencers at targeted accounts, prioritize accounts based on potential revenue opportunities, and develop personalized strategies for each account to generate leads.

A CRM system can give you a clear overview of everything in one place — a simple, customizable dashboard that can tell you a customer's previous history with you, the status of their orders, any outstanding customer service issues, and more.

Trade shows

Trade shows engage customers when they are most open to learning about new options. Bring your key influencers to the conference stage to demonstrate their endorsement. Using outspoken industry leaders gives you the benefit of association. Have them talk about industry trends to engage the audience, setting up your brand as a potential solution.

Use your trade show booth to directly engage with customers. Trade shows are an excellent chance for companies to acquire new leads, set up meetings with potential customers, and figure out how they can better target the right audience.

Integrated marketing approach

Ensure all the creative elements work together and drive a consistent message with a consistent look.

The thinking behind great marketing communications

The best marketing communications must balance being creatively **different** and strategically **smart**.

When your marketing communications effort is **smart but not different**, it gets lost in the clutter. It is natural for marketers to tense up when the creative work ends up being "too different."

In all parts of the business, marketers are trained to look for past proof as a sign something will work. However, when it comes to marketing communications, if the work looks too similar to what other brands have already done, then it will be at risk of boring your customers, so you never stand out enough to capture their attention. Push your comfort with creativity and take a chance to ensure your ad breaks through.

When marketing communications work is **different but not smart**, it will entertain customers, but do nothing for your brand. Your marketing communications must be smart enough to trigger the desired customer response to match your brand strategy.

Strategy (Smart ↑ / Not Smart)

Smart but not different
Solid strategy, but no creativity
Will do OK. Won't break through clutter to make a difference.

Different & smart
Creativity helps breakthrough.
Solid strategy motivates
Customers to take action

Not smart and not different
Brand is lost and floundering.
Conservative creative against a weak strategy.

Different but not smart
Creative for the sake of it.
Misses strategy: wrong target, message, or desired response.

Creativity (The same ← → Different)

How to predict marketing communications success

Let's take this creative thinking to a predictive marketing communications model, changing the creatively different to branded breakthrough, and the smart strategy becomes motivating customers.

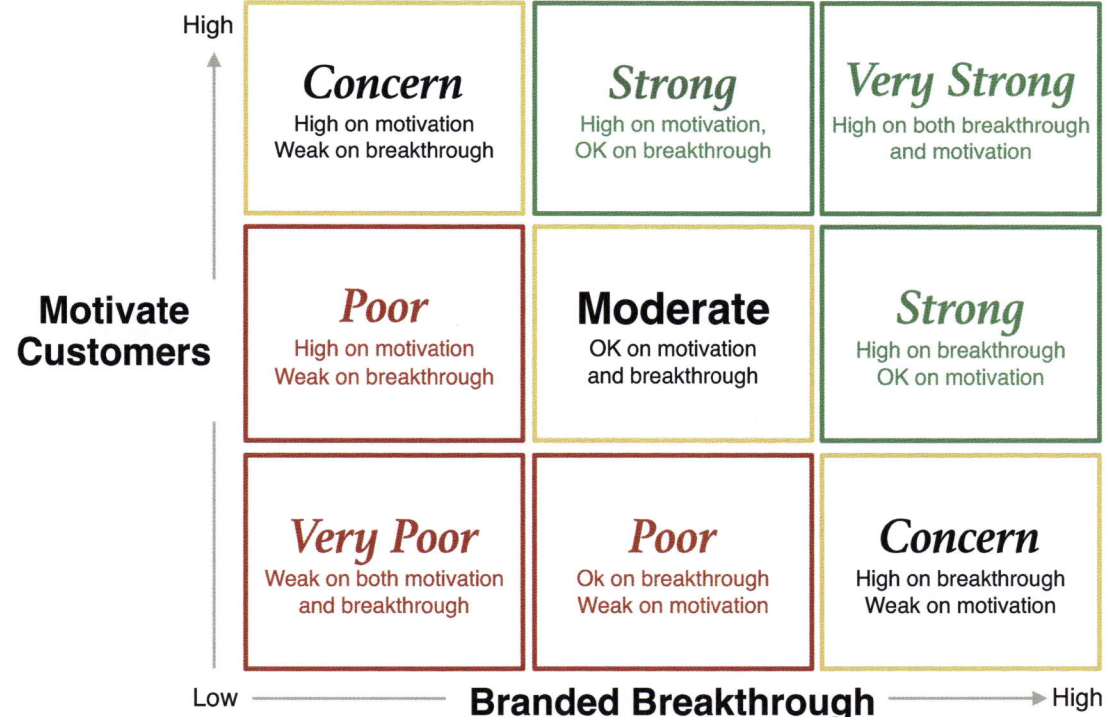

Branded Breakthrough + Motivate Customers =
Attention + Brand Link + Communication + Stickiness

Branded breakthrough is "how you say it." It uses creativity to capture the customer's attention within the clutter of the market while linking your brand closer to the story. The motivating message is "what you say."

Communicate the main message to connect with customers memorably, so the marketing communications work sticks enough to move customers to see, think, feel, or act differently than before they saw it.

Our Marketing PlayBox helps you focus on the best marketing execution ideas to provide feedback to your experts.

The best creative marketing ideas come through in-the-box creativity. As we introduced our Strategic ThinkBox to help you uncover the most significant key issues and strategies, we now turn to our Marketing PlayBox, with four dimensions to support our creative decision-making.

1. First, we want marketing ideas focused on the brand's desired target market.

2. Does the idea fit with the brand?

3. Does the idea express the brand's message?

4. Will the idea execute our strategy to move customers in ways that benefit our brand?

Our Marketing PlayBox works with marketing communication and product innovation.

The ABC's model for marketing execution decisions.

To achieve branded breakthrough, you need ideas that attract attention and link back to the brand. To motivate customers, you need ideas that communicates the message you know moves customers, and you need that message to stick in the mind of customers long enough to go through their path to purchase.

Our ABC's stands for Attention, Brand Link, Communication, and Stickiness.

When judging marketing communication, the most important thing I look for is to ensure the creative idea within the content will drive the attention, tell the brand story, communicates the main benefit and sticks in the customer's mind.

When you see a story, device, video, sell sheet, copy, or a visual that does not fit with the delivery, then you have a red flag. You run the risk that the creativity works against your objectives.

✓ Is it the creative idea that earns the customer's **attention** for the ad?
✓ Is the creative idea helping to drive maximum **brand** involvement?
✓ Is the creative idea setting up the **communication** of the main customer benefit?
✓ Is the creative idea memorable enough to **stick** in the customer's mind and move them to purchase?

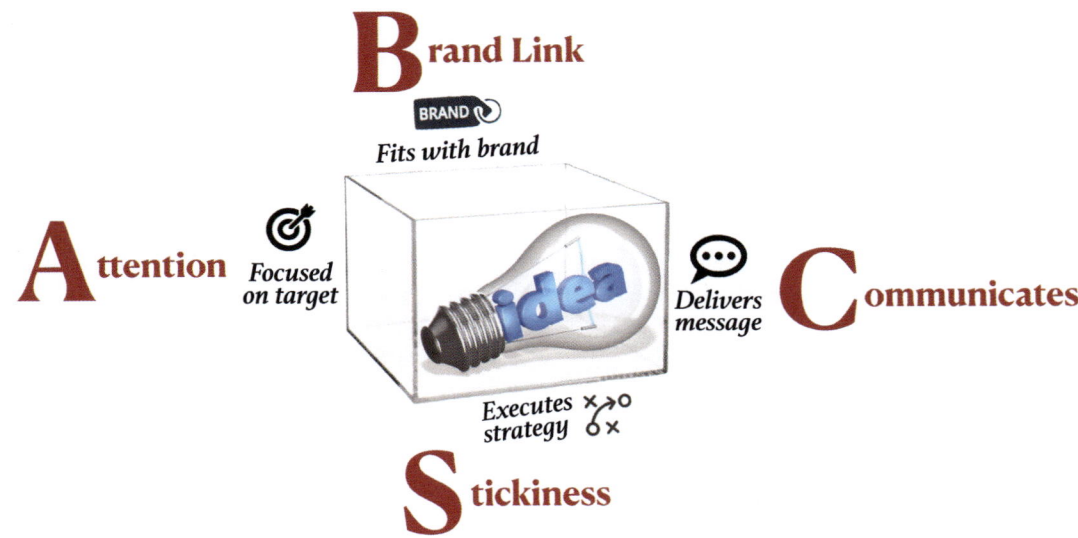

As you see creative marketing execution, we come back to the Marketing PlayBox to set up our Creative Checklist.

When you see the creative marketing ideas come back from your experts, our Creative Checklist will identify any gaps that you have with the work. Specifically, what do you see that is outside of the Marketing PlayBox?

Then, use your feedback to to steer the ideas back in-the-box. Highlight the gaps you see, while avoiding providing a solution. Let your creative marketing execution experts use their in-the-box creativity to figure out new solutions that will fit the box.

A reminder that our Marketing PlayBox focuses on four dimensions. We want our marketing execution work to be focused on our target, fit with the brand, deliver the message, and execute the strategy. We can use our ABC'S to help guide us through our checklist.

1. **Will the marketing idea capture the attention of the target? (A)**
   - You want marketing communications that helps build a bond with customer. First, ask if it speak directly to the target. Then, does it leverage customer insights to connect? Next, will the marketing idea deepen the bond with the customers? Finally, can the ad help build memories and rituals?

2. **Will customers link the marketing idea back to the brand? (B)**
   - Look for marketing ideas that fit with the brand. First, does the marketing idea deliver the brand idea? Second, does it leverage your creative assets? Third, is there a fit with the tone of the brand? Finally, does the marketing idea meet brand book standards.

3. **Does marketing idea communicate the message to customers? (C)**
   - You want marketing execution that has a motivating message. First, is the communication of the main benefit easy for customers to understand? Second, does the idea naturally set up the main message? Finally, will the main message move customers to see, think, act, feel, or whisper?
   - Does the creative marketing execution help distinguish the brand? Indeed, you want work to communicate the functional or emotional benefits. Importantly, the creative marketing execution should help the brand own a competitive space that is motivating to customers.

4. **Will the marketing idea stick in the minds of customers long enough to help move customers along their purchase journey?**
   - Find marketing ideas that delivers the strategy. First, does the marketing idea match up to the objective of the brief, from your brand plan? Then, does it achieve the desired customer response? Will it have an expected market impact and brand performance?

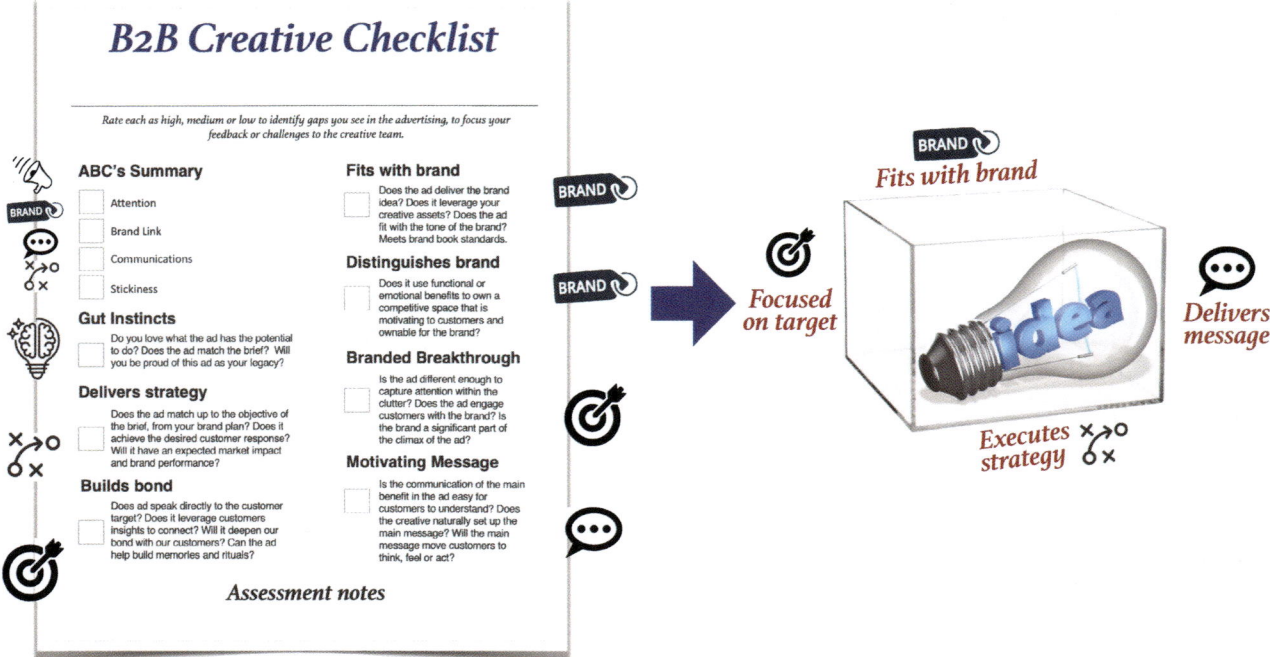

How to handle yourself at the creative meeting

In your next creative meeting, you should think fast with your instincts while trying to represent your customers. View the work through the eyes of your customers. I would not even let my agency do a setup of the work. I said, "Just show me the work as my customer sees it." I felt any setup or explanation clouded my judgment and impacted my instincts. As you are sitting in that decision-making hot seat at a creative meeting, here are challenging questions to ask yourself.

What does your gut instinct say? You might be coming from a three-hour meeting and it is hard to change speeds as you head into a creative meeting. Relax, find your creative energy, let it soak in, and use your quick-twitch instincts. Do you love what the marketing communications work has the potential to do? Will you be proud of it as your legacy?

Does the work deliver the strategy? Slow down with some thinking time after the meeting. In a quiet place alone, reflect to make sure it delivers your strategy. Does it match the objective in the creative brief? Does it achieve the desired customer response? Will it have an expected market impact and brand performance? Don't overthink and talk yourself out of something that works.

Will the work build a bond with customers? Will it speak directly to the customer target, leverage insights to connect, deepen our bond with our customers, or build memories and rituals?

Does the marketing communications fit with the brand and distinguish it in the market? Will it deliver the brand idea, leverage your creative assets, and fit with the tone of the brand? Does it use the functional or emotional benefits to own a competitive space that is motivating to customers and ownable for the brand? Is it different enough to capture attention within the clutter? Does the creative naturally set up the main message and move customers to think, feel, or act?

Making marketing communications decisions

As the brand leader seeing new work, you have three choices: Approve, reject, or change the work. From my experience, brand leaders rarely approve creative ideas outright. There also seems a reluctance or fear to reject outright.

So marketers mistakenly assume their role is to change the marketing communication ideas coming from your agency.

Approve the work **Reject the work** **Change the work**

I see too many marketers come to the creative meeting with a pen and paper and start to write feverishly all the recommended changes they have for each idea.

The problem is if we marketers are not talented enough to come up with the ideas in the first place, why do we think we are talented enough to change the work? You are a generalist, surrounded by experts. Use your experts.

Next time you go into a creative meeting, use the checklist, and score each point high, medium, or low. Look at the most significant gaps. Then take those gaps and create directional feedback to move the creative team. Stop giving the creative team your solutions, and give them new problems.

Think of your feedback as a game, where you want to move the creative work into a better space, without giving them the exact answer. If the creative brief is a "box" that creates a problem for the creative team to figure out, then use your feedback to create a new "box" for them to solve. Use your feedback to challenge and create a new problem for your agency to figure out the solution.

The best creative people I know would rather be pushed to do better work than held back to settle for OK work. Our greatness as a brand leader has to come from the experts we engage, so they will be inspired to reach for their own greatness and apply it to our brand.

Case Study: Gray's Dental Instruments

Our case study will judge the creative work of a B2B professional sell sheet.

The brand will use the sell sheet in a face-to-face sales call using an iPad, or it could be a drop-off print brochure for the dental professional to review.

Based on the creative brief, Gray's is trying to attract younger dentists by focusing on a new positioning where Gray's will help the dental professional deliver a better experience to their clients.
The main message we need to see in the creative work is that "Gray's dental instruments provide a noticeably gentler client experience that reminds you that you are using the best."

Most dentists realize that poor tools make for a poor client experience. With weaker tools, their hands get tired at the end of a long shift, and it becomes harder to remove the plaque and tartar on the teeth.

First creative meeting

At the first creative meeting, the agency comes back with a two-page spread for the sell sheet. The idea is to tell the dentist that they spend so much money on a dental chair, yet then connect back to why it makes sense to invest in better tools.

My first instinct is that it puts the dentist on the spot and is not where we want to be. I want to draw the dentist in by showing we understand what they go through and opening them up to engage.

I have no issue with how they have laid out the facts on the second page, so my feedback will focus on finding the right visual that connects with our younger dentists.

The agency's first attempt for Gray's Dental

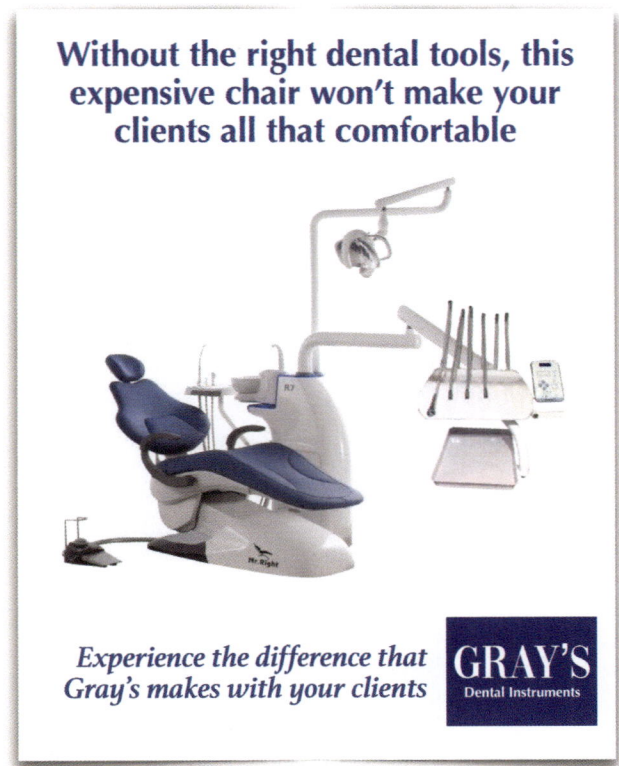

Use our creative checklist to see how the creative works for us

Attention

It is OK, but feels overly safe, and I don't think it will break through the clutter of messages that dentists see every day.

Brand Link

There is enough branding in the ad. However, the visual is a complete miss for us, as it looks like it's an ad for a dental chair and takes a while to get us back on track. If the dentist does not engage with page one, they miss out on the brand information on page two.

Communication

The chair gets in the way of our message. It looks like we are borrowing how they feel about their chair and trying to wedge our message in, but it is one degree more than I want. The second page does a great job of communicating the differences.

B2B Creative Checklist

Dental Chair ad

Rate each as high, medium or low to identify gaps you see in the advertising, to focus your feedback or challenges to the creative team.

ABC's Summary

 Attention

 Brand Link

 Communications

 Stickiness

Gut Instincts

 Do you love what the ad has the potential to do? Does the ad match the brief? Will you be proud of this ad as your legacy?

Delivers strategy

 Does the ad match up to the objective of the brief, from your brand plan? Does it achieve the desired customer response? Will it have an expected market impact and brand performance?

Builds bond

 Does ad speak directly to the customer target? Does it leverage customers insights to connect? Will it deepen our bond with our customers? Can the ad help build memories and rituals?

Fits with brand

 Does the ad deliver the brand idea? Does it leverage your creative assets? Does the ad fit with the tone of the brand? Meets brand book standards.

Distinguishes brand

 Does it use functional or emotional benefits to own a competitive space that is motivating to customers and ownable for the brand?

Branded Breakthrough

 Is the ad different enough to capture attention within the clutter? Does the ad engage customers with the brand? Is the brand a significant part of the climax of the ad?

Motivating Message

L Is the communication of the main benefit in the ad easy for customers to understand? Does the creative naturally set up the main message? Will the main message move customers to think, feel or act?

Assessment notes

Page two communication works well in communicating our brand positioning. Keeps things simple for our sales people to take their customers through the messages. However, the front page is a miss. It's the wrong visual—neither attention getting or the right communication.

Stickiness

This ad has no big creative idea, and it will not stick over time. We wouldn't want to keep comparing ourselves to the chair.

Gut instincts

It's an ok ad at best. Nothing new. It looks like something Gray's could have run the last 30-40 years resting on their laurels as the #1 brand.

Delivers the strategy

It will not capture younger dentists and fails to project a new brand positioning for Gray's. We need something much more personal.

Builds a bond with the customer?

The ad is too impersonal, not engaging our enemy or insights. It will fall flat with our younger audience.

Fits with the brand

The tagline of "Experience the difference that Gray's makes with your clients" delivers the brand idea. The visual is not helping. The second page does a fantastic job of communicating our brand.

Distinguishes the brand

Page one Doesn't do enough to position Gray's as the "gentler" clean. Page two does a great job separating Gray's from the competitors and projecting the new positioning.

Branded breakthrough and motivating message

The visual of the chair won't attract our customers, and likely won't move over to page two. If we look at our grid, it lands in the poor zone.

Identify the gaps we see and turn those into direction for the agency

- The second page is excellent as it will be easy for our sales reps to work with. The insight on page two is perfect, but how can we convey that equally on the first page?
- The chair visual on page one is not working for us. We want to connect with our dental professionals and link closer to the insight that "gentler hands means a gentler experience."
- We need a more engaging visual to project and build our brand positioning. We need to show our customers that we understand them.

Round 2 creative: Tired Dentist

As we move into round two, the agency visual and message gets closer for me. An exhausted dentist and speaks very personally to the inside of tired hands.

I'd score this High on awareness, stickiness, delivers the strategy, and builds a bond.

With all other scores at medium, I'm ready to approve the creative and move forward.

My checklist also allows me to sell the work to my boss and socialize it with the sales leadership.

Try out the Creative Checklist on something you are working on.

Thoughts on organizing the creative

Sales material should project the benefits/features to move customers through their purchase journey. Sales material includes brochures, flyers, sell sheets, iPad sell sheets, web content, price lists, emails, and newsletters. In collaboration with your sales team, you project your brand story to highlight the points of difference you can win on. You can promote products or services to specific target profiles.

- Find a captivating headline and visual to help the sales rep trigger a conversation with the customer
- For a sub headline or the headline on page two, use the main benefit from your brand concept
- Highlight a customer insight that says we understand you and allows the salesperson to connect with their customer. Provide some insight data to keep that conversation going.
- Bring the two key features to life with a visual and checklist
- Use a motivating call-to-action that reenforces the main benefit

Structuring your B2B communications

Challenge yourself to get better at marketing communications

1. **Be your best:** If you realized that how you show up as a client is the most significant factor in getting better marketing communications, would you show up differently? If so, then show up right.

2. **Be one of your agency's favorite clients:** Never treat anyone like they have to work on your business. Inspire everyone to want to work on your brand.

3. **Focus:** Stay focused on one target, one strategy, one customer benefit, and one brand idea. Avoid the just in case list or adding one more thing.

4. **Let go of control:** When writing a creative brief or providing feedback, resist controlling the creative outcome. Give your creative person your problems, not your solutions. Trust your creative team's expertise.

5. **Fight for what's right:** Be willing to fight anyone in the way of great work – even your boss. You will start to see everyone on the team fight for you.

6. **LOVE your marketing:** Never settle for OK. Never approve OK marketing work that feels safe. What signal do you think it sends everyone involved?

The ABC's of Product Innovation

While inventions are random, the best innovations must be well-planned. It is crucial to make innovation planning a core practice within your organization and embed an innovative spirit into the culture.

As we did with marketing communications ideas, we want innovative ideas that fit our Marketing PlayBox.

We can twist our ABC's tool to ensure the best innovations attract customers **(A)**, build on the brand's strengths **(B)**, communicate the brand idea **(C)**, and achieve a successful entry into the market **(S)**.

1. Does the innovation idea attract customers to create enough desire? (A)

- Focus on ideas that generate enough customers demand to help the innovation reach volume thresholds to impact both the category and the brand significantly. It must create a market impact that will tighten the brand's bond with customers, moves customers along their journey, or adds to the brand's reputation.

2. Does the innovation idea build on the brand's strengths? (B)

- Focus on ideas that build on the brand's manufacturing or servicing processes to ensure higher profitability and less reliance on partnerships to cover weaknesses. Pick ideas that match the go-to-market abilities of your current sales team and fit with the distribution, warehousing, and shipping.

3. Does the innovation idea communicate the brand idea? (C)

- Focus on ideas that communicate your brand idea so that you can continue to differentiate your brand in the customer's mind. When it fits with the brand idea, you can generate early trial from your brand's most loyal customers to help provide an easy entry for the innovation.

4. Does the innovation provide a successful entry into the marketplace? (S)

- Focus on ideas that provide profitable units you can sell to generate initial success, prevent competitors from duplicating your new offering, and lead to a long-term return on investment and effort.

Innovation Process

- Identify **new opportunities** through continually observing and finding unmet customer needs, market trends, and pain points, which new product ideas can solve. Use regular brainstorming to build a robust pipeline of ideas.

- From the best innovation ideas, develop concepts to test with customers, measuring new ideas on uniqueness, motivation to purchase, ownability, potential size, and strategic fit with the brand. Listen to customer feedback to optimize, adjust, or pivot the learning into new ideas.

- Build an **innovation pipeline,** pushing the best ideas through concept refinement, using market testing and a decision process with management. Approvals include execution plan and milestones from production to launch.

- Drive a robust pipeline, with a balance of lower risk launches and higher risk exploratory ideas. On the next page, I introduce our Innovation checklist that allows you to capture the key decision-making factors to consider when judging whether innovation will be successful.

- Create a **go-to-market launch plan** with project management, including name, logos, packaging, production, and channels. Build marketing support for marketing communications, launch presentations, and distributor plans.

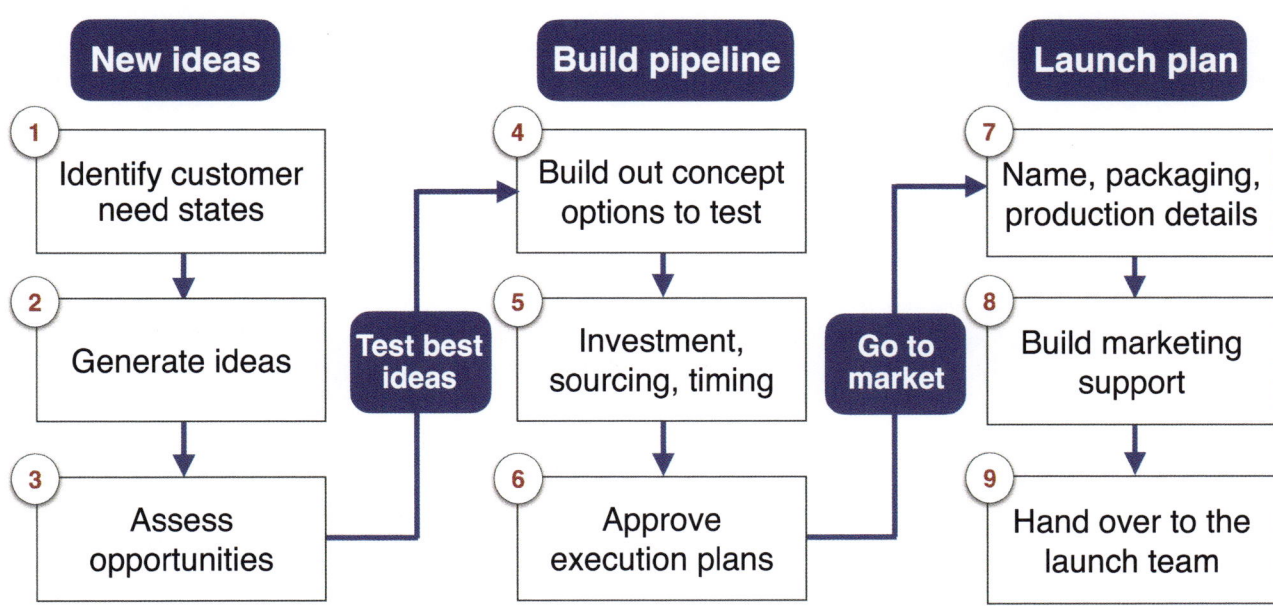

Different types of innovation

- **Product extensions:** Identify new customer need states that your brand can easily handle. Use to broaden your portfolio to help neutralize competitive advantages or use to gain share of shelf. Help to build continuous news that keeps brand momentum going with new benefits, flavors, and sizes.

- **Product improvements:** Identify where you are losing customers; help isolate flaws and gaps in your brand that need fixing so that your brand moves ahead or catches up to competitors.

- **New formats:** Stretch the brand into new subcategories/adjacencies or parts of the value chain. New formats help get your brand into new distribution channels or new usage occasions with customers.

- **Brand stretching:** Take the assets of the brand and move into new business opportunities—bringing your loyal user base and brand reputation.

- **Game-changing technology:** R&D driven invention needs to be matched up to reconfigure the invention to fit the needs of the customer.

- **Blue ocean exploratory areas:** These are completely exploratory ideas that combine your technical capabilities, matched to pure unexplored customer need states to create game-changing launches that move your brand into fully protected blue ocean–type competitive positions

Balance your Innovation Portfolio

While we all love the big ideas, small easy innovation plays a role of adding revenue/profit to keep pushing for those super-big ideas. Balance your innovation investment with both high risk / high reward ideas and the easier / smaller ideas to keep your brand fresh. The smaller ideas can help fund future investment to find those big ideas.

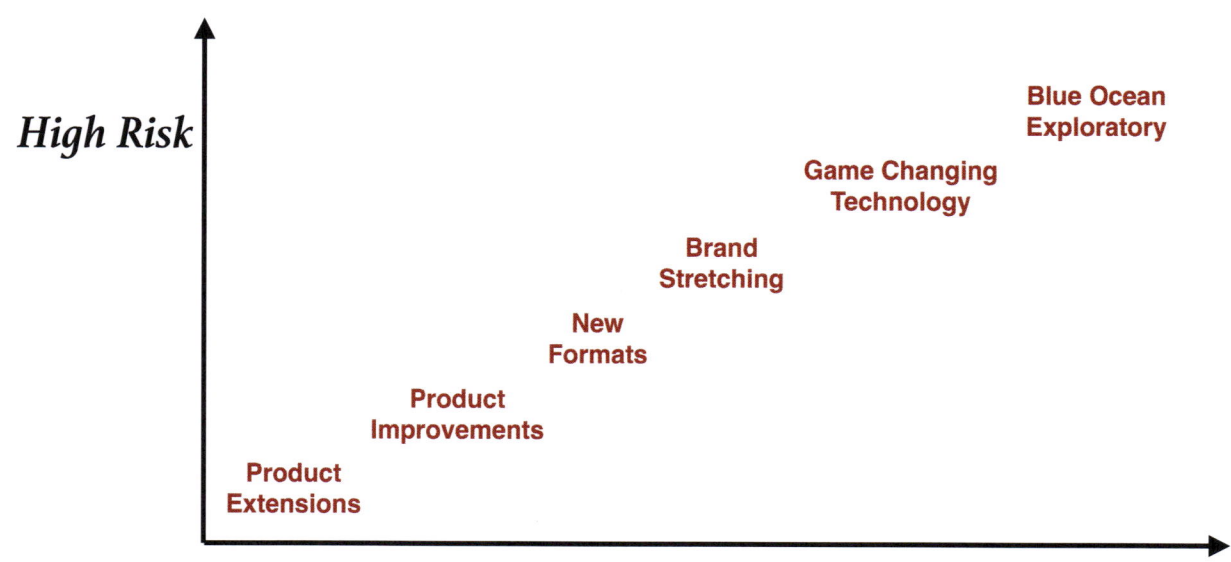

Examples of the different types of innovation for Gray's Dental.

Product Extensions

Gray's Slimline

GRAY'S — New 2022 line up

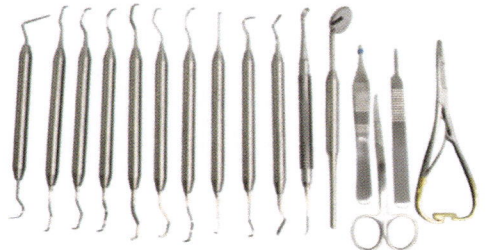

New formats

GRAY'S — Root Canal Specialty

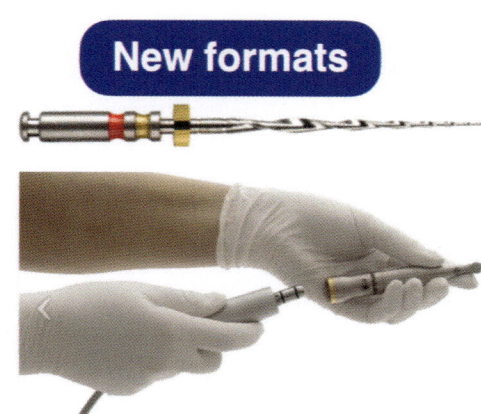

Product Improvements

GRAY'S — Titanium Steel

Gray's titanium nitride coating is 40 harder than stainless steel and testing has proven it to be the bes nonstick surface for placement, shaping and carving of composites

Brand Stretching

GRAY'S — Dental Sterilization

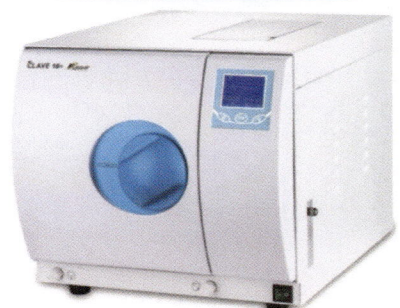

Game Changing Technology

GRAY'S — Intra-oral camera

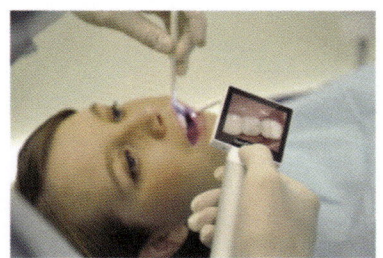

Blue Ocean Exploration

GRAY'S — Vet Line

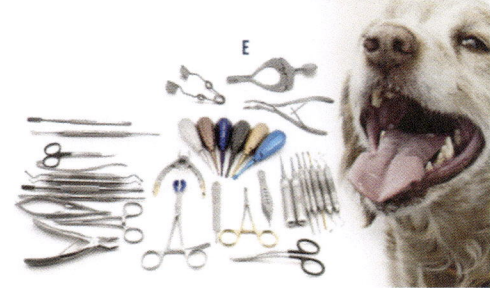

Innovation checklist to stay on strategy

To help judge the various innovation options, we use an Innovation Checklist to stay on strategy and deliver the ABC's. Our checklist looks at these seven factors:

- ✓ Customer demand to achieve volume thresholds
- ✓ Leverages brand idea to make for an easy entry
- ✓ Builds on your strengths of manufacturing or servicing
- ✓ Matches up with go-to-market of sales and distribution
- ✓ Profit payback and margin fit within the portfolio
- ✓ Competitive intensity of the category you enter
- ✓ Ability to be successful in the long run

GRAY'S
Dental Sterilization

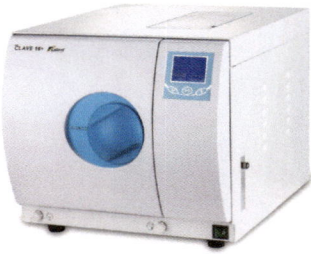

Innovation Checklist
Dental Sterilization

When facing multiple ideas, use the checklist to narrow down the list to potential winners to explore further. Rate each as high, medium or low to identify gaps you see in each innovation, to evaluate whether to the move forward, reject, or seek solutions where there are gaps.

Financial Projection

Year 1 revenue $5 MILLION

Margin %   50%

Investment needed $12 MILLION

Added headcount   20 production

Customer demand
L — Consumer response leads you to believe to trial/repeat will help achieve volume thresholds, making a significant impact on both the category and company.

Ownable for the brand
M — Consumers see fit with your brand idea and ownable for the brand. Provides an easy entry to bring your most loyal brand fans to the new product to drive early trial.

Go to market
H — Uses sales team's talents, relationships, knowledge or experience. Distribution matches with your current methods for warehousing, shipping, and servicing.

Production / Processes
M — Fit with your current manufacturing so you can produce efficiently, to drive higher profits, needing fewer partners

Profitability
M — Meets ROI hurdles, margin rates match current portfolio. Profitability allows for continuous investment in new innovation.

Competitive intensity
H — Competitive intensity of the category you enter impacts your initial success, pricing, profits and the ability of competitors to duplicate your offering.

Long-run success
H — Looking at differentiation to help separate brand, ownability of the brand, sales and profits, and fit with the strengths of the brand.

Market Impact
L — Tightens consumer's bond with the brand, adds to the brand reputation. Sizeable opportunity to keep investing.

Assessment notes

Moderate revenue, but it is low tech, easy to do, good fit to our tools, and builds on our connection into the dental market. If we can make the investment payback work, this is a good profit generator for Gray's. Recommend moving to next level evaluation.

Marketing Execution work exercise

Using a piece of communications from the brand that you are working on, grab our creative advertising checklist to evaluate. For each dimension, give a score of H (high) M (medium) or L (low) to find the gaps

____ Attention

____ Brand Link

____ Communication

____ Stickiness

____ Gut Reaction

____ Delivers Strategy

____ Builds a customer bond

____ Fits with the brand

____ Distinguishes the brand

____ Branded Breakthrough

____ Motivating Message

Based on your scoring, now formulate your overall feedback on this ad you would give to the agency. List out your top 3 points you'd communicate to your agency.

Chapter Sixteen

How to conduct a deep-dive business review to uncover brand issues

Too many marketers are not taking the time to dig in on the analytics. There is no value in having access to data if you are not using it. The best brand leaders can tell strategic stories through analytics.

Conduct a deep-dive business review at least once a year on your brand. Otherwise, you are negligent of the brand, where you are investing all your resources. Dig in on the five specific sections—marketplace, customers, channels, competitors, and the brand—to draw conclusions to help set up your brand's key issues, which you answer in the brand plan.

1. **Marketplace:** Start by looking at the overall category performance to gain a macro view of all significant issues. Dig in on the factors impacting category growth, including economic indicators, customer behavior, technology changes, buying trends, and political regulations. Also look at what is happening in related categories, which could impact your category or replicate what you may see next.

2. **Customers:** Analyze your customer target to better understand the customer's underlying beliefs, buying habits, growth trends, and critical insights. Use the brand funnel analysis and leaky bucket analysis to uncover how they shop and how they make purchase decisions. Try to understand what they think when they buy or reject your brand at every stage of the customer's purchase journey. Uncover customer perceptions through tracking data, the voice of the customer, and market research.

3. **Channel partners:** Assess the performance of all potential distribution channels and the performance of every major partner you sell through. Understand their strategies, and how well your brand is using their available tools and programs. Your brand must align with your partner's strategies.

4. **Competitors:** Dissect your closest competitors by looking at their performance indicators, brand positioning, innovation pipeline, pricing strategies, distribution, and the customer's perceptions of these brands. To go even deeper, you can map out a strategic brand plan for significant competitors to predict what they might do next. Use that knowledge within your brand plan.

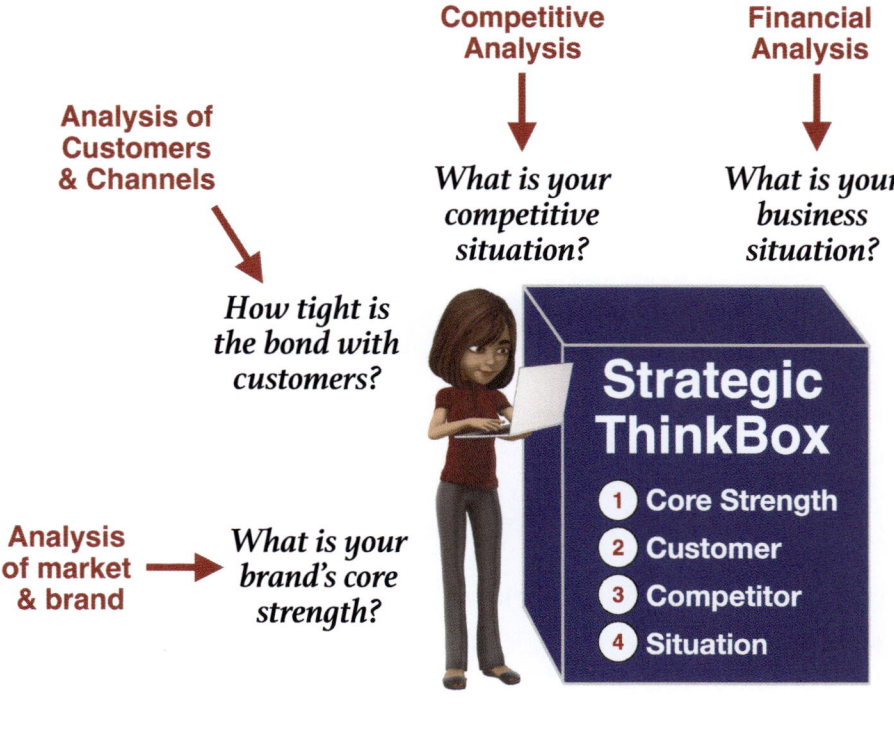

5. **Brand:** Analyze your brand through the lens of customers, channel partners, competitors, and employees. Use brand funnel data, market research, marketing program tracking results, pricing analysis, distribution gaps, and financial analysis. Focus on managing your brand's health and wealth.

6. **Summarize** your analysis to set up the key issues to tackle in your brand plan:

- **What's driving growth?** The top factors include your core strengths, positional power, or market inertia, with a proven link to driving your brand's growth. Your plan should continue to fuel these growth drivers.

- **What's inhibiting growth?** The most significant factors of weakness include unaddressed gaps or market friction you can prove to be holding back your brand's growth. Your plan should focus on reducing or reversing these inhibitors to growth.

- **Opportunities for growth:** Look at specific untapped areas in the market, which could fuel your brand's future growth, based on unfulfilled customer needs, new technologies on the horizon, potential regulation changes, new distribution channels, or the removal of trade barriers. Your plan should take advantage of these opportunities in the future so you can be where the market is going before your rivals get there.

- **Threats to future growth:** Changing circumstances, including customer needs, new technologies, competitive activity, distribution changes, an economic downturn, or potential barriers, which create potential risks to your brand's growth. Build your plan to minimize the impact of these risks.

1. The marketplace review

A. **Sales dollars vs. units:** First, look at the trend line for both sales dollars and sales units. Compare growth rates with the local economy or other similar categories. In this case, we see more dramatic double-digit growth rate swings between +19% and -13.5%. Compare the growth rates of dollars and units to see if there are differences.

Overall Category Sales

	2018	2019	2020	2021
Sales Dollars	878	760	791	803
% change	+19.1%	-13.5%	+4.8%	-0.7%
Units	134.0	117.5	119.5	122.7
% change	+28.3%	-12.35	+1.7%	+2.7%
Avg Price	$6.55	$6.47	$6.62	$6.54
% change	-6.4%	-2%	+3.1%	-1.9%

B. **Price vs. inflation:** Look at the trend line on price and compare it to inflation rates. In this case, the price has seen minor swings, which are less dramatic than volume swings.

C. **Regional growth:** The next critical dimension to look at is the regional performance. Start by understanding the size of each region and their relative growth rates. The combined size and growth rate may influence your investment in each region.

D. **Relative size:** Then look at the relative size of each region. Two ways to view the region is the share of the national business or use a development index relative to population or a bigger category (e.g. cereal to grocery).

Regional Category Sales Performance

	Northeast	Midwest	South	West
Regional Sales Dollars	350	50	100	302
Regional % change	+12%	-3%	+3%	-11%
Share of Nat'l Business	44%	6%	12%	38%
Development Index to pop	115	75	122	97
Brand Share	22%	9%	27%	23%
% brand growth	-2.4%	+11%	+2%	-1.9%

E. **Performance:** Finally, look at your brand's performance within each region. While this is still the macro category, it is useful to get a read on how your brand is doing at the macro level of the regions.

This process will help you decide on the regional activity, which either continues to drive growth or closes gaps that might exist. As a good practice, whenever you see a trend line, come up with the factors driving the category growth and the factors holding the category back. For each of the years, explain the major events and factors, which could explain the ups and downs.

There are many other aspects of the marketplace you should look at, including product formats (e.g., size, flavors, etc.), distribution channels, benefit segments, or competitors. With each element, look for breaks in the data to tell a story on the category. Each element adds to the story.

Use a **PEST analysis** of the macro trends impacting the category through political, economic, social, and technology trends.

- **Political trends:** The political elements look at changes in regulations, tax codes, trade restrictions, or the political climate, which could restrict or enhance your business. Consider local, national, and even international trends.

- **Economic trends:** Summarize economic factors, such as GDP growth, employment, inflation, interest rates, wages, interest rates, and foreign exchange rates. Understand how your brand reacts to any critical economic factors.

- **Social trends:** These factors include demographics, customer mindset changes, the use of media, or behavioral changes.

- **Technology trends:** These factors include advancements in the category, new scientific discoveries, formats, product deliveries, media (LinkedIn), and new distribution points (Amazon)..

To kickstart your review of the marketplace, here are 10 probing questions:

1. How is the category doing relative to the economy?
2. Look at the last five years and explain each of the ups and downs in the category.
3. What is driving category growth? What is holding the category back, the significant open opportunities you can use to your advantage, and the risks to the categories you see in the next few years?
4. What category segments are growing, declining, or emerging?
5. What are the macro trends influencing or changing this category?
6. What is the role of innovation? How fast does it change? Which innovations are transforming the category?
7. Which regional or geographic trends do you see?

8. Who holds the balance of power in the category: brands, suppliers, channels, or customers?
9. Look at other issues: Operations, inventory, mergers, technology, innovation, investments, global trade.
10. What is the overall value of the category? Any price changes? Major cost changes?

2. The customer review

In this section, I will show you how to use customer tracking data, the brand funnel analysis, and how it matches up to the brand love curve.

How to use customer tracking data

Tracking or household panel data helps you understand what's going on in the marketplace and will match up to what's happening at the store level.

As discussed in the strategy section, you are either trying to get more people to use your brand (drive penetration) or try to change the way they use your brand (drive purchase frequency). This tool uncovers the data; then you need to put a story to that data.

A. Penetration is the percentage of people who purchased your brand product at least once during a measured period.

B. Buying rate or sales per buyer is the total amount of product purchased by the average buying per person over an entire analysis period, expressed in dollars, units, or equivalent volume.

C. Purchase frequency or trips per buyer is the number of times the average buying per person of purchases your product over a time period (usually one year).

D. Purchase size or sales per trip is the average amount of product purchased on a single transaction by your average buyer. It can be calculated in dollars, units, or equivalent volume.

Sales = (Total Number of customers x Penetration) x Buying Rate

What's driving the sales of my brand?

A. Number of customers buying brand? (Penetration)

B. How much is each customer buying? (Buying Rate)

C. How often does each customer buy? (Frequency)

D. How much do customers buy each time? (per transaction)

How to analyze your brand using brand funnels

Every brand should understand the details of its brand funnel, the best tool for measuring your brand's underlying health. It is the equivalent to knowing your blood pressure or cholesterol scores. A classic brand funnel should measure awareness, familiarity, consideration, purchase, repeat, and loyalty.

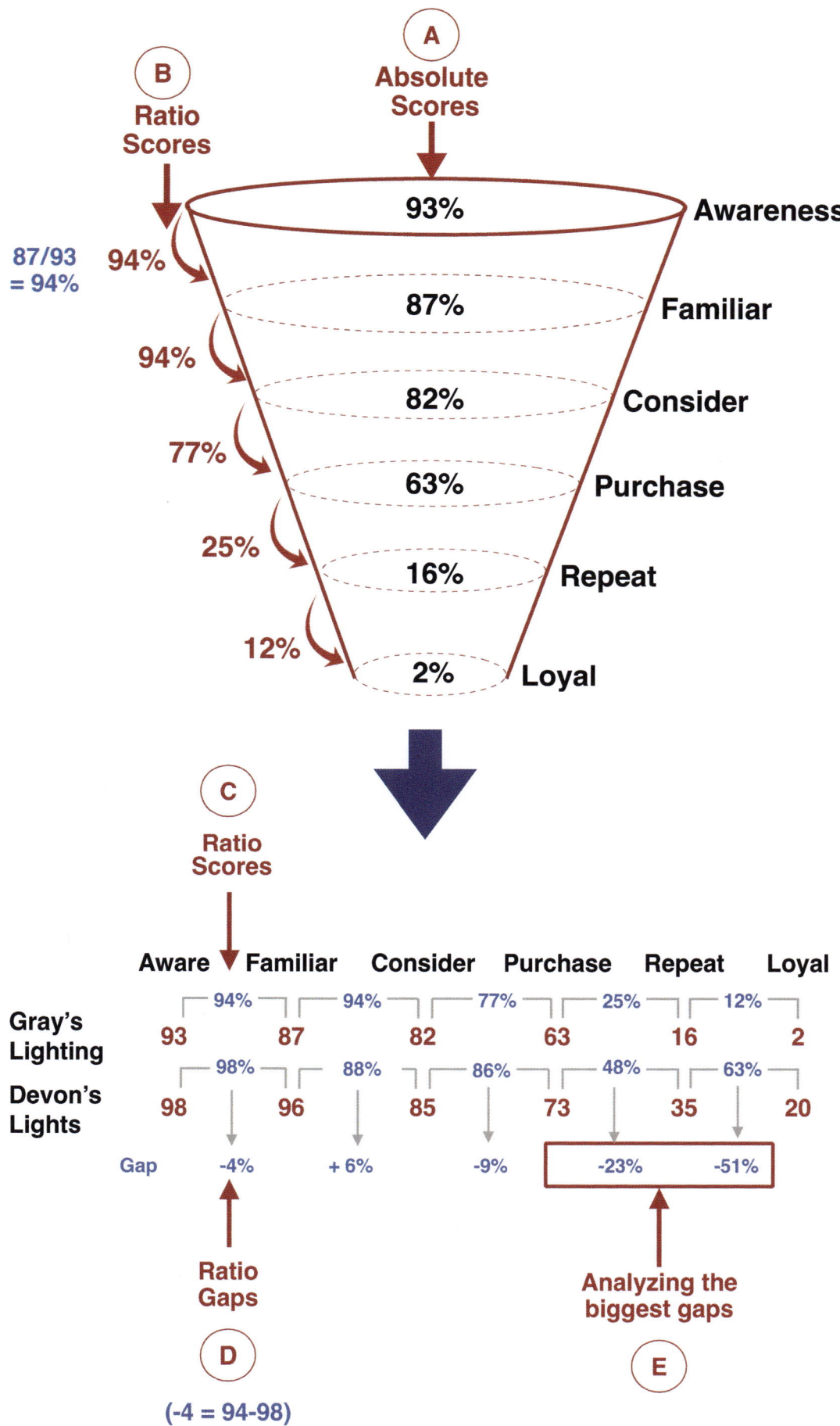

At the very least, you should measure awareness, purchase, and repeat. It is not just about understanding the absolute scores on the funnel but rather the ratios that explain how good of a job you are doing in moving customers from one stage of the funnel to the next.

I will show you how the robustness of your brand's funnel explains where your brand sits on the brand love curve. The broader the funnel, the better connected your brand is with customers.

Absolute brand funnel scores

A. Starting with the first chart, the first thing to do is look at the **absolute brand funnel scores**. There are many types of comparisons you can do, whether you compare to last year, competitors, or category norms.

B. Then look at the **brand funnel ratios**, which is the percentage score for how well your brand can convert customers from one stage of the funnel to the next. To create ratios, divide the absolute score by the score above it on the funnel. In the example above, take the familiar score of 87% and divide it by the awareness score of 93% to determine a conversion ratio of 91%. This means 91% of aware customers are familiar

Brand funnel ratios

C. For the chart below, lay out the absolute scores and the ratios in a horizontal way to allow a comparison. You will notice these are the same scores as "A" and "B" in the previous chart. The crucial numbers for Gray's Lighting are the **ratios** of 91%, 94%, 77%, 25%, and 12% at the top of the chart. Then bring in a close competitor (Bob's Lighting) with their absolute and ratios scores to allow a direct comparison.

D. Then find the **ratio gaps** by subtracting the competitor's ratio scores from your brand's ratio scores. In the example, the first ratio gap is -7% ratio gap (91% - 98%) which means Bob's does a 7% better job in converting customers from awareness to familiar than Gray's Lighting.

E. As you create ratio gaps along the bottom, you can see where your ratio is either stronger or weaker than the comparison brand. Finally, start analyzing the **significant gaps** between the two brands and tell a strategic story to explain each gap. Looking at the example, you can see Gray's and Bob's have similar scores at the top part of the Bob's, but Gray's starts to show real weakness (-23% and -51% gap) as it moves to repeat and loyalty. You need to address and fix these gaps with your brand plan.

Matching B2B customer analysis to the brand love curve

You can begin using your customer tracking, brand funnel, market share, and the voice of the customer to help explain where your brand sits on the brand love curve.

- **Indifferent brands** have skinny funnels, starting with inferior awareness scores. Customers have little to no opinion. Concerning performance, you will see low sales and poor margins. Your brand plan for indifferent brands should increase awareness and consideration to kickstart the funnel.

- **Like it brands** have funnels that are solid at the top but quickly narrow at the purchase stage. Customers see these brands as ordinary and purchase only on a deal. When they are not sold due to promotional price, sales fall off dramatically. These brands need to close potential leaks to build a loyal following behind happy experiences.
- **Love it brands** have a reasonably robust funnel but may have a smaller leak at loyal. They have stronger growth and margins. Look for ways to feed the love and turn repeat purchases into a ritual or routine.
- **Beloved brands** have the most robust brand funnels and positive customer views. These brands should continuously track their funnel and attack any weaknesses before competitors exploit them. Also, it is time to leverage that brand love to influence others.

	Indifferent	Like It	Love It	Beloved
Voice of the customer	No opinion, low interest, low importance. Do not care and have doubt. Have never bought.	Have a basic idea what brand stands for, but have no connection. See it as ordinary, not different.	See brand as better, High satisfaction, loyalty and frequency. Willing to recommend to their friends.	Outspoken fans who believes everything about the brand (product, experience, service) is better.
Market Indicators	Skinny brand funnel, market share squeeze, low unaided awareness. Low growth and shrinking margins.	Low conversion to sales, high percent bought on deal, low loyalty, strong private label share. Programs have low ROI	Robust brand funnel, healthy tracking scores, market share gains, high share of requirements.	Dominant share, net promoter scores, usage frequency and recommendations. High growth and profits.

Awareness
Consider
Purchase
Repeat
Loyal

10 probing questions to kickstart your review of the B2B customers:

1. Who are your possible target customer segments? Are they growing? How do you measure them?
2. Who are the customers most motivated by what you have to offer?
3. Who is your current target? How have you determined their role in the company, behavioral or psychographic, geographic, and usage occasion?
4. How is your brand performing against KEY segments? Share, sales, panel or funnel data, tracking scores? What about by channel or geography?
5. What drives customer choice? What are the primary need states? How do these customer needs line up to your brand assets? Where can you win with customers?
6. Map out the path to purchase and use brand funnels to assess your brand's performance in moving through each stage. Are customers changing at stages? Are you failing at stages?

7. What are the emerging customer trends? How does your brand match up to potentially exploit them? Where would your competitors win?
8. What are the customer's ideal brand experiences and unmet needs we can address?
9. What are the customer's emotional and functional need states? How does the brand perform against them? How are you doing in tracking studies to meet these benefits?
10. What is the customer's perceptions of your brand and your competitors? Voice of the customer.

3. The channel review

As we mentioned, you might be selling to a channel partner who then sells or serves the end customers. You want to gain an understanding of the channel partners you sell through. Then look for potential strengths to build upon or gaps to fix, including market share performance, listings, product knowledge, or sales by channel or by customer.

Start with a **distribution gap analysis** to determine where your brand has a presence with each customer. You can look at this by channel partners, then look at it for the overall brand or go right down to the specific product level.

Use a **"fair share index"** to find gaps. An index takes any measurement share and divides it by your overall market share. For instance, if you were getting 30% of display, yet your market share is 40%, your fair share index would be 0.75 (30% divided by 40%). Wherever your fair share index is below 1.0 represents an opportunity to close that gap.

Start at the macro level by looking at your brand's performance in each of the channels, looking at the fair share index for the overall distribution, then by region, then by customer. This analysis helps to determine where you might dig deeper.

Create customer scorecards for your biggest channel partners to track how well your brand is performing against that customer's tools. Start with how well that channel partner is performing by looking at that partner's share of the market and their growth rates.

Assess how your brand is performing with the customer, looking at your brand's share with the channel partner, share point change, and share index back to your overall share. Look at your brand's average pricing with that channel partner and compare to your average price or the customer's average category price. Align with your channel partner to lay out issues, opportunities, and risks to determine where your brand can have the biggest impact.

Here are ten probing questions to kickstart your channel partners review

1. How are each the channel partners performing? Are there regional differences by channel? Channel shifts?
2. Are there new and emerging channel partners? Are there channel partners on the horizon, not yet developed?

3. What are the strengths and weaknesses of each channel partners? How well do they know and understand the end customer?
4. Do you understand the strategies of your channel partners?
5. Do you have the competencies to service your channel partners?
6. Who are the top five channel partners? What are their strategies? How does our brand fit into that plan?
7. Who are your primary and secondary channel partners? Have you segmented and prioritized for growth versus opportunity? How large are they? What are their growth rates?
8. How is each channel partners performing? How profitable is that channel partner for your brand?
9. How is your brand doing within each channel partners? What are your brand's strength and weaknesses?
10. How is your relationship with the channel partners? How are the relationships with the channel partners and the top end customers?

4. The competitive review

Brands who think they **"don't have a competitor"** are naive. Assess your competitors' brand positioning to understand how well they are meeting the needs of customers.

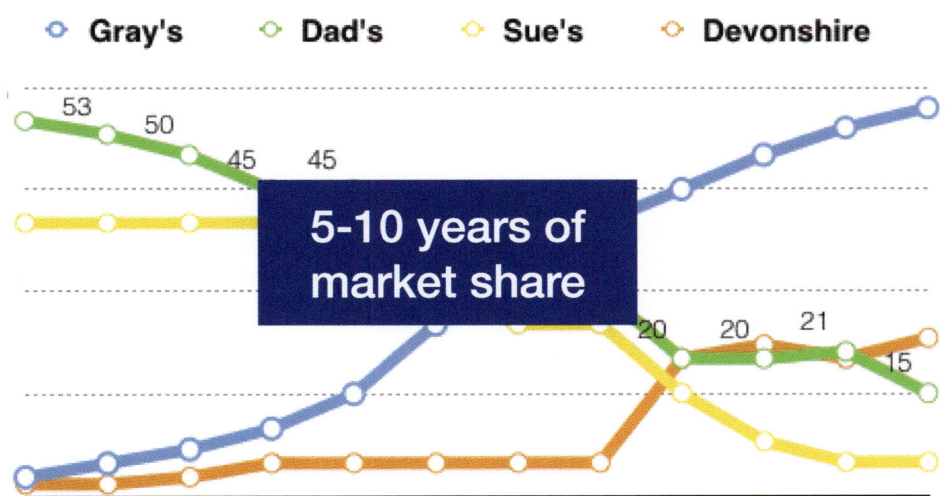

Who is their target, and what are their main benefit and reasons to believe? Do they have a brand idea, and how consistently do they deliver that big idea?

Look at your competitor's market share over the past five to ten years with explanations for the ups and downs, including new launches, distribution changes, significant investments, competitive dynamics, economic challenges, or impact of technology improvements.

Use any of the tools I have shown to dissect your closest competitors, looking at positioning, innovation pipeline, pricing, distribution, brand tracking, brand funnels, share, customer perception, and brand strategies.

Pricing

A. First, look at the **average price** and change versus a year ago for each competitor. Match up the data to what your sales partner says about the different prices for each channel.

B. Depending on channel/brand, you should look at the **deal pricing**, percent on deal, and coop ad (flyers). Compare both channels and customers to prior years.

When in a real competitive battle, complete your competitor's brand plan, laying out the vision, analysis, strategies, tactics, and even assumed budget levels. Getting in the shoes of your competitors will help you better understand their mindset, what moves they might make, and how they may attack you in the future. This war game process enables you to build a counterattack in your brand plan.

	Gray's	GE	Osram	Philips
Avg Price	$6.55	$6.47	$6.62	$6.54
% change vya	-6.4%	-2%	+3.1%	-1.9%
Avg Price on Deal	5.99	6.59	5.29	5.49
% change vya	+8.3%	-12.3%	+1.7%	+2.7%
% on deal	32%	22%	38%	20%
+/- vya	+7 pts	+1 pt	+10 pts	-2 pts

(A) — top two rows; (B) — middle rows

Here are 10 questions to kickstart your competitor review:

1. Who are your main competitors? How do they position themselves?
2. What are your competitor's use of communication, new products, and go-to-market strategy? How are they executing against each?
3. Describe your competitor's operating model, culture, and organization structure.
4. What are your competitor's strengths, weaknesses, opportunities, and threats?
5. How is your competitor doing regarding market share, customer market shares, investment, margins, innovation, culture, share of voice, or any regulatory advantage?
6. Map out the competitor's brand plan: vision, goals, key issues, strategies, and tactics.
7. What is the culture at your competitor and what is the role culture plays in their brand?
8. What is the investment stance and expected growth trajectory of your competitor's brand? How much and where do they invest? What are the marketing and commercial focus? What is their ROI?
9. What are your competitor's brand strengths, brand assets, and reputation?
10. Are there any public materials about the competitor, including strategy and financial results?

5. The brand review

You need to do a complete view of your brand through the lens of customers, channel partners, competitors, and employees. Use brand funnel data, market research, program tracking results, pricing analysis, distribution gaps, and financial analysis.

You should use ad tracking data to look at aided and unaided awareness scores, and purchase scores, including the share of last five purchases, uniqueness, and purchase intention.Leaky bucket analysis

I created the leaky bucket analysis tool as a way to uncover problems for your brand. While the brand funnel analysis usually looks at how well you move customers from one stage to the next, the leaky bucket helps to explain why customers fall out of the purchase journey.

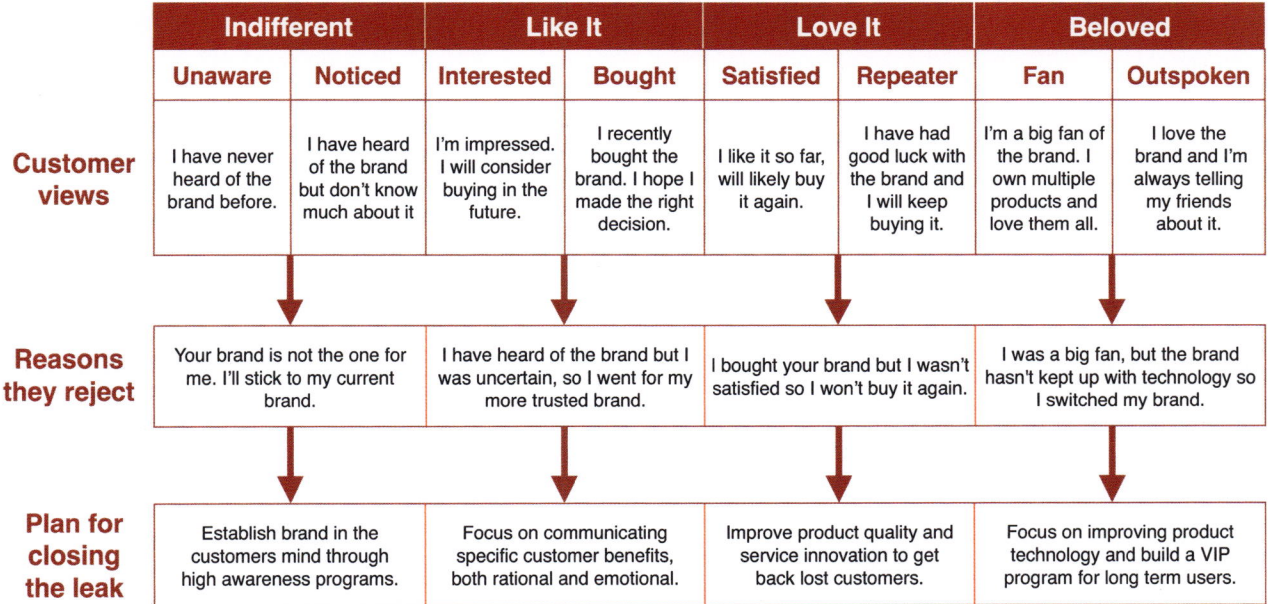

I have taken the four stages of the brand love curve and created **eight total stages of the customer purchase journey**, looking at: unaware, noticed, interested, bought, satisfied, repeater, fan, and outspoken. For each stage, map out how the customer sees the brand and the most significant reason customers reject the brand. Once you find the leak on your brand, you can build strategies to help **close those leaks**.

10 probing questions to assess your brand's performance:

1. What customer benefit can you win with, which is ownable, unique, and motivating for customers?

2. What is your biggest gain versus prior periods? What is your biggest gap?

3. What is your market share? Regionally? By channel? Where is your strength? Where is your gap?

4. How are you performing on key brand tracking data? Penetration? Frequency? Sales per buyer?
5. What are your brand's scores on the brand funnel?
6. How is your program tracking data doing? Where could you improve?
7. How far can you "stretch" your brand into other opportunities?
8. What is your current operating model?
9. What is your culture? Do you have alignment with the brand story and your employees?
10. What is the innovation process and capability of the organization?

How to build the ideal analytical slide

When telling your analytical story through a presentation, start every slide with an analytical conclusion statement as your headline, then have two to three key analytical support points for your conclusion.

Provide a supporting visual or graph to show the thinking underneath the analysis.

Finally, you must include an impact recommendation on every slide.

Never tell your management a data point without attaching your conclusion of what to do with that data.

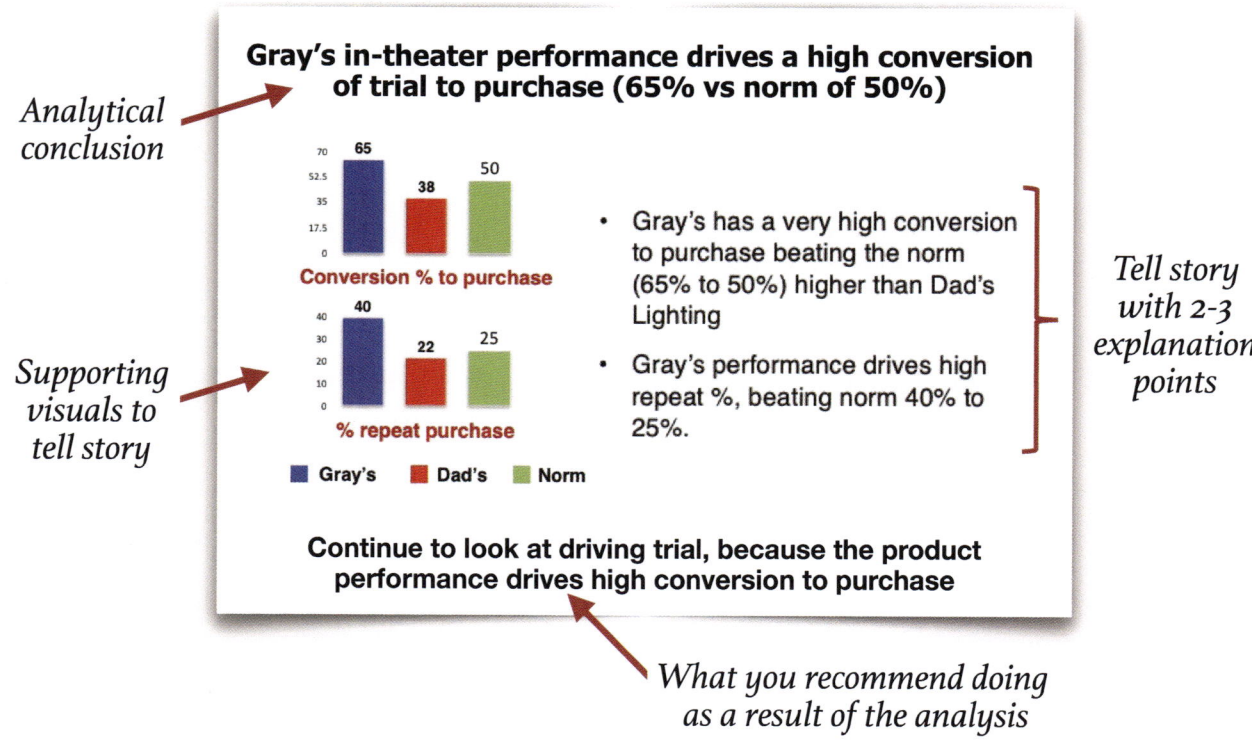

Putting together your business review

This process assumes you will put together a presentation for your management team. Each of the five sections you go deep on should have three to five ideal slides. The conclusion statement at the top of each slide gets carried forward to a summary page for each of the five sections.

You then draw out an overall conclusion statement for that section. You will have five conclusion statements, which you bring to the front of your presentation to form an overall summary page. Draw out one major brand challenge you see in the deep dive.

How to build each of the five analytical sections of the business review

A. For each of the 5 sections, lay out 3-5 key slides, that has a slide conclusion headline, key visual, 2-3 key points and a recommendation.

B. Each of the conclusion headlines should move to a summary slide, and then draw one section conclusion statement.

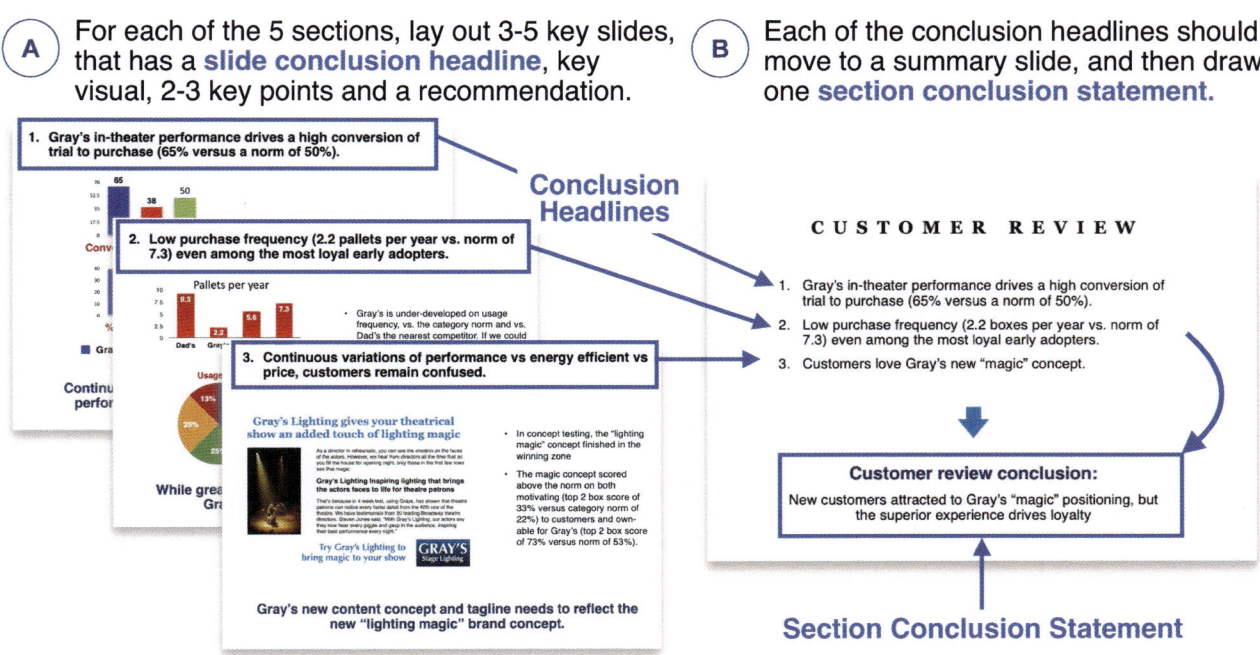

A. **Support your conclusions:** For each of the five sections of your deep dive business review, use all the data you have dug into to draw out the three hypothetical conclusions. Then build one ideal slide for each conclusion, adding the two to three critical support points, and layer in the supporting visual charts. This type of analysis is an iterative process where you have to keep modifying the conclusion headline and the support points to ensure they work together.

B. **Summarize your conclusions:** Once you have nailed the conclusion headline for each page, you should build a summary chart for each of the five sections, which takes those three conclusion statements and builds a section conclusion statement. The example above shows how to do it for the category, which you can replicate for the customers, channel partners, competitors, and the brand.

For each of the five sections, take each **section conclusion statement**, move them to an overall business review summary slide, and draw one big summary statement for each of the five sections. Use those section conclusion statements to draw out an overall **business review major issue**, which summarizes everything in the analysis.

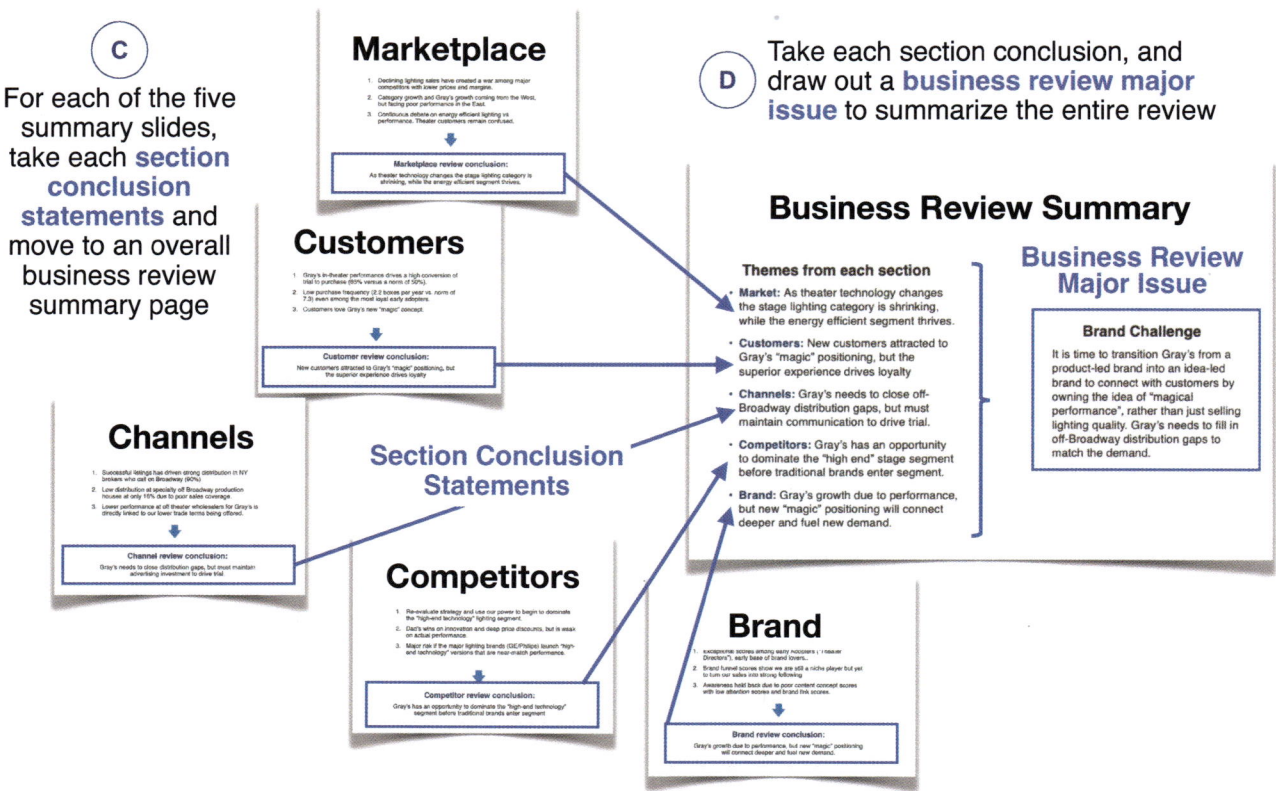

C. For each of the five sections, take each **section conclusion statement**, move them to an overall business review summary slide, and draw one big summary statement for each of the five sections.

D. Use those section conclusion statements to draw out an overall **business review major issue**, which summarizes everything in the analysis.

Work exercise #1: Dig deep into analysis

1. Using the brand that you are working on, review the marketplace questions and make an assumption of what you think are the top 3 analytical points

Marketplace Conclusion:

2. Review the customer questions and make an assumption of what you think are the top 3 analytical points

Customer Conclusion:

3. Review the competitor questions and make an assumption of what you think are the top 3 analytical points

Competitor Conclusion:

4. Review the channel customer questions and make an assumption of what you think are the top 3 analytical points

Channel Conclusion:

5. Review the brand questions and make an assumption of what you think are the top 3 analytical points

Brand Conclusion:

Work Exercise #2: Draw out conclusions of analysis

Take each conclusion statement from each section and draw out an overall challenge

- Marketplace
- Customers
- Channels
- Competitors
- Brand
- Overall Brand Challenge

Work Exercise #3: Analysis Summary

Shift your analysis into the top drivers and inhibitors your brand is facing now and the opportunities and threats your brand will face in the future

Drivers

Inhibitors

Opportunities

Threats

Chapter Seventeen

Marketing Finance 101 to help manage your brand's profitability

Anyone who does not include "profit" in their definition of a brand has never run a brand before. To me, a product is a basic commodity you sell. A brand creates a bond that leads to a power and profit beyond what the product alone can achieve.

If you want to succeed in brand management, you have to understand brand finance. After all, you are running a business. If you only like the activity of marketing, then you should become a subject matter expert because, if you cannot work the finances of your brand, you will not get promoted beyond brand manager.

I will go through everything you need to know so you can manage the profitability of your brands. I will include all the essential formulas you need to know with examples to help follow along. Even if you are not a natural at finance, my hope is this chapter will help make you smarter at brand finance.

Brand Financial Statement

	2025 $	2025 g%	2026 $	2026 g%	2027 $	2027 g%
Net Sales	**21,978**	**8%**	**24,616**	**12%**	**27,354**	**11%**
Cost of Goods Sold	12,496	9%	14,754	18%	17,129	16%
Gross Margin	**9,482**	**49%**	**9,862**	**4%**	**10,225**	**4%**
GM %	43%		40%		37%	
R&D	200	3%	352	76%	352	0%
Marketing Budget	**3,519**	**22%**	**4,266**	**21%**	**5,101**	**20%**
Communications	*2,000*	*22%*	*2,000*	*0%*	*2,712*	*36%*
Research	*125*	*55%*	*60*	*-52%*	*100*	*67%*
Packaging	*133*	*66%*	*30*	*-77%*	*50*	*67%*
Trade Expense	*250*	*44%*	*1,000*	*300%*	*1,250*	*25%*
Other SG&A	1,011	22%	1176	16%	989	-16%
Contribution Margin	**5,763**	**22%**	**5,244**	**-9%**	**4,772**	**-9%**
CM %	26%		21%		17%	

A quick dissection of the brand's financial statement

For many of us, we became marketers because we were attracted to the strategic, creative, and the psychological aspects of business. So if finance is not a natural skill, when your finance manager hands you the brand's profit and loss (P&L) statement, it can be intimidating. I come at this as a fellow marketer, not a finance expert.

To assess the performance of your brand, and begin knowing where to dig deeper, I recommend you break it down by looking at **four key numbers.**

1. **Growth rates:** As a leader of the brand, I start by trying to understand the growth rate. Most brand leaders have brand growth as their number one objective. You can do a quick calculation to figure out the average growth rate but, as you dig in, you should try to find out what happened each year to give you a better feel of the brand performance. There are two calculations you can use, either average growth rate or compound annual growth rate (CAGR).

   In this example, the average growth rate is 7%, and CAGR % is 9.1%, both of which are very high compared to the overall economic growth of 2-3%. My first instinct would be to look at the category growth to see if the brand is gaining or losing market share. Next, the year-by-year growth shows the growth rate has shot up to 12% over the past two years. I would make a mental note to expect to see this as an investment brand and determine whether the profit is paying off yet.

① Start with the overall sales line, and explain year-by-year growth rates

Explain growth rates of each year. We see a healthy average growth rate is 7%, and a strong compound growth rate is 9%.

	2016	2017	2018	2019	2020
Net Sales	19,483	20,383	21,978	24,616	27,569
Growth Rate		5%	8%	12%	12%

② Look at the Gross Margin %, by dividing the gross margin by Sales

Over the 3 years, the gross margin % is down from 43% to 37%. Either overall pricing has been cut or the costs are up.

	2018	2019	2020
Sales	21,978	24,616	27,569
Gross Margin	9,482	9,862	10,225
Gross Margin %	43%	40%	37%

③ Look at Contribution Margin %, dividing contribution margin by sales

Over the 3 years, the CM% fell from 26% to 17%. There a problem with the top-line margin, and gross margin is not covering off the increase in spend.

	2018	2019	2020
Sales	21,978	24,616	27,569
Contribution Margin	5,763	5,244	4,772
Contribution Margin %	26%	21%	17%

④ Compare the sales growth rate with the marketing spend growth rate

There was a significant spend increase, yet sales growth not keeping pace. Is it strategies, message, competitive activity or changing market dynamics?

	2017	2018	2019	2020
Sales Growth	5%	8%	12%	12%
Spend Growth	5%	22%	44%	11%

2. **Gross Margin Percent:** My eye is drawn immediately to figuring out the gross margin percentage, as a first signal of brand health or to try to understand the strategy behind the brand. Divide absolute gross margin by sales. Assess the brand's health by comparing the margin percent over time to see the trend line, with other brands in your portfolio to evaluate the opportunity cost, or with other competitive brands in the category.

   In this example, the gross margin percentage has fallen from 43% in 2018 to 37% in 2020, which should prompt you to go a layer deeper to look at price and cost of goods. Regarding **price**, dig around to see if there has been an average price decrease, then look to see if it is due to an increase in trade spend, a shift in the sales mix to lower-priced items, or even a shift to lower margin items.

3. **Contribution margin percentage:** Next, look at the contribution margin percentage, dividing the bottom line contribution income by the overall sales. Some cost factors are outside the brand's control, such as foreign exchange, raw material cost increases, duties, and transportation costs. However, look out for factors within the brand's control. Was there a strategic decision to change to a higher cost of raw material? Was there increased quality control at the manufacturing site? Did you switch to a more expensive supplier or change the location of your production?

   In the example, an alarm bell goes off when I see the contribution margin percentage has fallen from 26% to 17% in three years. My first observation is the sales are up dramatically, yet both the gross margin percentages and contribution margin percentages are down. While the gross margin percentage is down, the gross margin dollars increased. However, in this case, the contribution margin dollars have gone down from $5,763 to $4,772. After two years of investment, the brand is not responding fast enough to cover that spend level.

4. **Spending growth rate:** Look at the comparison between the sales growth rate and the spending growth rate.

   While sales are growing at 12% over the past two years, spending is up 22%. The brand is not covering the spending increase. Dig in to understand if the payback was expected to be slower. If not, I would dig in to explain why it is not paying back: not the right message, competitive activity, or market dynamics.

View each of these **four key numbers** as a starting point to dig in deeper and ask questions of the experts around you. From my experience, every P&L is as unique as a fingerprint. As the business leader, you run your brand's P&L.

There are eight ways you can drive brand profits

1. Premium pricing
2. Trade loyal customers up to a higher price
3. Lower cost of goods
4. Lower marketing and selling costs
5. Steal competitive users
6. Get loyal users to use more
7. Enter into new markets
8. Find new uses for the brand

Profit = (Price - Cost) x (Market Share x Market Size)*

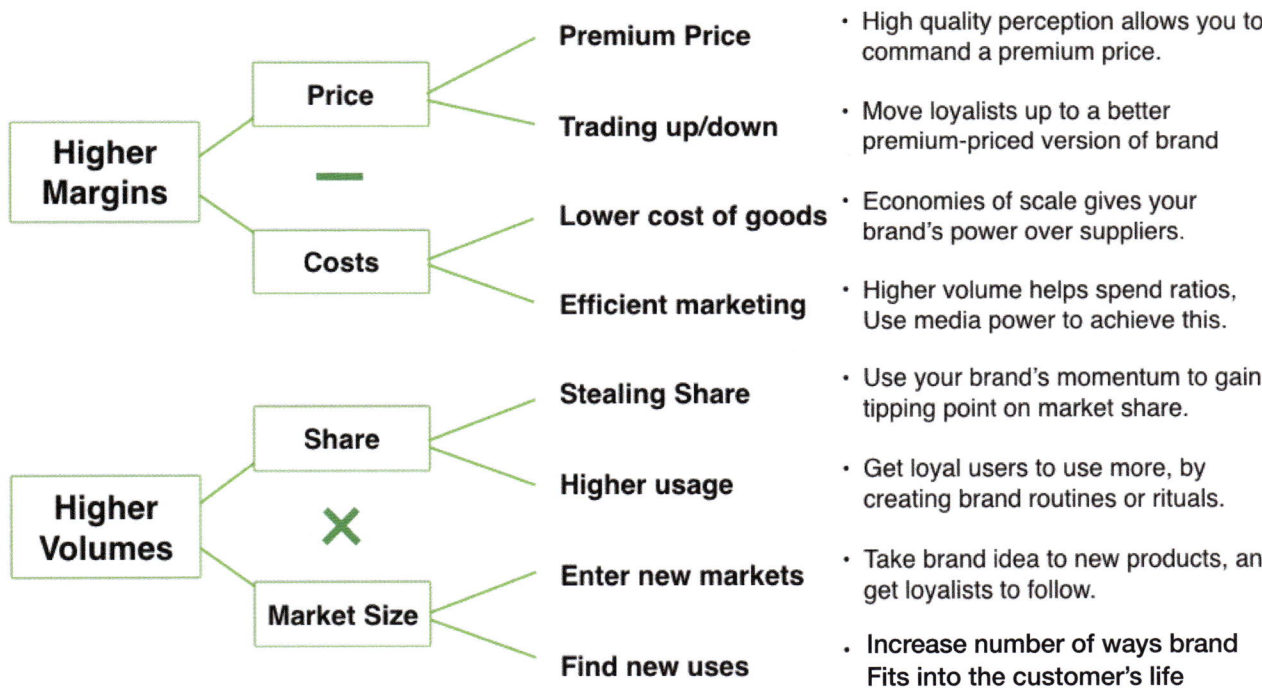

1. How to use premium pricing

While many marketers think of price as a defensive response to counter inflation or a competitive reaction at the retail shelf, the smartest brand leaders use price as a weapon to drive brand value.

It is crucial to understand the price/quality relationship of your brand and look for ways to increase the perception of quality. When you find a unique position, which you know motivates customers, it can differentiate you from competitors. Then you can use the motivation to tighten the bond with your customers.

The chart shows a relatively long-term direct correlation between perceived value and price. An indifferent brand has low perceived value and will end up with a much lower price point. A beloved brand can use its emotional connection to drive perceived value and ensure the price premium is perceived as good value.

For instance, customers are undoubtedly willing to pay $5 for a Starbucks latte, $500 for an iPad, or $100,000+ for a Mercedes. The same customers will price shop on brands where they have no feelings. A beloved brand has an inelastic price, which means the quantity demanded does not change very much when the price changes; customers will still keep buying from a beloved brand regardless of price fluctuations.

- **Price increase:** Simply put, brands can execute a price increase when the market or customers allow the brand to do so. A beloved B2B brand will have an easier time pushing through a price increase as it can use the power of its brand versus customers, competitors, or partners. When pushing a price increase through, brands usually require proof that the new price will work or that product costs have gone up. Factors that help the brand story include the health of the brand and the market conditions.

- **Price decrease:** Use this tactic when battling a competitor or in reaction to sluggish economic conditions. You can also use an aggressive price decrease when you have a cost advantage, whether that's manufacturing, materials or distribution, using that lower price to deplete the resources of your competitor.

Price changes always carry a risk of a competitive overreaction. Consider various potential competitive reactions when doing your financial analysis. Be careful. As difficult as it is to implement a price change, it is almost impossible to change it back.

2. Trade the customer up or down

Another strategy is to create a range of products at various price levels, with a good/better/best approach that allows the brand to reach up or down to a new segment of customers. Make sure that you are doing this for the right reason or it could backfire on you.

You can also create combinations of product and service levels to support a good/better/best strategy. This helps you focus on a total cost, rather than a line-by-line comparison cost versus a competitor.

- **Trading customers up on price:** Make sure your brand can carve out a meaningful difference to create a second or third tier, so customers can see an apparent reason to move up. Many brands will deploy a good/better/best approach to pricing. When your brand secures trust or a bond with the customer, it will be easier to use your brand reputation and product performance to move loyal customers up to the next level.

- **Trading customers down:** When the brand sees a potential unserved market, it can trade customers down when the move brings minimal damage to the brand image or reputation. In a tough economy, creating a lower-priced set of products can be a smarter strategy than lowering the overall price of your main brand. Once the economy bounces back, you can discontinue the lower-priced product option.

There are a few cautions around trying to trade customers up or down. Be careful not to lose your focus on the brand's core business or image.

Stay focused because brands struggle when they try to be all things to everyone. When trading down, try to take costs out of the product to ensure margins rates stay consistent.

Financial calculations for a price increase will impact both revenue and profits. You should do an elasticity market research test to find out how your brand will perform.

In this **example**, the price goes from $2.50 up to $2.75, only a 10% price increase. I assumed the cost of goods remained flat and I used a forecasted sales decline on units sold. The sales revenue falls slightly, but the profit goes up by $7,500 or by 4.6%.

Price Increase Formulas

	Current	New	Profit impact of a price increase
Price	$2.50	$2.75	**((New Price - COGs) x new unit volume)**
COGs	1.00	1.00	**MINUS ((Old Price - COGs) x old unit volume)**
Margin	1.50	1.75	
Margin %	60%	64%	= ((2.75-1.0) x 90,000) - ((2.5-1.0) x 100,000)
Unit Forcast	100,000	90,000	= $7,500
Revenue	$250,000	$247,500	With a 10% price increase against a 10% volume
Profit	$150,000	$157,500	decrease, you will generate $7,500 more profit.

3. Use product costs as a strategic weapon

Marketers usually assume that managing the cost of goods (COGs) is someone else's job. However, product costs can be a useful strategic weapon that marketers should utilize.

- **Decreasing the cost of goods:** There are a few ways to drive down COGs. First, you can use your brand power and higher volumes to negotiate with suppliers. You can choose to use lower-priced raw materials, drive process efficiencies, or explore offshore manufacturing.
- **Increasing the cost of goods:** Most significant reason to increase COGs is when upgrading to a premium market or an added benefit. Watch out for suppliers trying to pass along costs beyond inflationary rates.

When lowering your product costs, make sure the product change is not significantly noticeable. Where there is a noticeable product change, understand the potential impact on your brand's perceived performance or quality. When costs go up, make sure the increases can be covered through other parts of your profit statement, whether through price increases, volume increases, or cuts to your brand's marketing costs.

4. Control the marketing and selling costs

Marketers are protective of marketing budgets. They usually want as much money as possible to carry out the activities on their priority list. The strategic brand leader should act as the owner/CEO by using budgets to manage the profit rather than act like a subject-matter expert trying to protect their turf.

- **Marketing cost decrease:** Many times companies look at cost-cutting to counter short-term changes happening within other parts of the P&L (price, volume, or COGs). However, many of the best-run brands keep the investment strong, aligning with the longer-term strategy instead of a short-term situational need.

- **Marketing cost increase:** This scenario is often used when there is an opportunity to gain share against a competitor or as a defensive position trying to hold share. The brand should see an opportunity where significant revenue gains can offset the lower profit ratios.

Return on Investment (ROI) for a marketing investment

	Program	Formulas for ROI
Incremental Sales Volume	$5,000,000	
Cost of Goods Sold (COGS)	$3,000,000	**Gross Margin = Revenue - Cost of Goods Sold** $5 Million - $3 Million = $2 Million
Gross Margin	$2,000,000	
Gross Margin %	40%	**Contribution Margin = Gross Margin - Spend** $2 Million - $1.5 Million = $0.5 Million
Total Investment Spend	$1,500,000	**ROI = Contribution Margin divided by spend** $0.5 Million divided by $1.5 Million = 33%
Contribution Margin	$500,000	

Use your strategic thinking to determine your marketing budget level

How connected your brand is with customers determines where on the customer journey you will focus. For an **indifferent** or **liked** brand, you should focus on driving awareness and purchase, which are usually high in cost.

As you get to be more **loved**, you can concentrate on turning repeat purchases into routines. You can shift some of the marketing budgets over to create a superior customer experience to reward your loyal users. The more loved a brand, the better the spend-to-sales ratios you should realize.

The degree of **competitive warfare** should impact the size of your budget. Craft brands or disruptive brands are different enough to avoid competitive battles. When a brand takes on a challenger stance, the budget should go up. Be careful of competitive warfare situations, as a competitor may overreact, leading to spiralling spend escalations. Like a price war, marketing investment wars can also drain resources and will be viewed as a failure when there is very little market share change after the war.

Also, consider your brand's **core strength**. If you use a product-led or brand story-led strength, you will have to invest in marketing communication to show how your brand is better or different. These brands will require significant investment. However, an experience-led brand should put the brand's limited financial resources into creating a customer experience. Early on, you will have to rely on a slower build through word-of-mouth referrals rather than paid media.

Always bring an **ROI mindset** to your brand's marketing budget. In the example, the investment of $1.5 million generates a sales increase of $5 million. After subtracting the cost of goods and the marketing investment, your brand makes $500,000 in additional profit. To calculate the ROI, take the profit and divide it by the investment. In this example, the ROI is 33%; if it holds, the investment will take three years to pay back.

5. Steal other users

The share and volume game is a traditional tool for marketers. Be careful when trying to gain share. As discussed in the competitive strategy section, attacking competitors can prove challenging. Many times, an attack can result in a spend escalation with neither brand making any gains. When you lead a share war without a substantive competitive advantage, there may not be any winners, just losers.

- **Offensive share gains:** Look to gain share using a significant competitive advantage against an opportunity in the marketplace, whether that is a first-mover advantage into new technology, an unmet customer need, changing channels, or a chance to steal share, using your brand's superior performance against a vulnerable competitor.
- **Defensive share stance:** Hold your market share or minimize the share losses until your brand can catch up on technology. The best way to protect your brand is to feed your loyal base of customers who are less likely to switch.

6. Get users to use more

Going after usage frequency is a difficult strategy. It means convincing customers who have already decided how to use your brand to use your brand even more.
- **A higher share of requirements:** In many categories, even loyal customers will work within a competitive set of favorite brands. You need to provide a reason, through product superiority claims, consumer experiences, or

emotional benefits to persuade loyal consumers to use your brand for every occasion.
- **Get current users to use more:** Look for opportunities with loyal users to create a potential routine or ritual around your brand.

It is an excellent strategy to use when there is a real benefit to your customer to use your product more often. Otherwise, customers will see it as a shallow money grab by the brand. Driving routines or rituals can be difficult. Even with lifesaving medicines, the most prominent issue for frequency is compliance. The best frequency strategy is to link your brand to a part of their current work life or job performance.

Compound Annual Growth Rates (CAGR)

	Year 1	Year 2	Year 3	Year 4	Year 5
Sales	$500	$600	$650	$625	$800
Annual Growth		20%	8%	-4%	28%

CAGR = ((Y5/Y1) to the power of (1/4 years) -1
= ((800/500) to the power of 0.25) - 1 = 12.47%

Average Growth Rate = ((Y5 - Y1)/Y1)/4 years
= ((800-500)/500)/4) = 60/4 = 15%

When calculating revenue growth, you can use average growth rate, yet a compound annual growth rate is a much truer version of what is happening. In the example above, the average growth rate is 15%, but the more accurate compound growth rate is 12.47%. If you are scared off by math you can always use the CAGR calculator on the Investopedia website.

7. Enter new categories

When your brand has a strong base of loyal customers, and you see an opportunity to take those customers into a new peripheral category, you can open up new revenue streams for your brand. Make sure the new category fits with the brand idea, and you can transfer elements of your brand reputation into the new product. In terms of B2B brands, Apple has done a great job with desktops to MacBooks to iPhones to iPads.

When you enter a completely new category and complete a sales forecast, you may rely on market research projections or assumptions from prior launches. Use a combination of both numbers to build a brand funnel projection and populate the funnel to figure out your sales forecast.

Using the brand funnel to determine your sales forecast

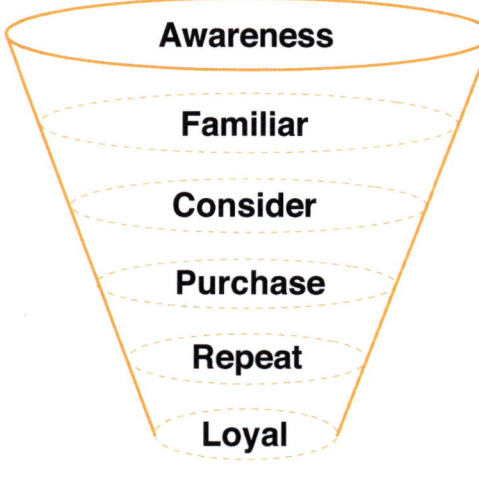

Assumptions		10 million people, $5 per item
Awareness	90%	9 million people aware
Familiar	75%	7.5 familiar
Consider	50%	Half of people consider
Purchase	25%	2.5 million first purchase at $5 per
Repeat	10%	1.0 million buy a 2nd time at $5 per
Loyal	2%	200k buy a 3rd time at $5 per

Using the funnel for a forecast

Purchase:	$12.5 Million
Repeat:	$ 5.0 Million
Loyal:	$. 1.0 Million
Total Sales	**$18.5 Million**

8. Create new uses

Take the brand and create similar experiences into a new format or new offering. You need to make sure your current brand is in order before you divert attention, funding, and focus on a potential blue ocean expansion area.

Be careful with this temptation because the legendary success stories (Arm & Hammer or one-a-day Aspirin) do not come along as often as you might hope.

Appreciation to Professor Ken Wong, who first introduced me to this financial model when I was in Marketing

10 financial questions to assess your brand's worth:

1. What is your brand's compound annual growth rate (CAGR)? Explain the ups and downs over the past five years.
2. What are your gross margins and contribution margins over the last five years? Can you break it out by product line? Is there more pressure from price or the cost of goods?
3. What is your brand's marketing budget breakout? Variable direct costs versus indirect fixed dollars? What is the break between media and creative production? Marketing spend versus trade spend?
4. Have you completed any pricing elasticity studies? What did you learn about your brand? If you did increase your price, what did you see in the marketplace?
5. How is your brand's overall strategy impacting your brand's profits? How do your decisions on your brand's core strength, customer connection, competitive pressures, and situation impact your financials?
6. How are your current brand/business performance metrics, brand's market goals, and financials linked?
7. Over the past five years, what are the programs that drive the highest and lowest ROI?
8. How does your business model impact your overall profit? What are you focusing on right now?
9. What are your forecasting error rates? Is there a seasonality impact? How do economic factors impact your brand's financials? How reasonable are your inventory levels?
10. What financial pressures do you face on an annual or quarterly basis?

© 2010-2020 Beloved Brands Inc., Graham Robertson, All rights reserved.

Our B2B toolkit has every PowerPoint slide that you need to run your brand

If you are running a B2B brand or you are a consultant looking after clients, our B2B Brand Toolkit has every PowerPoint slide you would need.

- The B2B brand plan template includes slides for your vision, purpose, analysis, key issues, strategies, and execution plans. In addition, we have separate slides for a sales forecast, financials, and activity calendar.

- Our B2B brand positioning template includes slides for your target profile, brand positioning statement, brand idea, brand concept, brand values, brand story, brand credo, and a creative brief.

- The B2B business review template includes slides for conducting a deep-dive business review that looks at the marketplace, customers, competitors, channels, and the brand.

https://beloved-brands.com/brand-management-templates/

Our B2B marketing training teaches how to think, define, plan, execute and analyze

Strategic Thinking:

Our B2B marketing training teaches brand leaders how to ask tough strategic questions to slow everyone down. They need to approach strategy in a thoughtful, analytical way. We created a Strategic ThinkBox that allows marketers to interrogate their brand.

Most importantly, it helps them look at the most important issues of the business. Furthermore, we force marketers to take a holistic look at their brand's core strength, competitive landscape, tightness of the customer bond, and business situation.

Brand Positioning:

Our brand positioning process starts by determining the ideal customer, whether a patient, B2B professional or B2B B2B leader. We show how to build customer profiles that use the customer's enemy, customer insights, and ways to play into accelerated need states.

We teach B2B marketers how to find the emotional and functional benefits their brand can deliver. Then, we show how to find the unique space for their brand that is interesting, simple, motivating, and ownable. Furthermore, we introduce our brand idea tool and show how to communicate that brand idea across the organization. In addition, marketers learn how to write a brand concept, brand story, and a brand credo document.

Marketing Plans:

The B2B marketing plan is a decision-making tool that communicates the expectations to everyone who works on the brand. We teach marketers how to put together the vision, purpose, goals, key issues, strategies and marketing execution plans.

Our B2B marketing training provides various tools including our one-page marketing plan and ideal presentation deck. Most importantly, we go into detail on how to write key issue questions and strategic statements that forms the foundation of the marketing plan.

Marketing Execution:

Our marketing execution training starts with the development of the creative brief, which serves as the bridge between the plan and execution. We review line-by-line of the creative brief and give you examples of the best and worst. Furthermore, we even provide participants with a checklist to make smarter decisions on your next marketing campaign.

We introduce our creative checklist to help make smarter decisions on creative communications. And, we emphasize how to match up media choices to the customer journey. Essentially, the skills will help your team get better work from their agency partners.

Brand Analytics:

Our comprehensive brand analytics sessions teach B2B marketers how to lead a deep-dive business review. They need to know how to assess their brand's performance, and set up smarter strategic thinking for their marketing plan.

As a result, we get marketers to look at the marketplace, customers, B2B professionals, channels of distribution, competitors or other brands in their industry category. Finally, we show how to lead an audit on the performance indicators of the brand.

Printed in Great Britain
by Amazon

ab1cb1e0-ac06-4051-b354-5b518398eb58R01